Perspectives
on
Presidential Selection

☆

Donald R. Matthews

EDITOR

☆

Perspectives
on
Presidential Selection

Studies in Presidential Selection
THE BROOKINGS INSTITUTION
Washington, D.C.

Copyright © 1973 by
THE BROOKINGS INSTITUTION
1775 Massachusetts Avenue, N.W., Washington, D.C. 20036

Library of Congress Cataloging in Publication Data:

Matthews, Donald R
  Perspectives on presidential selection.
  (Studies in presidential selection)
  Includes bibliographical references.
  1. Presidents—United States—Election.
2. Presidents—Election.   I. Title.   II. Series.
JK528.M33   329'.022   73-1078

ISBN 0-8157-5508-2
ISBN 0-8157-5507-4 (pbk.)

2 3 4 5 6 7 8 9

THE BROOKINGS INSTITUTION is an independent organization devoted to nonpartisan research, education, and publication in economics, government, foreign policy, and the social sciences generally. Its principal purposes are to aid in the development of sound public policies and to promote public understanding of issues of national importance.

The Institution was founded on December 8, 1927, to merge the activities of the Institute for Government Research, founded in 1916, the Institute of Economics, founded in 1922, and the Robert Brookings Graduate School of Economics and Government, founded in 1924.

The Board of Trustees is responsible for the general administration of the Institution, while the immediate direction of the policies, program, and staff is vested in the President, assisted by an advisory committee of the officers and staff. The by-laws of the Institution state, "It is the function of the Trustees to make possible the conduct of scientific research, and publication, under the most favorable conditions, and to safeguard the independence of the research staff in the pursuit of their studies and in the publication of the results of such studies. It is not a part of their function to determine, control, or influence the conduct of particular investigations or the conclusions reached."

The President bears final responsibility for the decision to publish a manuscript as a Brookings book or staff paper. In reaching his judgment on the competence, accuracy, and objectivity of each study, the President is advised by the director of the appropriate research program and weighs the views of a panel of expert outside readers who report to him in confidence on the quality of the work. Publication of a work signifies that it is deemed to be a competent treatment worthy of public consideration; such publication does not imply endorsement of conclusions or recommendations contained in the study.

The Institution maintains its position of neutrality on issues of public policy in order to safeguard the intellectual freedom of the staff. Hence interpretations or conclusions in Brookings publications should be understood to be solely those of the author or authors and should not be attributed to the Institution, to its trustees, officers, or other staff members, or to the organizations that support its research.

Foreword

THE QUADRENNIAL SELECTION of a president of the United States is the single most important political decision the American people are called upon to make. This collective choice, of course, results from far more than how the votes are cast on election day; by then a long and complex chain of events has narrowed the alternatives to only two men with a realistic chance of winning. These early and unofficial stages of presidential choice are critically important to the final election. Few phenomena are more fascinating, or more influential in determining the quality of American public life.

Given its intrinsic interest and importance, the presidential selection process has not received in recent decades as much attention from scholars as one would have expected. While proposals to reform various aspects of the presidential selection process abound, systematic and disinterested inquiry into the workings of the process and the strengths and weaknesses of the present system compared to its alternatives has lagged behind.

The Brookings project on Presidential Selection seeks to contribute to a better understanding of the process in two ways. First, under the general supervision of Donald R. Matthews, the staff of the project is preparing a series of books on a number of aspects of presidential selection. Three have already been published: *Voting for President: The Electoral College and the American Political System*, by Wallace S. Sayre and Judith H. Parris; *Financing Presidential Campaigns*, by Delmer D. Dunn; and *The Convention Problem: Issues in Reform of Presidential Nominating Procedures*, by Judith H. Parris. Other volumes in this series are scheduled to appear in 1973 and 1974.

But the need for research on presidential selection will not be satisfied by this modest effort. An integral part of the presidential selection project has been an effort to stimulate more and better research on presidential selection by political scientists at colleges and universities. The present book was the vehicle adopted to promote this end. An open competition for original manuscripts by young students of politics on any aspect of presidential selection in the United States was announced in the summer of 1970. The best of these manuscripts were to be published as a book. The seven best articles received during this competition, along with an introductory essay by the editor, make up the contents of this volume. We hope readers will agree that these articles demonstrate that young academicians can contribute to the continuing debate over how best to select American presidents. And we hope and expect that the young scholars whose work is presented below will continue their research efforts in this field.

This project was directed by Mr. Matthews, a senior fellow in the Brookings Governmental Studies program, of which Gilbert Y. Steiner is director. A bipartisan public advisory council, whose members are listed in the front of this book, has offered practical comment and assistance for the series of studies in presidential selection. The editor also wishes to acknowledge the assistance of his colleagues in the presidential selection project—William R. Keech, Judith H. Parris, and Daniel A. Mazmanian—in evaluating manuscripts. Several anonymous readers provided invaluable aid in making the final selections. Edwin Watkins and Elizabeth H. Cross edited the manuscript; James W. Rowe prepared the index. Sara Sklar handled secretarial duties with exceptional dispatch and accuracy.

Financial support for the project of which this book is a part was provided by a grant from the Ford Foundation. The views, opinions, and interpretations in this book are solely those of the authors. They should not be attributed to the members of the public advisory council, to other staff members, officers, or trustees of the Brookings Institution, or to the Ford Foundation.

January 1973
Washington, D.C.

KERMIT GORDON
President

Contents

TABLES AND FIGURES

☆
Chapter One
☆

Introduction

DONALD R. MATTHEWS

ON TUESDAY, November 7, 1972, some 76 million Americans interrupted the ordinary round of their lives to mark a ballot or pull a lever indicating their preferences for president of the United States. This quietly dramatic act of collective choice—repeated quadrennially now for more than a century and a half—lies at the heart of the American system of government. If the president of the United States were chosen in some other way—by a council of notables (as intended by the framers of the Constitution of 1789), by legislators (as in most other modern democracies), by lot (Aristotle suggested this as the only "democratic" way)—our system of government would be very different. The way presidents are chosen affects the nature of the presidential office and in some measure predetermines the type of person chosen as well as his performance in office.

The process that culminates in the popular choice of a president begins years before election day, and a long sequence of events determines the alternatives from which the voters choose. At the end of this process the voters are presented with a simple forced choice; a small handful out of the millions of persons who meet the constitutional requirements for the office are listed on the ballot, and of these only two usually have a realistic chance of winning. How, and how well, the preliminary screening process works is thus at least as important as what happens on election day. The whole process by which a few candidates emerge and one is elected president we shall call the presidential selection process.

There is anxiety these days about how American presidents are selected. The vulgarity of the nominating conventions, escalating campaign costs, and the dubious arithmetic of the electoral college have been favorite targets of reformers for generations, but disquiet and discontent with the entire system became manifest in the 1960s. The educated young, the black, the poor, and the white South are already disaffected; now the more politically conscious and politically active segments of the voting public are becoming increasingly critical. If this loss of confidence should continue, it would have profoundly negative effects on the legitimacy and effectiveness of the presidential office. The result would be the same even if it could be demonstrated that the present system does in fact provide for the selection of well-qualified presidents—an assumption that a growing number of Americans view as either arguable or absurd.

Although, partly as a result of such discontent, the number of states holding presidential primaries jumped from sixteen in 1968 to twenty-three in 1972, few participants or observers were happy with the long, expensive, and confusing battle for the 1972 Democratic nomination that resulted. In another move, the Democratic party drastically reformed the organization and procedures of its convention in an effort to make the nominating conclave more "open" and "democratic," but whether the 1972 convention was successful or suicidal will remain in controversy for some time to come. Agitation for the reform of the national conventions of both parties will continue—and a serious campaign to eliminate conventions altogether in favor of a direct national primary must be expected. The Congress has passed new legislation limiting and regulating the financing of campaigns; efforts to revise the regulations began almost before they had been tried. The House of Representatives has recently passed, by a lopsided vote, a resolution to substitute the direct popular election of presidents for the present electoral college system. Eighteen- to twenty-one-year-olds have been enfranchised.

Significant changes in the mode of selecting presidents are now being made, and more can be expected in the future. It is critically important that any change be made responsibly, after a sober evaluation of the present system and with a full understanding of the probable costs and benefits of alternative arrangements.

The Genesis of This Book

Political scientists are now in a much better position to provide the kind of information and analysis needed for responsible decision making than in the past. A sizable body of new, general, and reasonably reliable information about politics and political behavior, along with more sophisticated and powerful methods of analysis, has been developed over the last twenty years. But these advances were purchased at the price of neglect of policy studies and questions of institutional reform. The time has arrived to apply the new findings and techniques of political science to the resolution of contemporary problems, chief among them the ultimate problem of American governance: how best to select our presidents.

This book is the result of an effort to encourage students of politics to improve both the quality and the quantity of research on this question. In June 1970 the Brookings Institution decided to publish a book of original articles on presidential selection by younger scholars, chosen on the basis of an open competition. Any aspect of the presidential selection process, with the single exception of analyses of voting, would be considered for inclusion. (The behavior of the electorate in presidential elections was, and still is, the most thoroughly and successfully analyzed portion of the total selection process, and hence did not seem to require additional emphasis.) Contributions could employ any methodology, be based on any kind of data, cover any time period, and take either an "applied" or a "theoretical" approach. No preconceived theme or mode of organization would be imposed on the book, but the editor would select contributions for their scholarly merit alone.

Notices of the competition were published in several journals of political science, and form letters were sent to more than eighty chairmen of college and university political science departments asking them to draw the competition to the attention of their junior staff members and graduate students. The result of these initiatives was a heartening if not overwhelming flow of research proposals, dissertations, seminar papers, and manuscripts in various stages of completion. All told, about sixty potential authors or sets of authors were heard from, although by no means all of them eventually submitted finished papers. Almost all the potential contributors were young, and few had previous records of publication. Manuscripts by established scholars were for the most part turned away, although the rule was relaxed to allow consideration of collaborations between younger and more established writers.

Early in 1972, the editor selected a dozen manuscripts to be read by several experts on American politics. Drawing upon their reports and his own evaluation, he then selected the seven articles published in this volume.

A book put together in this way tells us a good deal about the interests and research orientations of the younger generation of political scientists. Although there are talented junior scholars actively engaged in research on the presidential selection process, the number is small. Some critically important subjects have not so far received their attention; very few papers examining the nominating process were submitted, none on the reforms of the McGovern-Fraser Commission and the O'Hara Commission within the Democratic party. The few papers submitted on the role of money and the problem of campaign financing and on the political impact of the mass media were judged to be of insufficient quality to merit publication. The volume of good work is smaller and the range of topics narrower than had been hoped —but that can be said of political science research on many subjects. One of the purposes of this book is thus to encourage more and better research on some aspects of the presidential selection process.

If the papers chosen are a reliable guide, future research on the selection of presidents is likely to be far more comparative and far more theoretical than previous investigations in this field. Almost half the chapters that follow employ comparisons with other nations to illuminate presidential politics in the United States, and formal models and quasi-mathematical approaches are almost as conspicuous. Both emphases reflect recent developments within the discipline of political science. While the editor feels that the application of these new tools to the analysis of a subject previously approached in highly descriptive and ethnocentric ways is exciting, the reader must decide whether they improve his understanding of the American system of presidential selection.

Neither cross-national comparisons nor theoretical concerns seem likely to enhance the immediate applicability of political science research to the problems of the day. Readers who approach this book looking for quick and easy answers to the problems surrounding presidential selection will be disappointed. But the authors of these papers manifest a desire to be both more rigorous and more practical than previous students of politics. The goal is not easy, and there is still a long way to go, but these young men and women seem to have rejected both premature and ill-founded prescription and the pursuit of knowledge without concern for its practical utility. This is a start in the right direction. It is the aim of this book to encourage others to follow.

Comparative Approaches

The first three articles attempt to understand America by looking abroad, comparing the choice of chief executives in other modern democracies with that in the United States. While this approach is scarcely new—James Bryce contrasted the selection of United States presidents and British prime ministers in *The American Common-wealth*, published in 1893—the authors of this book have been able to penetrate beyond the obvious institutional and cultural differences to explore the less formal generic processes by which executive leaders are chosen. What is truly unique about the American system is thus brought into sharper focus.

Hugh Heclo's comparison of the selection of British prime ministers and American presidents provides an admirable example of the merits of this approach. It is important to realize from the start that Heclo's definition of the term "selection" is narrower than that of the other authors of this book. The selection of chief executives, by Heclo's definition, includes only those processes by which politicians become candidates for the office—party leaders in Britain and presidential nominees in the United States—and excludes the electoral processes by which a popular choice is subsequently made among those who have been selected. The failure to distinguish sharply between these two stages in the choice of chief executives, he argues, has been one of the major causes of distortion in most attempts to compare the British and American systems. His concern is with the first—and more important—step in the process.

The formal and institutional differences between the methods employed by the two nations to select their chief executives are common knowledge; less well understood is the manner in which these manifest differences, in combination with other factors, affect the process of selection and its outcome. Heclo's subtle analysis of these questions manages to isolate a number of essential similarities and differences between British and American practice. Most readers are likely to be struck by how many of the alleged differences between the two systems largely disappear upon close inspection.

But differences still remain, and Heclo suggests that they may have
significant consequences for the chief executive's capacity to govern.
While chief executives are selected in the United States at the onset of
election campaigns, there is no such connection between the selection
and election process in Britain. The capacity to win elections is thus
given far greater weight in American selection processes, although it
is by no means absent as a criterion in Britain. Selection as prime minister in Great Britain results from a successful apprenticeship, the
learning of the craft of governance under the "watchful eye of established masters" who ultimately decide who should be selected. The
selection of American presidents results, on the other hand, from the
open and public clash of competing political entrepreneurs, one of
whom succeeds in putting together a winning coalition at the national
party convention.

Both the apprenticeship and the entrepreneurial systems are inten-
sive learning experiences, although they teach different lessons. Prime
ministers are taught to be "team players," at home in an atmosphere
of collegial decision making, shared power, and responsibility. Presidential selection encourages individualistic and populistic perspectives, a view of the world as an all-powerful mass electorate and the
lonely presidential aspirant, surrounded not by colleagues but by em-
ployees. These differences in orientation may well be consistent with
the requirements of the two different offices—collegial skills are certainly more important to British prime ministers than to American
presidents, while the entrepreneurial lessons taught by American selection processes are more necessary to American presidents than to
prime ministers—and yet the fact cannot be escaped that selection in
the United States is heavily weighted toward electoral criteria rather
than presumed ability to perform in the White House. In Britain, future prime ministers advance by demonstrating ability to perform
within the same network of relationships they will confront in office.
Presidential nominations in the United States are a less direct test of
the capacity to govern, and may teach lessons that are counterproduc-
tive to effective performance, while raising expectations about the
leader's capacity to govern that may make credible performance
exceedingly difficult.

That a parliamentary system of government need not be combined
with the apprenticeship model of leadership selection is illustrated by
the case of Canada, where the British method was abandoned in 1919.

The reasons for the sharp departure from British practice were much the same as the ones that led the American parties to abandon the congressional caucus a century before—party caucuses of national legislators were insufficiently representative of the two sprawling nations to ensure the nomination of strong national candidates. In their place, Canadians adopted a convention system originally devised in the United States to meet the needs of a presidential form of government.

The Canadian leadership conventions, however, are far from slavish copies of their counterparts in the United States, as Carl and Ellen Baar demonstrate in their comparison of the internal organization and procedures of party conventions in the two countries. For one thing, the major Canadian parties seek to represent all segments of the party organization rather than provincial parties alone. They thus allocate votes at their national conventions to members of Parliament, members of provincial legislatures, and other public officials; to a variety of party officials at the federal, provincial, and local levels; to local constituency organizations; and to youth, women's, and student associations. In combination with voting rules that require a secret ballot and the elimination of the low man among the candidates after each ballot, this feature results in a weak system of "intermediate leadership" and "a lack of organized subgroups." In the United States, where convention votes are allocated only to state parties and delegates are organized by states, state party leaders become a powerful force whose interests are not identical with those of the candidates or of national party officers. Public roll calls of votes cast state-by-state with no limit to their number are an invitation to bargaining among the state party leaders in an effort to build—or block—a winning majority. The Baars liken Canadian conventions to a "mass society," a large set of individual delegates responding privately and individually to the appeals of competing candidates, with little lateral communication among themselves, while American conventions, with their relatively rich panoply of subgroups, leaders, and communications channels, are characterized by "intermediate leadership."

The reasons for the emergence and persistence of the two types of convention are not hard to find. The national parties in the United States are little more than temporary confederations of state parties for the purpose of electing a president, while in Canada the provincial parties play a secondary role in federal leadership selection. Moreover, the Canadian parliamentary system argues for a tighter articulation of the national conventions and the parliamentary party than seems appropriate in the United States, since the selection of a large number of delegates by the constituency organization of the parliamentary district and the ex officio representation of parliamentary figures reduces, although it has not entirely eliminated, the potential for conflict between the convention and the parliamentary party.

The Baars find distinct advantages in the "mass society" convention. A large number of minorities—women, youth, and racial and ethnic minorities—today demand direct representation in party affairs, and a nominating convention that does not include members of these groups in rough proportion to their numerical importance within the party is viewed by many as "undemocratic" and "illegitimate." The Canadian party conventions, by using organized subgroups as well as geographically defined constituencies as units of representation, have achieved greater direct minority representation than the American. While recent reforms of selection procedures in the Democratic party require that state delegations be demographically representative, their enforcement is difficult. Since American party reformers have insisted in addition that the selection of delegates be "open" and "democratic," with extensive participation by rank-and-file party members, there can be no assurance that demographically representative delegations will result; indeed, it is more plausible to assume that majority groups will be overrepresented among the winners of open and fair contests for delegate seats. Caught in this dilemma, the Democratic party in 1972 had to resolve an extraordinary number of bitter challenges to the seating of delegates. Ultimately, the presidential nomination hinged—or at least seemed to—upon which set of delegates from California was seated at the convention in Miami Beach. It is by no means clear that American parties can resolve such politically charged conflicts in ways that will retain popular support for the national convention as an institution. The conflict of principles— minority representation versus democratic majority rule—is obviously lost sight of as supporters of the competing candidates jockey for advantage. The Canadian parties have solved this problem.

The Canadian convention has a further advantage, according to the Baars: secret balloting and the "low-man-out" rule result in the automatic, rapid emergence of winners in a way that largely eliminates backroom "bargains" and "deals." The number of ballots at a Canadian convention is limited by the number of candidates. As candidates are eliminated, there is little opportunity to swing blocs of votes from one candidate to another because of the secret ballot and the absence of organized subgroups and subleaders. Lacking alternative cues, the delegates tend to drift toward the candidate who led on the first ballot. Deadlock is avoided as first, second, and third choices are combined until one candidate achieves majority support without private negotiations by leaders in "smoke-filled rooms."

The changes in Democratic party convention rules and delegate-selection procedures brought about by the McGovern-Fraser Commission (the Commission on Party Structure and Delegate Selection, headed first by Senator George McGovern, later by Representative Donald M. Fraser) and the Commission on Rules (chaired by Representative James O'Hara) seem quite modest from the Canadian perspective. Party conventions restructured along Canadian lines would have, the Baars believe, a better chance of simultaneously achieving "participatory democracy," direct representation of minority groups, and limited control over nominations by established party leaders, than the cumbersome attempts of party reformers in the United States to regulate the procedures of state parties. Even those who feel these goals are of dubious value, or the costs of achieving them exorbitantly high, can learn much about how and why party conventions operate as they do from the Baars' stimulating analysis.

The final paper that uses a comparative approach to the problem of presidential selection is Elijah Kaminsky's analysis of the "nomination" of candidates for president in the Fifth French Republic. The word nomination has been placed in quotation marks advisedly, since there are no institutionalized procedures for preselecting candidates in France (except that candidates must obtain a hundred signatures from a panel of eligible sponsors, a requirement that seems to eliminate only the most frivolous of candidacies), and "no specific event denotes completion of nominations and the beginning of the main campaign." Nonetheless, some preselection of candidates must occur before a nationwide popular election is possible: the nominating *function* must be performed somehow. How and how well this function is performed in France and the United States is Kaminsky's subject.

In the United States presidential nominations are made every four years by well-established, if extra-constitutional, institutions. The vote-getting prowess of presidential hopefuls is regularly tested by contests for lesser office—candidates include state governors, U.S.

senators, and mayors of the nation's larger cities—and many a presidential campaign has been launched by an impressive showing in one of these elections. Presidential primaries, some held many months in advance of the party convention, add substantially to the complexity, duration, and strenuousness of the nominating process.

In France, none of these conditions holds. The dates of presidential elections are unpredictable and the lead time in which support can be built up for a few strong contenders varies from seven years to a matter of days. Subelections in which aspiring politicians can prove themselves are much less frequent, and the time between them and presidential elections is unpredictable. Presidential primaries are, of course, a strictly American invention. While French parties hold regular conventions, an endorsement by one of them does not indicate that the candidate has the massive support needed to win a Democratic or Republican nomination in the United States. In addition, the French two-ballot election system, which provides that if no candidate receives an absolute majority on the first ballot, the two top candidates after withdrawals run against each other two weeks later, does not offer an adequate parallel to an American nomination. The runoff encourages multiple candidacies and limited aggregation of support in the first election, and two weeks are inadequate for the reaggregation of support after the weaker candidates have been eliminated.

If the American system of nominations is highly decentralized and fluid in comparison with the British, it at least has a regularity and degree of institutionalization that are lacking in France. In the absence of nominating institutions, Kaminsky argues, "only the mass media, public opinion polls, and negotiation among politicians remain as channels for presidential nomination." His brief description of presidential nominating politics in France since 1962 would seem to bear out his point.

Although the American system has many merits, at least in comparison with a system that has yet to devise an institutionalized presidential nominating process, the institutions that Kaminsky argues are of critical importance to the American process are under sharp attack, in danger of losing their legitimacy unless they are substantially reformed. One returns to the disturbing query raised by Heclo's comparison of the American system with the British: does the American system result in the selection of men who are *able to govern?* Or does it attach more importance to electoral criteria than to demonstrated competence in office, raise false hopes about what the president can do, and instill attitudes in a candidate which, once he is in the White House, will make effective performance difficult?

Although the three articles contain no final answers to these questions, they emphasize their importance for students of American politics.

American Party Conventions: Behavioral Approaches

The small number of papers of high quality that dealt directly with presidential nominating politics in the United States was one of the unhappy surprises of the competition. Nevertheless, the next two papers are more than just the best of a small lot. They are genuinely fresh analyses of party conventions.

The first of these, "A Theory of Presidential Nominations, with a 1968 Illustration," by James P. Zais and John H. Kessel, views the presidential nominating process as a special instance of coalition formation and draws upon formal-mathematical theory developed in recent years. Proposing a theory of how delegates arrive at decisions, Zais and Kessel test it by comparing predictions derived from it with the actual performance of the Republican national convention of 1968. This approach to the study of politics is not universally understood or admired. But this paper makes a good case for its promise as a way of studying presidential nominating politics in the United States.

Zais and Kessel's theory can be briefly stated. The probability that a national convention delegate will join the coalition of supporters of one of the presidential candidates will be the product of the size of the candidates' coalition (relative to the size needed to win) times the extent of ideological agreement between the delegate and the coalition.

This formulation has much appeal to an intuitive understanding of the process. It is true that delegate votes are sometimes affected by the candidates' chance of winning; but if this were the sole determinant, the leading candidate would always win, the happy beneficiary of an automatic and irresistible bandwagon effect. It is also true that delegate votes are in part affected by their policy preferences; but if this were the sole determinant, conventions would be static affairs, prone to deadlock unless there were dramatic shifts in the candidates' policy positions, and stampedes toward the ultimate winner would be impossible. The common sense of the equation also illuminates the pre-

convention campaign: at the beginning of the process of coalition formation, candidates must appeal primarily to their "natural" friends—
those who agree with them ideologically—since the size of their coalitions is too small to have any significant appeal. As their coalitions
grow in size, the strength of their ideological appeal to the remaining
delegates diminishes; their main attraction becomes the prospect of
victory.

The authors assess the validity of the model in a computer simulation of the 1968 Republican convention. Because the inadequacy of
data and the imperatives of computer technology required a number
of simplifying assumptions and arbitrary definitions, however, the
operational application of the theory diverges from the model of delegate decision making described above in a number of important respects. The unit of analysis becomes the state delegation rather than
the individual, state delegations are assumed to act in unison, presidential candidates are given all the votes from their home states and
states in which they have won primaries as an assured base of support
from which to begin building coalitions, and the deviations of the ideological positions of candidates from those of state delegations are estimated by the authors. A degree of error and unreality is thus introduced into the simulation in addition to that inherent in the initial
theory—an inevitable problem in computer simulations that compli-
cates the task of evaluating their results.

Nonetheless, there is reasonable congruence between the simulated
results and the actual outcome of the Republican convention of 1968,
and the plausibility of the model of coalition formation at national
conventions is strengthened. Of course, their theory is far from
"proven" by a rough simulation of a single convention. But a theory,
no matter how inadequate or difficult to test it may be, is a beginning.

The 1972 Democratic national convention has been widely viewed
as unique in that eight of every ten delegates had never before been to
a national nominating convention. A study by Loch Johnson and Harlan
Hahn, "Delegate Turnover at National Party Conventions, 1944–
1968," provides both historical and theoretical perspective on this
phenomenon.

Johnson and Hahn begin with the observation that the stability—or
instability—of personnel is one of the most significant attributes of
any institution, especially of political parties. Since parties flourish

only by winning elections, they are compelled to attract new supporters continuously; yet organizational maintenance and efficiency are best served by stable personnel.

Johnson and Hahn point out that of more than 50,000 delegates and alternates to the major party conventions from 1940 through 1968, 63 percent of the Democratic and 65 percent of the Republican delegates had not attended a prior convention. Of the more experienced delegates, most had been to only one earlier convention. The pattern varies little between the parties or from year to year; instability of convention personnel seems to be a stable fact of life. The uniqueness of the Democrats' 1972 convention, in this respect, can thus be exaggerated.

The pattern of instability varies, however, from state to state, and an examination of the differences in convention turnover rates results in some interesting findings. States with two-party systems and/or relatively centralized party structures choose delegations that are more experienced than those from less competitive and less centralized parties. And the presidential primary—adopted in part to keep "boss"-dominated state conventions from sending "party hacks" to national conventions—has not had that effect: presidential primary states usually send more experienced people to national conventions than do states using the convention system of choosing delegates.

What difference does the permeability of party conventions make in their decisions? Examining the relation between the prior convention experience of delegations and their collective voting records, Johnson and Hahn find that relatively high proportions of inexperienced delegates characterized delegations that voted for such challengers as Stassen in 1948, Kefauver in 1952, and McCarthy in 1968, while the more experienced delegations voted disproportionately for Truman, Harriman, Stevenson, Kennedy, Taft, and Rockefeller. On the whole, they find the more experienced state delegations clustered around the center of the Democratic party and at the ideological extremes of the Republican party.

The high rate of delegate turnover, Johnson and Hahn conclude, has advantages and disadvantages. The delegates' typical lack of experience can make them either "the pawns of party leaders or incorrigible mavericks." On the other hand, they continue, high levels of turnover at the national conventions may "enhance the legitimacy of leadership selection in America" if the continuous stream of new party activists attending them is genuinely representative of the American public.

The qualifying clause is important, for on this point Johnson and Hahn's data are silent and the record of the conventions is mixed. At least since the advent of public opinion polling, however, we know that the party conventions have almost invariably nominated their party's most popular candidate; in this extremely important respect, the conventions have proved to be successful representative institutions. In the past, however, this result has been achieved in ways that discriminated against the choice of delegates from minority groups—women, young people, blacks, and others. The "continuous stream of new party activists" which Johnson and Hahn document so well came from a limited segment of the society. Those who have been left out now want to get in, and in 1972 were successful, to a large degree, in achieving direct representation among the delegates to the Democratic convention. The liberal representation of these minorities among the Democratic delegates at Miami Beach in 1972, rather than the delegates' lack of experience, was the genuinely radical departure from the past.

The challenge both major parties still face is how to make conventions more broadly and equitably representative in this sense without sacrificing the capacity to choose the strongest candidate the party can field in a fashion that enhances, rather than weakens, his chances for victory in November. A policy requiring delegations to contain women, young people, blacks, and Mexican-Americans in approximate proportion to their numbers within the party as a whole is a standing invitation to other self-conscious minorities—the poor, Jews, the aged, those of Polish ancestry, middle-aged WASP males, and so forth—to demand their "fair share." Achieving such a "balanced" convention through open and democratic procedures is no mean feat, to say nothing of arriving at agreement on the single strongest candidate when the balkanized convention is convened for a few short days in a single hall.

The Electoral College Debate

The debate over the electoral college is as old as the institution itself. Since January 6, 1797, when the first constitutional amendment proposing a reform of the electoral college was introduced in the House of Representatives, hardly a session of Congress has passed without one or more such proposals. Untold numbers of books, articles, and debates have addressed themselves to its merits and problems. It was a pleasant surprise to discover, in judging the manuscripts on presidential selection submitted to the Brookings Institution, that fresh research is being conducted by young political scientists on this well-worn subject.

Much of the controversy about the electoral college has revolved around an empirical question: who really derives advantage from this unusual way of counting votes? John H. Yunker and Lawrence D. Longley, in "The Biases of the Electoral College," resolve the contradictory assessments of the impact of the institution more satisfactorily than anyone has done heretofore—if still not definitively.

The authors expand upon the work of John F. Banzhaf, who has established power indices for voters in each state under the electoral college and various alternative systems. Banzhaf defines voting power as "the ability to affect decisions through the process of voting": if all voters have an equal chance to affect the outcome, they have equal voting power. This pivotal-vote approach to the measurement of power, an analysis derived from the mathematical theory of games, requires several calculations before it can be applied to the electoral college. The analysis first computes the chance each state has of casting the pivotal vote in the electoral college, then the chance that a voter can, by altering his vote, change the way in which his state's electoral votes are cast. Finally, the results of these two steps are combined in a single measure of the chance that an individual voter has of affecting the electoral college outcome.

The analysis concludes that, under the electoral college system, a voter in New York is 3.312 times more likely to determine the outcome of a presidential election than one in the District of Columbia. By this criterion, the voters in the seven largest states in the country have more than the average amount of voting power, while those in the other forty-three states and the District of Columbia are disadvantaged. The relation between the size of a state and the voting power of its inhabitants, however, is not linear. Because two electoral votes are automatically assigned to each state, the citizens of the very smallest states have a relative voting power considerably larger than that of states of moderate size. Both those who argue that the electoral college favors the large states and those who claim that it favors the small ones are thus partly correct. Applying the same approach to two of the most popular alternatives to the electoral college—the proportional plan and the district plan—Yunker and Longley find that both would have substantial biases in favor of the smaller states. Of course, if the electoral college were abandoned in favor of a direct popular vote, the power of all voters would be equal, since all would have an equal chance of casting the pivotal vote.

The authors then compute the average voting power of various demographic groups and compare it with the average voting power of the whole population. On the whole, the results tend to support the view that urban-ethnic groups are somewhat favored by the present system. The findings for two groups, however, partially contradict this conclusion: black voters have less than average voting power because they are concentrated in small and medium-sized states in the South, in the District of Columbia, as well as in the central cities of large states, and suburban residents have a slight advantage over residents of central cities.

The authors conclude with a critique of the pivotal-vote approach to the measurement of relative power. The definition of power as the opportunity to cast the deciding vote rests on a number of unrealistic assumptions. Moreover, the power indices derived by this approach reflect inequalities built into the system—ignoring such factors as voter turnout or one-party dominance in a state—that may substantially affect the voter's opportunity to cast the deciding vote in a presidential election. The analysis simply assumes that these factors vary from election to election and will tend to cancel one another out over a long series of elections.

Certain causes of inequality in voting power are, however, relatively stable and predictable. In the final portion of the article, the authors discuss some of the causes of error in their estimates and ways in which they might be eliminated.

The final paper, by Max S. Power, is an impressive analysis of the controversy over the electoral college and its principal alternative, direct popular election of presidents.

Advocates of popular election base their case on the principles of popular sovereignty and majority rule, but rarely specify precisely what these abstractions mean in the context of democratic elections. Drawing upon the mathematical literature on collective choice, Power explains the necessary and sufficient conditions for simple majority choice between two alternatives and then compares these with the electoral college and direct election systems. So long as there are only two candidates for the presidency, direct popular elections meet all these criteria, while the electoral college system, like other indirect systems, falls short. But when there are more than two candidates there is no way of assuring that even direct popular elections will meet the requirements of popular sovereignty and majority rule. Faced with this objection, the advocates of direct election fall back on the requirement of a plurality, provided the leading candidate attracts a specified minimum level of support, usually 40 percent. But the logical case for this type of popular election is not particularly compelling, and other extraneous values—especially the desirability of a two-party system and presidential legitimacy—become central issues.

While advocates of direct popular election rely primarily on highly abstract and deductive arguments, defenders of the present system are concerned primarily with practical political consequences. The existing system, they argue, works. It also has a number of side effects which they view as beneficial—disproportionate power for urban-ethnic minorities, the preservation of a two-party system, and the enhanced legitimacy of the presidency which, they claim, follows the inflation of the victor's margin of victory by the electoral college. None of these side effects, however, has been conclusively demonstrated to result from the electoral college mechanism, and the first two are subject to differing evaluations: proponents of direct election contend that inequalities in voting power are never morally justifiable, and deny that weakening the two-party system is inherently bad. Both sides agree, however, that the method by which presidents are chosen should enhance the legitimacy of the office, although they disagree about the system that will achieve this goal. Here, perhaps, is the basic empirical question that remains unanswered: would a president selected strictly according to the rules of popular sovereignty and political equality enjoy more popular support than a president selected by a system that, although it falls short of these standards, magnifies his apparent margin of victory?

In the end, Power concludes, the debate over electoral college reform boils down to "a clash of philosophical perspectives." The proponents of reform are devotees of a rationalistic-deductive mode of thought who insist that the legitimacy of political institutions stems from "the logically correct application of first principles." The defenders of the status quo, with their empirical-pragmatic cast of mind, insist that reforms "ought to be evaluated in terms of their effects, not their logic." Political institutions, they argue, are legitimate if the people think they are; the electoral college's long and successful history contributes to that end. Perhaps this difference in intellectual style explains why this debate has gone on for more than 180 years, and why the controversy is unlikely to end soon.

Chapter Two

Presidential and Prime Ministerial Selection

HUGH HECLO

AMERICAN PRESIDENTS and British prime ministers have often been compared in analyses of the presidency, not least by writers who are critical of the selection process in the United States. Lord Bryce, in a chapter entitled "Why Great Men Are Not Chosen President," argued that the method of choice naturally tends to exclude "great" men from reaching the top. To support this view, he cited seven or eight prime ministers and only four presidents whom he considered "of the first rank," along with eight presidents and six prime ministers who were "personally insignificant." Building upon Bryce's analysis, Ostrogorski pointed out that even Gladstone would have been excluded from the presidency by residency requirements.[1]

By and large, such comparisons have suffered from oversimplifications imported to confirm a distaste for the noisiness, disorganization, and vulgarity of the method of selection used in the United States. Worse, the actual operation of political recruitment in the United States is usually contrasted with the ideal operation of the British system, to the disadvantage of the former. Modern writers have devoted little attention to the comparative study of top leadership choice, and the literature is particularly thin in Britain. Most of the studies are monographic, noncumulative, and belletristic.[2]

Note. I wish to thank James Douglas, Anthony King, Richard Rose, and Aaron Wildavsky for their helpful comments on this paper.

1. Lord Bryce, *The American Commonwealth*, Vol. 1 (London: Macmillan, 1893), Chap. 8. Chapters 5–9 concern the presidency and still repay rereading. M. Ostrogorski, *Democracy and the Organization of Political Parties*, Vol. 2 (Haskell, 1964).

2. For a review of approaches, see L. Edinger (ed.), *Political Leadership in Industrialized Societies* (Wiley, 1967); Elmer Cornwell (ed.), *The American Presidency* (Scott, Foresman, 1966). Among the more useful books on the prime ministership are Anthony King (ed.), *The British Prime Minister* (London: Macmillan, 1969); Byrum Carter, *The Office of Prime Minister* (London: Faber and Faber, 1956), Chap. 2, "The Selection of Prime Ministers"; *British Prime Ministers* (London: Allan Wingate, 1953), a collection of articles that originally appeared in *History Today*; Lewis Broad, *The Path to Power* (London: Muller, 1965); Lucille Iremonger, *The Fiery Chariot* (London: Secker and Warburg, 1970).

Despite its possible abuses, the comparative technique remains of great value. Viewed as a special case of political socialization and recruitment, presidential selection is susceptible to comparison, if not to one-to-one comparison, with the process of executive selection in Britain. This is in no way to discount social and political differences between the two nations. The formal institutional differences are well known: unitary, parliamentary government with well-organized national parties in Britain, versus federal, presidential government with poorly organized parties in the United States. The challenge is to make such familiar institutional factors speak to the more informal processes, and in particular to the political recruitment of executive leadership. While the essence of parliamentary government, for example, is the election of the executive from within the legislature, the essence of presidential government is his choice by a general electorate. What is not clear is the effect of such institutional differences on informal executive *selection* as well as formal *election*. Far from overlooking political differences, a comparative approach offers the only means of distinguishing unique from more generic phenomena. Like depth perception in optics, political depth perception often depends on a set of partly contrasting, partly overlapping images. Investigation from this bifocal perspective leads one to revise a number of accepted stereotypes concerning the selection of presidents and prime ministers, and perhaps to a clearer view of each.

In the following sections, the American and British selection processes will be compared in five categories: recruitment continuity and timing, selection sites, mobility patterns, selection criteria, and degree of openness to the public. Inasmuch as the United States has no party leaders in the British sense of the term, the comparison will be based on the population of presidential nominees and British party leaders— who are, roughly speaking, nominees to the prime ministership. The analysis will be limited to changes in party leadership since 1900, a period especially significant in British politics since it marks the time of changes in Conservative party selection procedures, the last stages of relevant Liberal party selections, and the beginning of Labour party selections.[3] The leader of the Labour party, in the simplest

3. Bonar Law's selection for the Conservative leadership in 1911 was the first "independent" election of the leader by Conservative M.P.s since 1846; in the interim all subsequent Conservative leaders in the House of Commons had begun as the virtual nominees of a peer who was the recognized leader of the party. On general selection procedures in Britain, see R. T. McKenzie, *British Political Parties* (London: Heinemann, 1963).

terms, has always been selected by majority vote of the parliamentary Labour party. Until 1965, the Conservative leaders arose through a less formal process of emergence with the blessing of party elders; on February 25, 1965, a new and complicated procedure was instituted by which the leader is formally elected by the parliamentary party. Throughout this period, selections by both parties in the United States have been made by nominating conventions of state party representatives.

Selection versus Election

In both Britain and the United States the key locus of choice is in the preelection selection process. Though more dramatic and publicized, the election itself is far less important—in the sense of the number of alternatives eliminated—than the selection, when one from a large number of potential candidates is designated. As a systems analyst once said, "If I can set the options, I don't care who makes the choice." The distinction requires a careful use of terms. By "selection" I mean the initial picking out from a group (the Latin *seligere*, to separate by culling out); "election" will refer to the effective choosing by vote for office (*eligere*, to choose). Election is thus a clearly delimited public act, defined procedurally by voting, while selection is a vaguer form of private choice that may be carried out by a variety of procedures; selection results in nomination to office, election in the holding of office. One of the most common confusions in the popular conceptions of the presidency and prime ministership is the identification of the election, and its attendant campaign activity, with the prior selection process. The result is usually overemphasis on or misidentification of the differences between the two recruitment patterns.

This distinction may, for example, elucidate the question of continuity in leadership. The British system is usually considered conducive to stability of party leadership, while the United States, with its constitutionally required quadrennial elections, is considered subject to greater fluctuations.[4] This view is difficult to substantiate. Since 1900, there have been nineteen general elections in Britain and eighteen in the United States, and a total of fifteen prime ministers and thirteen presidents. Average presidential tenure has been six

---

4. Since 1911, except for wartime emergencies, the legal requirement in Britain is an election at least once every five years.

years (5.4 years if Franklin D. Roosevelt is excluded), that of prime ministers slightly less than five. During the same time, there have been eleven changes of Conservative and thirteen of Labour party leadership in Britain. If one regards the choice of a presidential nominee as roughly equivalent to the choice of a British party leader, there have been eleven changes of Republican and nine of Democratic leadership. If anything, the continuity of executive leadership and of those selected for potential leadership has been not less but greater in the United States than in Britain.

What is the source of the common belief to the contrary? The answer probably lies in the differing relation of the selection process to elections. The difference between the two nations lies not in the absolute length of tenure but in the timing of selection. Selection in the United States is directly and inextricably tied to forthcoming elections, and candidates are chosen for their actual or predicted election performance. As Bryce put it, "Now to a party it is more important that its nominee should be a good candidate than that he should turn out a good President."[5] The remarkable orientation to "election success" of the American selection process—and the basis for the assumed longevity of British political leadership—is also suggested by surveying the candidates who have been defeated in elections. Since 1900, Richard M. Nixon is the only defeated candidate who has remained sufficiently attractive to be elected president later. On only five other occasions has a defeated presidential candidate been renominated; and only four other defeated candidates have been given the courtesy of a significant number of votes at a subsequent national convention (James M. Cox in 1924, Alfred E. Smith in 1932, Adlai E. Stevenson in 1960, and Hubert H. Humphrey in 1972). By comparison, the beneficiary of selection in Britain seems highly impervious to electoral defeat. During this century, in the Conservative and Labour parties, there have been no fewer than fourteen occasions (seven in each party) on which the designated leaders have continued to lead their parties after electoral defeats. This is not to say that pressures have not arisen following such defeats: Arthur Balfour was virtually pushed out in 1911, but only after three lost elections; Stanley Baldwin had to fight to regain control after the 1923 and 1929 defeats; and Sir Alec Douglas-Home's position was greatly weakened after the

5. Lord Bryce, *American Commonwealth*, Vol. 1, p. 80.

electoral defeat of 1964.[6] But these cases stand out precisely because of their exceptional nature. Paradoxically, although the American presidential nominee may be far less a party leader than the British prime-minister-designate, he is in effect held far more accountable for electoral defeats.

If the relation of selection to election performance is much less direct in Britain than in the United States, so too is the relative timetable. Without exception, presidential selection is made in the period immediately preceding elections, while British selections generally show little systematic relation to elections. Figure 1 summarizes the electoral intervals at which selections of party leaders have occurred, and illustrates the exceptional and frequently overlooked position of the United States.

There appears to be a tendency in postwar Britain for selections to precede elections more closely than earlier in the century, but there is still a great gap between Britain and the United States.[7] In no sense is selection in Britain the inescapable prologue to election; a good indicator of the difference is found in the assumptions of election analysts in the two nations. Theodore White's analysis of the 1964 American election, for example, devotes more than half its content to the pre-election selection process in each party, while the standard study of the 1964 British general election devotes two paragraphs to the nine-month struggle over the Conservative leadership in 1963 and only three sentences to the Labour party's selection of Hugh Gaitskell's successor in the same year.[8]

The difference in the relation of selection to electoral performance and timing is derived from the nature of government institutions and party organization. While parties supply the personnel for selection,

6. In general, see Robert Blake, *The Conservative Party from Peel to Churchill* (London: Eyre and Spottiswoode, 1970); on Home's selection and replacement, Anthony King, "Britain: The Search for Leadership," in William Andrews (ed.), *European Politics*, Vol. 1 (Van Nostrand, 1966).

7. Attlee was clearly chosen in 1935 with a view to Lansbury's inadequacy to lead the party in the forthcoming election two months away; the timing of Eden's and Gaitskell's successions in 1955 was predetermined, in Eden's case for more than a decade. In the background of Heath's selection in August 1965 was the knowledge that, because of the delicate parliamentary balance, an election could not be too far away—seven months, as it turned out.

8. Theodore H. White, *The Making of the President 1964* (Atheneum, 1965); D. E. Butler and Anthony King, *The British General Election of 1964* (London: Macmillan, 1965).

FIGURE 1. *Time at Which Party Leaders Were Selected in Relation to the Elections Preceding and Following Their Selection, Conservative Party, 1902–65, and Labour Party, 1911–64*

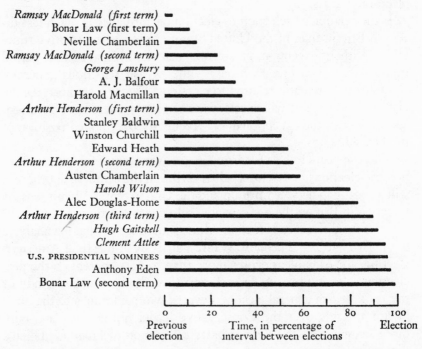

Party leader and party affiliation[a]

Source: David Butler and Jennie Freeman, *British Political Facts, 1900–1967* (2d ed. London: Macmillan, 1968).

a. Names of Conservative party leaders are in roman type; those of Labour party leaders are in italics.

government institutions determine how this personnel will be structured; personnel and structure together define the nature of the selectorate. By further distinguishing the "selective" from the "elective" operations of these bodies, some of the other accepted truths concerning executive selection can better be questioned, or at least refined.

The Locus of Selection

One can scarcely conceive of a modern political system that does not require some sort of preelection winnowing, no matter how inchoate the process. The central characteristic of the executive recruit is that of a "group actor"; designation of a nominee to the highest political office in both Britain and the United States occurs through, and by virtue of, participation in limited political groups. Although designation to the British prime ministership may be far less formal than nomination for the American presidency, identifiable selection procedures in the two countries can be compared in terms of these differing group structures and personnel.

The most important group is of course the political party; the obvious fact, which is nevertheless easily overlooked, is that the personnel of the selectorate are party members. No man in either nation during this century has attained nomination to supreme office without a clear profession of party allegiance. Even the seeming exceptions only serve to emphasize the point. Both Wendell Willkie in 1940 and Dwight Eisenhower in 1952 were required to confirm their party credentials before nomination; the one recent attempt at a nonparty draft—Democratic Senator Claude Pepper's proposal in July 1948 that Eisenhower be adopted as a national candidate and that Democrats confine themselves to subnational elections—was stillborn. In Britain, Winston Churchill suffered several decades of suspicion for his "ratting and reratting" on the Conservative party; the collapse of David Lloyd George's coalition government in 1921 left him a leader without a party, while the creation of a National Government under Ramsay MacDonald in 1931 temporarily left Labour as a party without a leader. By the Second World War, Churchill had learned enough of the importance of party allegiance, even at the height of a struggle for national survival, to insist upon eventually taking up the leadership of the Conservative party.[9]

The parties in each nation shape themselves to the structures of government, both in central institutions and in national-local divisions of power. The well-worn distinction between the unitary British state with a parliamentary-cabinet government and the federal United States with separated powers remains the most useful shorthand expression for the extremely complex differences. Such institutional dif-

9. Winston S. Churchill, *Their Finest Hour* (Houghton Mifflin, 1949), p. 496: "I should have found it impossible to conduct the war if I had to procure the agreement . . . not only of the leaders of the two minority parties, but of the leaders of the Conservative majority. Whoever had been chosen and whatever his self-denying virtues, he would have had the real political power. For me there would have been only executive responsibility."

ferences will be of concern here only insofar as they are molding forces through which the party groups operate to select national leaders.

At risk of oversimplification, one may say that the central-local party structure in the United States is characterized by a disparate confederacy of state and local party organizations, which intermittently coalesce for the specific purpose of nominating a presidential candidate. One of the oldest observations on the subject remains valid: the central task at the nominating convention is the search for an election "winner," for it is only through striving for such victory that the heterogeneous party can be brought together.[10] The national nominating convention is an extreme device used to meet extreme party decentralization, a contrivance which has since its beginning been rather a consequence than a cause of the incoherent nature of America's national parties. The intimate tie between selection and election is thus due not to the unique nature of the presidency but to the decentralization of the parties, which find that the selection of a national election winner is the one common cause in which they can at least temporarily unite. But for this centripetal force, the selection process might well occur long before the elections.

In Britain, on the other hand, the parties are more continuously unified national organizations, without a regular timetable for choosing party leaders and potential prime ministers. When the succession in party leadership has been disputed, local party organizations have made their voices heard, but usually in the negative form of complaints and grumbles rather than in the expression of positive preferences.[11] The unified national party selectorate thus aims not so much to create party unity, as in the United States, as to preserve it.

The ease with which, when strong central party leadership is absent, the British selection process can come to resemble the American was demonstrated in 1963. Until this time the Conservative party had been cited as the model of coherent party organization, with a smoothly operating, emergence style of leadership recruitment. From the mo-

10. See, for example, Lord Bryce, *American Commonwealth*, Vol. 1, Chap. 8; Pendleton Herring, *The Politics of Democracy* (Norton, 1965); and Nelson W. Polsby and Aaron B. Wildavsky, *Presidential Elections: Strategies of American Electoral Politics* (Scribner's, 1964), pp. 60 ff.

11. On the independent power of several Northern "bosses," see Randolph Churchill, *Lord Derby, King of Lancashire* (London: Heinemann, 1959); and Stanley Salvidge, *Salvidge of Liverpool* (London: Hodder and Stoughton, 1934).

ment of the surprise announcement of Prime Minister Harold Macmillan's serious illness and impending retirement, the usually stolid Conservative party conference of local constituency organizations began to resemble an inchoate national nominating convention, with all the attendant intrigues, gossipmongering, and deals. The "candidate" whom many considered the most likely successful election performer, Lord Hailsham, was given warm and rousing receptions. The maneuvering became, as in the United States, heated, public, and exaggerated. *The Times* wrote disdainfully: "The atmosphere there is unhealthy. With all the hob-nobbing in hotel rooms, the gossip, and rumours, the conference is resembling an American nomination convention. The Cabinet is said to have one candidate, the Parliamentary party another, and the constituency associations a third."[12] The point worth noting is the ease with which the question of selection came to dominate an assembly of localists who suddenly felt that they might be allowed to have a say in the designation of the next leader. While the 1963 Conservative controversy demonstrated that a swing in the American direction is possible, its denouement was equally revealing: the choice of a new leader fell neither to the party conference nor to the local constituency organizations. After the hyperthyroid interlude of the conference, a "process of consultation," managed by Macmillan from his hospital room, led to the selection of the modest Home.[13]

Important consequences for executive selection flow from such differences in party structure and centralization. Selection in the United States depends on creating from the large number of local-party power centers the confederal alliances necessary to sway the nominating convention. Yet if the fragmentation is greater in the United States, so too is the room for maneuver, both in the number of potential candidates and in their strategies. The very diversity of party groups in the United States provides a combinatorial richness and a range of choice far wider than that produced through the British party structure. One can predict with a probability approaching certainty that the British leader selected will be an experienced party man with long membership in Parliament and a long career of ascent through junior ministerial, ministerial, and cabinet positions. Of the American candidate one can say only that he will be a figure with "some" position of

12. *The Times* (London), Oct. 11, 1963.
13. A full account is given by King, "Britain: The Search for Leadership."

national prominence.[14] Those who seriously enter into contention sometimes lack long party backgrounds, legislative experience, or tenure in a national executive office. The "strategic environment" of both selection and election is a jungle of voting blocs, interest groups, local leaders, money and information resources, and public appeals. Strategies may range from hoping to win by popular acclaim by running first and hardest in primaries to waiting quietly for a deadlocked convention.

The breadth of competition in the American system is indicated by the number of contenders for office. While the United States since 1900 has held fewer national elections than Britain and has experienced longer executive tenure and slightly fewer changes in party leadership, it has had approximately 50 percent more contenders under serious consideration for selection. A review of the limited literature available shows that for the twenty-four British changes in party leadership roughly thirty-six contenders have been considered, while for the twenty-two changes of presidential nominees there have been fifty-five contenders.[15] This is not to claim an innate superiority for the American process; but on the assumption that there is a reservoir of political talent spread throughout the political system, the American selection process casts the net somewhat more widely than the British.[16]

The overall differences may be summarized by saying that the selection process in Britain is an "apprenticeship" system, as contrasted with the "entrepreneurial" system of recruitment in the United States. Apprenticeship may be understood in its usual meaning of "learning a craft," the result of which is gradual advancement into

14. A brief comparison is made in James Douglas, "The Nixon Changeover," *New Society*, Feb. 6, 1969. For one author's difficulty in setting out the U.S. parties' test of a candidate, see Grant McConnell, *The Modern Presidency* (St. Martin's, 1966); on the strategic environment, see Polsby and Wildavsky, *Presidential Elections*.

15. Serious contenders in Britain are counted as those who have received backing for the leadership from some segment of party opinion; in the United States, they are those who have received at least 10 percent of the votes in national conventions or have made significant primary challenges and been eliminated before the convention, such as Willkie in 1944 and Kefauver in 1956.

16. Even when he reaches Parliament, the politician is in a very narrow catchment area. Guttsman, for example, can dismiss in one footnote the M.P.'s chance of becoming prime minister; odds against the M.P.'s getting into the cabinet are, historically, fifteen to one, and the "chance of becoming Prime Minister is so absolutely remote as not to come seriously within the purview of calculable chance for the aspiring politician." W. L. Guttsman, *The British Political Elite* (London: MacGibbon, 1964), pp. 198 and 203.

professional ranks under the watchful eye of established masters. "Entrepreneur" has a rather precise meaning in economics that may also be enlightening in politics: one who creates new combinations in the means of production and credit. The entrepreneur's creativity is characterized by innovative rearrangements and the calling forth of new resources rather than by simple "management" of existing combinations; his is not usually a permanent profession but consists in a temporary ad hoc manipulation of the forces at hand. Although the flux and combinatorial richness of forces in the American selection process suggest the label "entrepreneurial," this is not to say that the entrepreneur is an independent, free-standing capitalist; new combinations may be created, and usually are, by those who are part of an organization and draw upon credit and capital other than their own.[17] The distinction between the apprenticeship and entrepreneurial systems is highlighted by a look at the place of political experience in the two nations' selection processes.

Political Experience and Mobility Patterns

Probably the most common generalization is the claim that the prime ministerial system excels because it requires greater governmental experience in the eventual nominee. Bryce, for example, compared the "natural selection" of the English Parliament with the "artificial selection" of American politics.[18]

There can be no doubt that greater parliamentary experience is required by a nonfederal system of unified executive and legislative powers than by the American system. The British selection process appears "natural" in the sense that it provides for apprenticeship from parliamentary ranks to cabinet office. Of the eighteen British party leaders and twenty-five presidential nominees of this century (through 1972), all the British had had parliamentary experience—a total of 364 years, for an average of 20.2—at the time of their selection, while only eleven presidential nominees had had congressional experience— a total of 109 years, for an average of 9.9. The facile conclusion that

17. The discussion of entrepreneurial activity is of course based on J. A. Schumpeter's *The Theory of Economic Development* (Harvard University Press, 1961), pp. 74 ff. Unlike the economic entrepreneur, however, the political entrepreneur has involved his own "capital" and is necessarily a "risk-bearer."

18. Lord Bryce, *American Commonwealth*, Vol. 1, p. 85.

British leaders have had more experience in government has always
been only a short step away.

Mere membership in Parliament, however, is a poor indicator of
real experience in government, especially in view of the limited legislative role of Parliament in comparison both with its role in earlier
centuries and with the role of Congress in this century. For a more accurate measure of substantive experience in governing, one might
look not at the bare number of years a man has spent in Parliament
but at the government offices he has held; such an analysis shows that
the relation is the opposite of what is usually assumed. Table 1 compares the government experience of presidents and party leaders. A
survey of tenure in offices above the level of parliamentary private
secretary shows that the average experience of British party leaders at
the time of their selection was 8.4 years, with a high of 20 years for
Churchill in 1940 and none for MacDonald in 1924. Rather than being
less experienced, presidential nominees at the time of their selection
had spent an average of 10.2 years in government offices apart from
Congress. (This also disregards Eisenhower's career, which, if not
formally political, was also not without experience in a significant
area of public affairs.) In the postwar period legislative experience
has become as prominent in the United States as in Britain.

The important distinction between the two nations, however, rests
not in the length but in the variety of government experience of designated leaders. Almost without exception, potential prime ministers
have advanced along the single route from junior minister to minister,
from minister to major cabinet figure, but even this rule has not, on
occasion, prevented party leadership, and thus potential national
leadership, from falling on extremely inexperienced men. Mac-
Donald was not the only leader with little experience in national government; Bonar Law had had three years in an executive government
position when he was selected party leader in 1911, and Clement
Attlee had had two years at the time of his selection in 1935.[19] In the
United States, without a direct legislative-executive link, the presidential selection process has brought forth a set of men with an astonishing range of political experience.

19. In both nations, a party in opposition for extended periods may become long removed from government experience. After thirteen years in opposition, the Labour party
in 1964 formed a government of whose members few except Wilson had had previous
high-level experience in government. Similarly, recent Republican administrations have
been short of experienced national politicians.

TABLE I. *Political Experience of U.S. Presidential Nominees and British Party Leaders at Time of Selection*

Number of years

Nominee or party leader	National legislature	National executive office	State or local assembly	State or local executive office	Administrative appointment	Judicial
Presidential nominee						
Theodore Roosevelt	—	2	2	3	6	—
William Jennings Bryan	4	—	—	—	—	—
Alton B. Parker	—	—	—	8	—	16
William H. Taft	—	8	—	—	2	10
Woodrow Wilson	—	—	—	2	—	—
Charles Evans Hughes	—	—	—	3	—	6
Warren G. Harding	6	—	4	2	—	—
James M. Cox	4	—	—	6	—	—
Calvin Coolidge	—	3	5	6	—	4
John W. Davis	2	—	—	—	8	—
Herbert C. Hoover	—	7	—	—	5	—
Alfred E. Smith	—	—	12	8	—	—
Franklin D. Roosevelt	—	7	2	4	—	—
Alfred M. Landon	—	—	—	4	—	—
Wendell L. Willkie	—	—	—	—	—	—
Thomas E. Dewey	—	—	—	8	—	—
Harry S. Truman	10	2	—	—	10	10
Dwight D. Eisenhower	—	—	—	—	—	—
Adlai E. Stevenson	—	4	—	4	6	—
Richard M. Nixon	6	8	—	—	—	—
John F. Kennedy	13	—	—	—	—	—
Barry M. Goldwater	11	—	3	—	—	—
Lyndon B. Johnson	24	3	—	—	2	—
Hubert H. Humphrey	15	4	—	3	3	—
George McGovern	14	2	—	—	—	—
Party leader						
A. J. Balfour	18	6	—	—	—	—
Henry Campbell-Bannerman	32	12	—	—	—	—
H. H. Asquith	18	4	—	—	—	—
David Lloyd George	26	12	—	—	—	—
Austen Chamberlain	30	16	—	—	—	—
Bonar Law	12	4	—	—	—	—
Stanley Baldwin	16	6	—	—	—	—
Ramsay MacDonald	16	—	4	—	—	—
George Lansbury	12	2	16	2	—	—
Neville Chamberlain	18	12	6	2	2	—

TABLE 1 *(continued)*

Nominee or party leader	National legis-lature	National execu-tive office	State or local assem-bly	State or local execu-tive office	Ad-minis-trative appoint-ment	Judicial
Winston Churchill	40	24	—	—	—	—
Clement Attlee	14	2	4	2	—	—
Hugh Gaitskell	10	6	—	—	6	—
Anthony Eden	20	8	—	—	—	—
Harold Macmillan	34	12	—	—	—	—
Alec Douglas-Home	32	14	—	—	—	—
Harold Wilson	18	6	—	—	2	—
Edward Heath	16	10	—	—	—	—

Sources: David Butler and Jennie Freeman, *British Political Facts, 1900–1967* (2d ed. London: Macmillan, 1968); J. N. Kane (ed.), *Facts about the Presidents* (Wilson, 1968).

More than half the presidential nominees have, for example, had some experience in nonelective government office, while in Britain only Neville Chamberlain, Gaitskell, and Harold Wilson meet the criterion. Two-thirds of presidential nominees have had subnational government experience, in contrast with Chamberlain and the three Labour leaders who served on local government councils. Nowhere in Britain is there evidence of anything like the wide catchment area being drawn upon in the United States: governors, administrators, legislators, and the occasional nonprofessional politician. The evidence suggests that those selected for the presidency are not less politically experienced, but that they are less restricted than British leaders to one level—the national—and to one institution—the legislature. One can of course argue that the offices in the two nations are by nature different, and that many of the offices held by presidential nominees cannot be equated with British cabinet posts as sources of political experience. On the other hand, one may rightfully justify subnational political experience as preparation for leadership and point to the parochialism found in the rarefied atmosphere of political capitals. At a time when central government is increasingly criticized for its lack of perspective and responsiveness, alternative career routes and varying political experience are assets to a political system.

The difference in recruitment in apprenticeship and entrepreneur systems is not simply a question of the distinction between ascription and achievement typically used to describe mobility patterns. Neither nation yields more than a few instances of leaders who have been successfully designated by their predecessors; Balfour and Sir Anthony Eden in Britain and William H. Taft and Nixon (1960) in the United States would be the prime examples. More useful is the distinction between sponsored and contested mobility.[20] Roughly speaking, the British apprentice moves upward by ingratiating himself with his guild masters; the American entrepreneur moves through a wide-ranging series of contests against other largely isolated contenders attempting to arrange their own combinations of political resources. For purposes of his own advancement, the apprentice's constituency is largely internal; the scrutineers in his selectorate are his own political superiors in Parliament, while the American entrepreneur looks far more to an outside constituency of disparate party leaders whose self-interest must be mobilized on his behalf. The apprentice's guild operates smoothly by retaining its exclusiveness, but the entrepreneur thrives as his market for potential support becomes more extensive. Thus though the wide-ranging selection process typically serves as a centripetal force in the decentralized American system, it can easily prove centrifugal in a tightly centralized party structure. After the trauma of 1963, the Conservative party was not long in establishing a formal selection procedure, which, as in the Labour party, explicitly lays responsibility on the parliamentary party and seeks to quarantine the disruptive forces of selection.

Selection Criteria and Personality

I have already touched briefly on the question of selection criteria. Although unfortunately there is little direct evidence from which the actual criteria used in either the United States or Britain can be determined, several points stand out. The fact that selection in the British apprenticeship system seeks to preserve rather than to create unity suggests a concern for more cooperative and less openly combative qualities; a capacity not to rock the boat typically takes precedence

20. See, for example, T. Parson and E. Shils (eds.), *Toward a General Theory of Action* (Harvard University Press, 1951); G. A. Almond and J. S. Coleman, *Politics and Developing Areas* (Princeton University Press, 1960); and Ralph H. Turner, "Sponsored and Contest Mobility and the School System," *American Sociological Review*, Vol. 25 (December 1960), p. 855.

over ability to rally the troops. Although individual classifications are disputable, there are certain categories into which recruits can be grouped.[21]

In Great Britain, of eighteen party leaders selected,

• seven, or 39 percent, were strong contenders who won a factional fight (Lloyd George, Baldwin, MacDonald, Gaitskell, Macmillan, Wilson, Heath);
• three, or 17 percent, were compromise candidates between strong candidates (Campbell-Bannerman, Law, Home);
• eight, or 44 percent, emerged without a factional fight (Balfour, Asquith, Austen Chamberlain, Lansbury, Neville Chamberlain, Churchill, Attlee, Eden).

In the United States, of twenty-seven nominations (involving twenty-four different nominees),

• fifteen, or 56 percent, were strong contenders who won a factional fight (Parker, Wilson, Cox, Franklin D. Roosevelt, Willkie, Dewey [1944, 1948], Eisenhower, Stevenson [1952, 1956], Kennedy, Goldwater, Nixon [1968], Humphrey, McGovern);
• two, or 7 percent, were compromise candidates between strong candidates (Harding, Davis);
• six, or 22 percent, emerged without a factional fight (Taft [1908], Hughes, Hoover, Landon, Smith, Nixon [1960]);
• four, or 15 percent, came to office as succeeding vice-presidents (Theodore Roosevelt, Coolidge, Truman, Johnson).

The recruit who emerges "peacefully," or serves as a compromise between factious contenders, appears more frequently in Britain than in the United States.[22] In both nations there is a contemporary tendency toward an increase in the number of selection contests, but

21. The U.S. list excludes Bryan's third nomination and the renomination of elected presidents. British figures are for the Conservative party, 1900–65; the Liberal party, 1900–18; and the Labour party, 1921–65. General histories of the struggles for selection are (for Britain) Lewis Broad, *The Path to Power* (London: Muller, 1965); and (for the United States) Herbert Eaton, *Presidential Timber: A History of Nominating Conventions 1868–1960* (Macmillan, 1964).

22. The significant number of selections that have occurred automatically through succeeding vice-presidents should be noted. Little reliable research has been done on the subject, but it is doubtful that qualifications for the presidency have often played an important part in vice-presidential selection.

Britain has not gone as far in this direction as the United States. The details of the Conservative selection procedure established in February 1965 are revealing in this regard. The first draft plan called for a straight election with ranked preferences, but party leaders objected that this would not encourage the emergence of compromise candidates and would involve selectors in hypothetical choices rather than realistic comparisons. The voting rules eventually decided upon deliberately seek to avoid sharp distinctions and to encourage the emergence of a consensus leader.[23]

A second criterion is the candidate's electoral appeal. One might reasonably hypothesize that different selectors have different criteria, and that the unified national selectorate of Britain will not necessarily have the same touchstones as a conference of localists. In trying to mobilize the self-interest of decentralized power centers, the American entrepreneur has one common coin in which to deal: the electoral aid he can bring to state and local tickets. Local delegates can more reasonably be expected to respond to this appeal than to the claims of a semiexistent presidential party.

In Britain a comparable force is at work in the selection process, regardless of what champions of the more "natural" British ideal may say. Thus during the 1963 selection controversy, the joint chairman of the Conservative party, and many others, backed Lord Hailsham "as the man to win the election."[24] The point is that this admittedly important consideration was only one of the criteria the British guild selectorate could be expected to use. The background against which the apprentice is evaluated includes not only an indefinite future election but also many years' performance as a parliamentary and cabinet colleague. Although a convention in the United States may register the entrepreneur's ability to "deal well" with others, it presumes a great deal on the perspicacity of localists to expect them to judge a

23. Each candidate must indicate on the nomination paper that he is prepared to accept nomination; names of both proposer and seconder remain confidential. The first ballot allows only one choice for each voter, and results in a decision only if the candidate has a majority plus 15 percent over any other candidate. Two to four days are allowed for discussions before the second ballot, on which the candidate must receive an overall majority. If still no decision is reached, a third ballot of the top three candidates of the second ballot is held. Each voter is given two preference votes; the candidate with the lowest number of first preferences is eliminated, his second preferences redistributed among the remaining two candidates, and the majority candidate declared elected.

24. Quoted in Lord Butler's memoirs, *The Art of the Possible* (London: Hamish Hamilton, 1972).

man on his ability to cooperate and "work well" with party colleagues. The multidimensional nature of British criteria was reflected in a comment of the Conservative chief whip in the House of Lords during the 1963 polling of preferences for leader. Lord Montgomery had replied by asking what was wanted, the best prime minister or a man to win the election; to which the chief whip replied matter-of-factly, "We want both."[25]

Perhaps the most frequently cited difference is the part played in the two nations by personal images. Although the deep psychological personality forces at work cannot be probed here, when one notices that more than one-third of the presidents and more than half the prime ministers since the eighteenth century had lost one or both parents before reaching seventeen years,[26] the field for investigation certainly appears fertile. Selection of prime ministers is said to be less personality-oriented than the selection of presidents, in the sense that there is less concentration on the leader's public image, its packaging and marketing. When the hoary arguments are advanced that prime ministers are becoming increasingly like presidents, the discussion typically centers on the growing force of the leader's personality as opposed to the supposedly greater anonymity prevailing in the past.[27]

Again, such distinctions tend to confuse electoral campaign publicity with the more vital preelection selection process. There can be no question that the appeal of a prospective candidate's public image is an important factor in the search for an American presidential nominee. One of the first professional publicity buildups in a selection struggle was given to Wendell Willkie before the 1940 Republican convention—with the now familiar coterie of public relations experts, family magazine profiles, and intimate portraits of the "real" man. This treatment has been used as a tool of persuasion by prospective nominees ever since. Yet compared with the selling job done on behalf of the "Princeton schoolmaster" by Colonel George Harvey of *Harper's Weekly*, and with William Randolph Hearst's efforts to make Alfred M. Landon the "best-loved family man in America," these

25. Quoted in Randolph Churchill, *The Fight for the Tory Leadership* (London: Heinemann, 1964), p. 135.

26. Iremonger, *Fiery Chariot*, Fig. 15; and J. N. Kane (ed.), *Facts about the Presidents* (Wilson, 1968).

27. See, for example, F. W. G. Benemy, *The Elected Monarch* (London: George Harrup, 1965).

later developments amounted to a difference of technique rather than of kind.

Attention to personal images is hardly peculiar to the United States. Butler and Stokes found that although the voters' views of party leaders significantly affected their party choice in the period from 1963 to 1966, attitudes toward the party itself were more important. Yet this did not prevent a general agreement during the 1960s that if a party was to be electorally successful, its leader should be more popular than the opposition party leader and his own party.[28] Thus one of the important factors weakening Home's position among party leaders in 1965, and strengthening Wilson's among his own supporters, was Home's consistently low public-image rating. The last poll before Home's resignation showed him trailing Wilson in every favorable characteristic about which opinions were asked ("tough, sincere, straightforward, progressive"). Even more disturbing was the fact that among Conservative supporters Home badly trailed Wilson's ratings for toughness, being in touch with ordinary people, speaking ability, and capacity to deal with the unions. Six months after succeeding Home, Edward Heath was still trailing Wilson among the general population, but among Conservative supporters was rated second only in his capacity to deal with the unions.[29]

If anything, the monopoly of Parliament as the locus within which British selection takes place ensures that personal acceptability will play a greater part than in the United States; the difference is that while in the open American market attention will be directed at second hand to the entrepreneur as a popular product, the Westminster guild will turn more directly to the candidate's personal qualities as a colleague. In the hothouse atmosphere of Parliament, assessments of the working relationships established over the decades are inescapable. The result in Britain is likely to be an extremely intimate and pervasive attention to the nuances of personality in a selection process aiming to preserve unity. Nor should one confuse a new technology for making this assessment, such as polls, with the fact that such assessments have always been made. The Conservative party in 1911 chose as its leader the little-known Bonar Law, rather than either of

28. D. E. Butler and Donald Stokes, *Political Change in Britain* (London: Macmillan, 1969), pp. 383–88; and Richard Hodder-Williams, *Public Opinion Polls and British Politics* (London: Routledge and Kegan Paul, 1970), p. 91.

29. National Opinion Polls, July 1965 and January 1966.

the two leading and more illustrious contenders, Austen Chamberlain and Walter Long, because Long and Chamberlain so detested each other that they threatened to split the party in a fight for the leadership. Chamberlain summed up the feeling when he said of Long, "I made a step toward him and had it on my lips to tell him he was a cad and to slap him across the face."[30] In comparison with the "pompous," "vain," and "weak" Chamberlain, and the verbose and impetuous Long—and these were the terms of analysis used at the time—Bonar Law was characterized as firm, modest, and straightforward. In the end, rather than give ascendancy to an archenemy, Long and Chamberlain both withdrew in Law's favor.[31]

For much the same reason, Baldwin was chosen as leader in 1923 over the much more formally qualified Lord Curzon. According to one close observer, this selection, now widely given as an example of the disqualification of peers from the leadership, was in fact "made mainly on the issue of the personal acceptability of the two candidates."[32] Compared to the brilliant, experienced, but also imperious and arrogant Curzon, Baldwin was a modest but agreeable colleague to promote.

The cases could be multiplied at length—William Harcourt, Lloyd George, Macmillan, Herbert Morrison, Attlee, George Brown, and others providing examples of the strong part played by intimate assessments of personal images. In the United States, the political entrepreneur is relatively free to trade in varying personal images with slightly known local leaders; the British apprentice depends directly on the continued esteem and respect of that small group for and with whom he is serving his apprenticeship. This in turn raises the question of how democratic and open the two systems are.

---

30. Quoted in Robert Blake, *The Unknown Prime Minister* (London: Eyre and Spottiswoode, 1955), p. 78.

31. Sir Charles Petrie, *Walter Long and His Times* (London: Hutchinson. 1936), pp. 170 ff.; Sir Austen Chamberlain, *Politics from the Inside* (London: Cassell, 1936), pp. 345, 373, 387–89; and Blake, *Unknown Prime Minister*, Chap. 4.

32. Leopold Amery, *Thoughts on the Constitution* (Oxford University Press, 1948), p. 22. On Curzon's personality see Harold Nicolson, *Curzon: The Last Phase* (Houghton Mifflin, 1934), Chap. 1. For similar incidents, see Lord Kilmur, *Political Adventure* (London: Weidenfeld and Nicolson, 1964), p. 286. An admittedly biased source described the exclusion of Butler in 1957 as "the most squalid political maneuver that I have ever been aware of." Lord Lambton, quoted in Anthony Sampson, *Macmillan: A Study in Ambiguity* (London: Allen Lane, 1967), p. 124.

Public Participation

There has been much discussion in Britain and the United States of the degree of democratic openness in the two selection processes. The more public nature of selection in the American system is often considered a counter to its admitted disadvantages, while the lack of public participation in Britain is the one drawback commonly cited in the British system.[33] There is, of course, an unjustified inferential leap in the suggestion that the less public process is necessarily the less democratic; the essential issue is the extent to which public participation effectively enters into the selection of presidential and prime-ministerial candidates.

Evidence of a sort is provided by the proportion of contested selections in each country, on the assumption that a contest is more likely to be amenable to outside public influences than selection by some form of prior understanding in the selectorate. By this standard, the British in fact appear more openly competitive, for while about one-half of American convention selections have gone uncontested, only about one-third of the eighteen British selections discussed in this study have occurred without a plurality of "candidates" appealing to various elements of the party. This difference is explained of course by the large number of incumbent presidents renominated, without which the proportion of uncontested selections in the United States drops to 23 percent. One might in fact say that in such cases "selection" is a misnomer for the perfunctory formalities of renomination wrought by the regular election cycle. Still, the near certainty during this century of an incumbent president's renomination should not be neglected by advocates of popular participation.

There are, to be sure, no statistics on the numbers of people consulted on changes of leadership in each country, but if one counts the number who indicate a preference through the medium of American primaries, British experience clearly offers nothing comparable. During this century the linkage between election campaigns and the selection process has been further strengthened by the incorporation of preelection elections, in the form of primaries, into the actual selection process.

Again, one must beware of stereotypes, and of the facile conclusion

33. Louis Koenig, *The Chief Executive* (Harcourt, Brace, 1964); see esp. Chap. 15.

that the use of presidential primaries in the United States automatically ensures a more "democratic" selection process. While the direct public impact in Britain is minimal, there is also little evidence that the *direct* public voice in the United States has been successful in influencing the selection of candidates. In fact, American candidates who have relied largely on a strategy of primaries and popular acclaim have been notably unsuccessful in finally gaining nomination; more often than not, those most successful in primaries have not been selected. In 1912, for example, Theodore Roosevelt won 221 of the 388 delegates elected by primaries to the Republican convention, and Robert M. La Follette won substantially more states than Taft—all to no avail. On the Democratic side in the same year, Champ Clark had won as many contests as Woodrow Wilson and had 413 delegates to Wilson's 274 by the start of the convention. If primaries had been a guide, the 1920 Republican nomination would have gone to Leonard Wood or Hiram Johnson, not to Warren G. Harding, and the Democratic nomination in 1924 to William G. McAdoo, not to John W. Davis. In 1932, primary victories by former Senator Joseph I. France of Maryland demonstrated that almost any Republican leader was more popular than Hoover, but Hoover was renominated. Even Franklin D. Roosevelt in 1932, despite a string of primary victories, went on to demonstrate serious popular weakness by losing such weathervane states as Massachusetts and Pennsylvania to Smith, and California to Garner (by 216,000 votes to 170,000). In 1948, Harold E. Stassen assembled impressive primary victories over Thomas E. Dewey in Wisconsin, Nebraska, and Pennsylvania, and lost the supposedly decisive Oregon primary to Dewey by only 9,000 votes. Robert A. Taft in 1952 won five primaries to Eisenhower's four, taking Illinois by seven to one and winning 458 delegates to Eisenhower's 406 by convention time. In 1952, Estes Kefauver beat President Harry S. Truman in the New Hampshire primary, won eight other primaries, and had the largest number of pledged delegates at the convention's opening, only to lose to Stevenson. In the 1964 struggle for the Republican nomination, Henry Cabot Lodge won in New Hampshire; Nelson Rockefeller beat Barry Goldwater by almost two to one in Oregon and fell only 3.2 percent of the vote behind Goldwater in California. Nor was there very much positive direction from the polls: Goldwater was the first choice among Republican voters during most of 1963, trailed Lodge and Nixon during early 1964, and was virtually even with Nixon and Scranton as the convention assembled. Polls during much of 1968 showed that Rockefeller was clearly preferred to the eventual nominee, Nixon.

While presidential primaries may not be the "eyewash" President Truman called them in 1952, it nevertheless seems that their direct influence on the selection process can easily be overestimated. Their importance has lain not in their direct linkage to selection but in their indirect effect on those making the selection. Campaigns that have most successfully used primaries in the selection process, such as Roosevelt's in 1932 and John F. Kennedy's in 1960, have not relied on the results of the primaries as such, but have used their results as indicators of popular preferences in order to influence party selectors. Arnold Rose, for example, contrasts Kennedy's strategy of appealing to the general public, as an instrumental device in seeking the support of party delegates, with Lyndon B. Johnson's and Stuart Symington's use of the "British technique" of endorsement by party elders.[34] Obviously, the importance of the West Virginia primary lay not in the state's convention votes but in its demonstration to party leaders that Kennedy could overcome the religious issue.

If such is the case, it is difficult to substantiate the claim that the *indirect* role of the public is any more decisive in the United States than in Britain. By-elections have always served such purposes, and, particularly within the last twenty years, public opinion polls have occasionally come into play in the deliberations surrounding the choice of new leaders—even in the supposedly undemocratic Conservative party. In the spring of 1931, Baldwin came under heavy pressure to resign the Conservative leadership because of the reports coming in from the Principal Agent concerning opinion at Central Office and among party officials; most other agents were also reporting that poor feeling about the leadership prevailed locally. Baldwin fought back through the indirect use of public preferences. At first he considered standing for an election himself, but eventually instead gave explicit backing to Alfred Duff Cooper in the St. George's by-election; success in this test of public approval was decisive in Baldwin's retaining the leadership.[35]

The events surrounding Home's resignation as Conservative leader

34. Arnold Rose, *The Power Structure* (Oxford University Press, 1967).
35. See K. Middlemas and J. Barnes, *Baldwin* (London: Weidenfeld and Nicholson, 1969), Chap. 22.

in July 1965 show a limited but similar indirect responsiveness to public opinion. After the 1964 Conservative election defeat, reports from the constituencies showed a recurring and rising tide of local discontent. In March 1965, an unexpected Conservative by-election defeat at Roxburgh intensified the discontent and, since it took place next door to Home's own constituency, was interpreted as a blow to his leadership. A further report from National Opinion Polls on July 15 showed Labour's lead increasing from 2.0 percent to 4.6 percent and Home trailing even further behind Wilson than before. Amid mounting reports of discontent, and "shaken by the opinion poll," Home retired to his country estate and emerged a few days later to announce his resignation as leader.[36]

Although indicators of public preference are a limited but important negative force, it is difficult to argue that in either nation they have been decisive positive forces, at least not in the sense of clearly designating the candidate to be selected. We have already referred to the ambiguous or disregarded signals of public preference in America; much the same thing happens in Britain. After Home's resignation, the Conservative leadership went to Heath, who until his selection had at best been a distant second choice for succession of both the general public and Conservative supporters.[37] After his selection, the polls shifted back to show that Heath was preferred. The same sequence occurred in the Labour party during 1963 on the occasion of Harold Wilson's selection as successor to Gaitskell. In January, Wilson trailed George Brown with both the general public and Labour supporters; one month later, more than four-fifths of both groups approved of Wilson's selection.[38] In the face of such mercurial public guidance, it is not surprising that even those most concerned with the election potential of recruits should hesitate to base their judgments directly on the latest poll or primary result.

Thus although there is no reliable evidence to demonstrate how far by-elections, polls, and constituency reports have influenced leaders

36. D. E. Butler and Anthony King, *The British General Election of 1966* (London: Macmillan, 1966), p. 51; for accounts of the events, see "The Birth of a Campaign to Oust Sir Alec," *The Times* (London), April 5, 1965; "Insight on the Tory Leadership," *Sunday Times* (London), July 25, 1965; and Alan Watkins, "How Heath Pulled It Off," *Spectator*, July 30, 1965.

37. See Gallup polls for January 15–20, 1965; March 5–9, 1965; and National Opinion Polls, February 1965 and July 25–26, 1965.

38. National Opinion Polls, January and February 1963.

in Britain, it would seem rash to suppose that politicians' indirect assessments of public preference have been any more important in the geographically patchy and intermittent American primary system than in Britain. Because of the direct tie between selection and election, indicators of public preference will be given greater publicity by prospective candidates in the United States. But to say that British deliberations are less publicized is not necessarily to say they are less sensitive to public opinion, and there is even less justification in extending this to say that they are therefore less democratic. The distinctiveness of the American selection process lies in the variety and manipulability of such public soundings. As a by-product of the decentralization and diversity of the American selectorate, political entrepreneurs find countless opportunities to mobilize or manufacture indications of indirect public impact. What shall be the standard of public preferences—performance in Congress? Governorship? The last margin of victory in the candidate's own constituency? Primary victories in certain parts of the nation? State party convention decisions? Public opinion polls? In a typical contest, all these and other indicators will be cited against each other. By contrast, British assessment of public preference takes on a highly coherent and aggregated form at the hands of a limited number of persons in the party organization assumed to be knowledgeable.

Behavioral Links

I have tried to show that through a comparative approach much of what might otherwise be thought unique in American presidential selection can also be found in Britain. The predominant place of the party as the group within which claims to leadership are advanced, the insulation of selection from direct public influence (but also with considerable indirect influence through anticipation of public response), the extended government experience required of nominees, the attention paid to questions of personal image—all these phenomena may be observed in both countries. At the same time, American selection has been distinguished by its very intimate ties to electoral criteria, by the incoherence of party groups, by its extended areas of recruitment, and by the resulting increase in room for maneuver, coalition-building, and publicity appeals. One of these processes has been described as an "apprenticeship," the other as "entrepreneurial."

This is, however, only the point of departure for any discussion of executive selection in the two countries. Probably the greatest lack at present in the study of executive recruitment is the failure to establish any reliable connection between different selection processes and the winners' subsequent behavior in office. The question is of course not the effect of idiosyncratic recruitment experiences on a particular officeholder, but rather the possible consistent effects of broadly differing selection processes.

The current neglect of this question is curious, in view of its centrality in traditional democratic thought in the last several centuries. Both proponents and opponents of the extension of democratic procedures have identified selection with election and have usually assumed both to have a direct effect on output: the leader was expected to implement the wishes of those who chose him for office; he would at least act consistently with those wishes, and at a very minimum would anticipate what those wishes would be. Since experience has shown that these easy democratic assumptions do not work out as neatly as had been supposed, the hope of identifying behavioral linkages between selection and performance in office seems to have been largely abandoned.

Clearly, the difficulties in tracing such linkages are formidable. Considering the wide varieties of leadership manifest in each of the two countries during this century, one would be justified in concluding that variations in behavior are greater within than between the two political milieus. Yet the imprecision and indeterminacy of the search for more general causal links should not excuse the neglect of an issue of such obvious importance.

Behavior in office is a complex variable that can be disentangled in a variety of ways. One aspect of behavior reflects substantive policy preferences; at present, however, there appears no obvious or easily testable connection between such preferences and methods of selection. Perhaps more amenable to analysis is leadership style. The labels "entrepreneurial" and "apprenticeship" should not be taken to imply that learning takes place in one system and not in the other. In both systems, the nature and constraints of the group interaction leading to selection for leadership play a crucial part in socializing the future executive. Erwin Hargrove has hypothesized that "the styles of leadership seen in the chief political executive are usually learned at lower political levels of the political elite. An important socialization process for leaders takes place in the years of ascent to the top."[39] Learning takes place in both entrepreneurial and apprenticeship systems, the difference being in the type of behavior that is rewarded. The challenge, to which I can offer only a preliminary response here, is to specify the kinds of behavior that are rewarded differently in the two systems.

In the first place, one need not accept Bryce's argument about the natural mediocrity of presidents to appreciate that selections in the United States will give relatively heavy weight to characteristics of palpable public appeal. The extremely close correspondence between the criteria for selection and election suggests a bias in favor of men who are thought of, possible superficially, as election winners. British leaders have of course been chosen with an eye to winning elections, and the older view that the constraints imposed on presidential selection lead to selection of nullities is clearly wrong. A significant difference between the entrepreneurial and apprenticeship systems is the greater unpredictability in the behavioral characteristics of presidents. Selection by the American process seems more likely than the British to result in the election of unknown quantities, whose appeal lay in their supposed electoral strength and whose operational character apart from this strength was relatively disregarded. Especially if one accepts the view of a more "personalized" politics in the United States, it is paradoxical that so little will be known of the nominee eventually selected, even by those who have selected him. What is likely to prevail, both before and during the election campaign, is a series of campaign images, carefully assessed, to be sure, but assessed largely in terms of a preoccupation with the forthcoming election.

A more predictable aspect of behavior is the officeholder's response to the constraints and supports of his strategic environment. Although it is unlikely that any presidential or prime-ministerial "type" is evolved by the selection processes, distinctive behavioral dispositions are probably learned on the route to office. Thus the close tie between election and selection suggests that a president will have been conditioned to pay greater attention to public preferences in justifying his actions than a prime minister. Presidential actions will quite probably be more heavily influenced by consideration of whether they will receive immediate public approval, the touchstone that was judged so

39. Erwin C. Hargrove, "Popular Leadership in the Anglo-American Democracies," in Edinger, *Political Leadership*, p. 218.

important in securing selection in the first place. The difference may easily be exaggerated; no British prime minister has ever deliberately sought public disfavor. But a president who knows that the justification for his preeminence rests heavily upon past and expected plebiscitary success, rather than upon apprenticeship among colleagues, must have a more consistently populist perspective than is likely in prime ministers.

From the nature of the group struggle, it also seems reasonable to suppose that upon entering office a president will have learned an individualistic rather than a prime minister's collegial perspective. The future prime minister has advanced through a muted, nonzero-sum struggle requiring cooperation with sponsors and colleagues; his fate has been inextricably tied to the collective fate of his selectorate, both as government and opposition. Even if the working political life of the future president has been spent in an interdependent group, his selection for the highest office has probably taken place through a zero-sum struggle with other political entrepreneurs trying to mold winning alliances in a disorganized party. The formal constitutional separation of powers is of course consistent with such a view, but even without this separation, the president would have been predisposed by the real-life recruitment struggle to view his actions and those of his staff as independently justified and legitimate rather than as requiring agreement of his colleagues or party. This perspective goes beyond a simple lack of rapport with Congress, which, without the British parliamentary locus of selection, is natural enough. By the time of his arrival in office, a president is likely to have undergone one of the most unusual learning experiences in the world. He is likely to have absorbed not simply an individualistic but a tribunal perspective—a psychological terrain in which the outstanding features are the all-powerful but indeterminate people and himself as their chosen leader. This is a strange and heroic world, an illimitable, misty sea on which the president is the sole argonaut. As he enters the White House, the new president has already gone a long way toward learning to be "the loneliest man in the world."

By the same token, the president, unlike the prime minister, will have learned to seek assistance from fairly wide circles of political and social leadership rather than exclusively from the legislative and civil service fields. Yet no matter what staff is assembled in the executive branch, they will be seen most readily as individualistic cadres rather than as a working collectivity. While the prime minister is more limited in his top appointments, he will be surer of having a united group which is able to work together. In the United States, staff allegiance, responsibility, and consequently fates will be individual and contingent upon electoral success. While the president will need be much less concerned than the prime minister with maneuverings in cabinet, legislature, and party, he can for this reason allow himself to be isolated from these vital sources of feedback. As long as he is in office, his party's selection process is virtually terminated; there remains only his towering position and the vague, all-powerful voting public. By the same token, the defeated candidate's army of supporters fades away; he is not a party leader in the British sense of the term; no shadow-cabinet position unites the leader and his colleagues in the new tasks of opposition. Nothing remains. If the president is the loneliest officeholder in the world, the defeated candidate is the world's loneliest nonofficeholder. The successful candidate remains supreme with his associates, but they are his placemen and beyond the court there is little but the election and the nothingness attached to electoral defeat.

The behavioral inheritances from the selection process suggest no absolute standards on which to judge one nation's recruitment procedure "better" than that of another. At a minimum, however, the requirements for selection should be consistent with the requirements of the office. Given the separation of national institutions, the federal diffusions of power, and the regularly recurring congressional and presidential elections, entrepreneurial lessons are probably as appropriate and important to the president of the United States as are acquired collegial skills to the British prime minister. There is much force in the argument that the selection process socializes the future president in ways in which he would in any event be socialized by the constitutional structure of the nation. Yet this should not obscure the fact that selection in the United States is heavily weighted toward electoral rather than other performance criteria. In Britain the successful apprentice has advanced through exactly the working relationships by which he will one day govern; this may not always help win the election, but it will help him in office. In the United States, the party coalition that was sufficient to win nomination and the electoral coalition that was sufficient to win office will not necessarily be sufficient to govern. If the president's problems involved simply building rather than also using a winning coalition, if the likelihood of popular acclaim were a touchstone of sensible action, if policy were susceptible to single, neat, decisive outcomes, then electoral entrepreneurship would suffice. But life is not that simple. The temporary, if dramatic, creation of unity in American presidential selection offers little guidance for the preservation of unity and even less preparation on how to work through the confederation of departments within the executive itself. By fleetingly raising expectations concerning the leader's unifying and governing powers, the selection process in the United States may actually make credible government all the more difficult. In popular conception the president is selected to reign in supreme command; in reality he will often be pulling strings and hoping that something somewhere will jump.

Chapter Three

Party and Convention Organization and Leadership Selection in Canada and the United States

CARL BAAR *and* ELLEN BAAR

IN 1967 and 1968, the Progressive Conservative and the Liberal parties in Canada each held national conventions for the primary purpose of selecting leaders for their parties in the federal House of Commons. Canada is "the only country in the British parliamentary tradition" whose major parties use national conventions for leadership selection.[1] The convention tradition, half a century old, is frequently criticized by Canadians as an incursion of the U.S. style of politics in a setting of parliamentary cabinet government. It is argued that selection of leadership by national convention rather than by parliamentary caucus is incompatible with parliamentary government. For example,

The Australian cabinet and senate recently quietly selected a new leader. They were the only people truly qualified to judge the man they consider responsible enough to take this onerous position.

The ballyhoo we have here of a leadership convention closely follows the American example of more and more people, more and more noise, but little real business.

Note. The authors wish to thank Victor Hoar, director of the Committee of Canadian-American Studies at Michigan State University, and Theodore Lowi for their encouragement and assistance; and Lawrence LeDuc, Jr., Hugh Thorburn, John Courtney, and Ralph Goldman for their comments and criticisms of an earlier draft of this paper prepared for delivery at the 1970 annual meeting of the American Political Science Association, Los Angeles, California. A faculty research grant from the University of British Columbia allowed Carl Baar to attend the 1968 Liberal convention as an official observer.
 1. D. V. Smiley, "The National Party Leadership Convention in Canada: A Preliminary Analysis," *Canadian Journal of Political Science*, Vol. 1 (December 1968), p. 373.

What could be more confusing than a number of seekers for political leadership, of whom the delegates really know very little personally, trying to sell themselves at a political convention, their qualifications being that they look good, or speak well, dress well, etc., and spend thousands of dollars on propaganda?

Only the men who work closely with these elected representatives really know who is best respected and qualified to lead the country.

Why don't we in Canada continue with this advantage of the parliamentary system and have our leaders elected in a dignified manner by those best qualified to judge?

Let us send the balloons and animals south of our border where, although they seem to have a lot of fun, they have a lot to learn about stable government.[2]

In Canada, as in the United States, the use of national conventions for leadership selection arose as a result of the inability of intragovernmental party apparatus—the parliamentary caucus and the congressional caucus—to reflect the variety of interests within large, diverse federal polities. In both countries national conventions arose as extragovernmental institutions for leadership selection when the earlier methods no longer reflected the political base required for a successful national party. The first Canadian leadership convention was held by the Liberal party in 1919, when, as a result of conflicts over Canadian participation in World War I, the Liberal caucus in Parliament was reduced to eighty-two members, sixty-two of whom were from the Province of Quebec. Extragovernmental leadership selection was essential to reestablish the Liberals as a national party. The convention therefore had to represent the nation rather than the limited segment of the nation supporting the party at that time. In the United States, national party conventions were first used just before the election of 1832, a reflection of the breakdown of the congressional caucus system in the election of 1824, the accession to power of Andrew Jackson, Jackson's effort to replace Vice-President John Calhoun with Secretary of State Martin Van Buren, and the efforts of the short-lived Anti-Masonic party to appeal "to voters in areas where the party had not yet won any elections."[3]

Since political parties in both Canada and the United States use na-

2. "Voice of the People," *Toronto Daily Star*, Jan. 13, 1968.
3. Paul T. David, Ralph M. Goldman, and Richard C. Bain, *The Politics of National Party Conventions* (Brookings Institution, 1960), pp. 15–19.

tional conventions to broaden participation in the leadership selection process, there are many outward similarities between the conventions. In both systems, the conventions have evolved into large bodies which function as decision-making and decision-legitimating organizations and as giant campaign rallies. Consider two recent Canadian leadership conventions. In September 1967, more than 2,000 delegates to the Progressive Conservative convention met for five days at Maple Leaf Gardens in Toronto. Robert L. Stanfield, premier of Nova Scotia, was elected leader over Duff Roblin, premier of Manitoba, and two members of the federal Parliament and former cabinet ministers, E. Davie Fulton of British Columbia and George Hees of Ontario. In April 1968, more than 2,000 delegates to the Liberal convention met for three days at the Civic Centre in Ottawa. Pierre Trudeau of Quebec, federal attorney general and minister of justice, was elected leader over Robert Winters of Ontario, who had served almost eleven years in the federal cabinet. Three other ministers, Paul Hellyer, John Turner, and Paul Martin, also received widespread delegate support.[4]

The two Canadian leadership conventions also displayed outward contrasts with recent American national party conventions. The Conservative leadership race had eleven contenders, eight of whom received more than 120 delegate votes, and took five ballots to decide. The Liberal convention featured nine candidates, eight of whom received more than 100 delegate votes, and took four ballots to decide. Not since the Republicans nominated Wendell Willkie on six ballots in 1940 has either party in the United States gone beyond three ballots to pick a presidential candidate. Furthermore, one of the Conservative leadership candidates was the incumbent leader, former Prime Minister John G. Diefenbaker, who finished fifth on the first ballot with only 12 percent of the votes cast. And the two Liberal leadership candidates with longest established ties with party officials, Martin and Hellyer, received a combined total of 25.7 percent of the votes

4. In April 1971, the Canadian New Democratic party (NDP) held a national leadership convention for four days in Ottawa. The 1,700 delegates elected Ontario M.P. David Lewis as party leader on the fourth ballot. A number of characteristics of NDP party and convention organization differed from those of the Liberals and Conservatives, although similar convention voting rules made the dynamics of leadership selection quite similar. Since this paper was drafted before the NDP convention, statements on Canadian practice apply to the conventions of the Liberals and Conservatives, while the analysis of the NDP, an important task, has been left to a separate paper.

cast, and withdrew on the first and third ballots respectively. Such candidacies could expect more substantial support and a greater likelihood of success in Democratic and Republican conventions in the United States.[5]

Further exploration of Canadian and American national party conventions will indicate that, in a number of important respects, the conventions of Canada's two largest parties are strikingly similar to each other and different from their counterparts in the United States. In both systems, the convention has enabled extension of the national party's support within the existing organizational structure. Therefore, differences in the organization and procedure of Canadian and American political conventions can be analyzed as a product of differences in the organizational framework of Canadian and American political parties; and the interaction between party and convention organization in the two countries can be related to cross-national differences in patterns of leadership selection.

To support the argument and develop the analysis proposed here, this paper will focus on the organizational characteristics of party conventions, rather than on the perceptions of individual delegates and party leaders, in order to generate and evaluate propositions about the structure and operation of national party leadership conventions in Canada and the United States. Succeeding sections of this chapter will focus on delegate apportionment, voting rules, and the degree of subgroup organization in the party conventions of the two countries. In each case, cross-national differences will be analyzed as a product of differences between the party systems, which in turn reinforce these differences and affect the process of national leadership selection.

5. For example, the parallels to Diefenbaker's defeat are few. Since 1896 the only former Democratic standard bearers whose candidacies were rejected in convention were Hubert Humphrey (1972), Adlai Stevenson (1960), Alfred E. Smith (1932), and James M. Cox (1924), none of whom had ever served as chief of state. On the other hand, William Jennings Bryan twice sought and received renomination (1900 and 1908), Stevenson won renomination in 1956, and every incumbent Democratic president who sought either nomination (Harry S. Truman in 1948 and Lyndon B. Johnson in 1964) or renomination (Woodrow Wilson in 1916, Franklin D. Roosevelt in 1936, 1940, and 1944) were successful. On the Republican side, the only former standard bearer rejected in convention was Theodore Roosevelt in 1912, when he challenged an incumbent Republican president. Losing candidates awarded renomination include Thomas E. Dewey (1948) and Richard M. Nixon (1968). For complete convention voting records see Richard C. Bain and Judith H. Parris, *Convention Decisions and Voting Records* (2d ed., Brookings Institution, 1973), App. C.

Delegate Apportionment

The apportionment of delegates to the various party conventions is determined in each case by a formula enunciated by the party's national committee. The apportionment formulas that applied in 1967 and 1968 are presented in the appendix; some of their effects on delegate composition are presented in Table 1.

Since party conventions in both countries seek, among other things, to extend or maintain a base of national party support, all four parties showed a tendency to apportion delegates by population rather than in proportion to party voters. Both Liberals and Conservatives allocated an equal number of delegates to each constituency association without

TABLE 1. *Vote Apportionment in Canadian and American Political Conventions, as Established by National Party Committees*

| | Party[a] | | | |
| | Canada | | United States | |
Source of designation[b]	Progressive Conservative (1967)	Liberal (1968)	Democratic (1968)[c]	Republican (1968)
Ex officio by virtue of public office or candidacy for public office	340	502	—	—
National	(150)	(344)	—	—
State/provincial	(190)	(158)	—	—
Ex officio by virtue of party office	201	256	102	—
State/provincial/territorial party organization	356	—	2,520	1,333
Constituency organizations of federal legislative district level	1,320	1,584	—	—
Other party organizations (e.g., youth, women's, and student associations)	212	130	—	
Total	2,429	2,472	2,622	1,333
Percentage in largest category	54.3	64.0	96.1	100.0

a. The appendix to this chapter contains the apportionment formulas by party.

b. Omitted from this table are the requirements of Canadian parties that at least one delegate from each of the 264 constituency organizations be a woman, and at least one a person under thirty; and any requirements of American state parties that delegates be selected by county or district caucuses, or apportioned ex officio to state party officials or officeholders. Certain Canadian delegates are ex officio by virtue of holding more than one office. For purposes of this table, such delegates are counted only once.

c. Figures for the Democratic party represent votes, not delegates. In 1968, 3,084 delegates cast 2,622 votes.

regard for the percentage of popular vote given to the party in the previous federal election. The Liberals not only named their 131 members of Parliament as delegates ex officio, but gave the same status to 126 candidates defeated in the previous federal election, no matter how few votes they may have received.[6] The Conservatives apportioned delegates-at-large to provinces without regard for the number of Conservative seats held in the province. The Republican party allocated delegates partly in relation to votes cast in previous elections, but did so through the use of two congressional district cutoff points which would not tend to differentiate sharply between states on the basis of relative party strength. The Democratic party gave the greatest weight to party voting, but its apportionment formula allocated 1,614 delegates (62 percent of all delegates) to the states on the basis of electoral college vote rather than the popular votes received by party candidates.[7] Although the apportionment by population is somewhat skewed toward the smaller states and provinces in all four parties, all use delegate-apportionment formulas to favor leaders with national appeal.

The basic difference between the delegate-apportionment formulas in Canada and in the United States is that the Canadian formulas provide direct representation for public officials, party officials, constituency organizations, and interests that might otherwise be underrepresented in these three categories. On the other hand, American formulas provide direct representation for state delegations alone. Representation of the segments of American parties that have traditionally been underrepresented—women, youth, minorities—has been and continues to be indirect rather than direct. The increased representation of these groups in 1972 was achieved not by having the national parties allocate a percentage of delegate positions to women, youth, and minorities, but by urging the state parties to assure them

6. The Progressive Conservatives accredited defeated candidates for Parliament in the 1929 and 1938 conventions but have not done so since then. At the 1967 convention, candidates nominated for the forthcoming election were named delegates ex officio, but apparently only eight persons were accredited on that basis. See Michael Vineberg, "The Progressive Conservative Leadership Convention of 1967" (Master's thesis, McGill University, 1968), pp. 33–34 and App. D. The authors wish to thank Brian Armstrong of the Progressive Conservative party's Ottawa office for bringing Vineberg's thesis to their attention.

7. For the apportionment formula used by the Democrats and Republicans in 1972, see the appendix to this chapter.

adequate representation. The formulas in the United States reflect an attempt to build a national party by involving state party organizations in leadership selection, those in Canada an attempt to build a national party by involving representatives of all segments of the party organization in the process of leadership selection. Because leadership conventions in Canada are designed to represent all segments of the party organization rather than provincial parties alone, the national party committees in Canada take a more active role in defining the composition of convention delegates. Both the Liberal and Conservative national party committees provided for methods of delegate selection that assured representation of both federal and provincial party organizations, all federal candidates, elected federal officials, and a substantial number of elected provincial officials. Representation was granted directly to student party groups on university campuses. Representation of youth and women was assured through the requirement that each of the 264 federal constituencies include one person from each category. In the United States, the Democratic and Republican National Committees determined the allocation of votes among state parties, but representation of federal party associations, federal candidates and elected officials, youth, women, or college students was left to the discretion of the state party organizations. In 1972, this discretion was limited by the encouragement of state delegations to take affirmative action to ensure that underrepresented segments of the party be represented on state delegations.

As a result of these differences in delegate apportionment, Canadian leadership conventions show a much closer articulation with elected officials than do the party conventions in the United States. All federal members of Parliament were designated ex officio delegates by their respective parties.[8] In the United States, senators and representatives do not serve as delegates unless chosen by state parties. The resulting participation in recent national party conventions is shown in Table 2, which indicates that while a substantial percentage of senators from both parties serve as convention delegates, a much smaller percentage of representatives do so. For both houses, the Democratic percentage has been considerably higher than the Re-

8. Both Liberals and Conservatives have designated federal M.P.s and senators delegates ex officio from their first leadership conventions. See Vineberg, "Progressive Conservative Convention," pp. 33–34.

TABLE 2. *U.S. Senators and Representatives Serving as Delegates to Selected National Party Conventions, 1948–72*
Percent

Year	Senators serving as delegates		Representatives serving as delegates	
	Democrat	Republican	Democrat	Republican
1948	57.8	41.2	15.1	5.3
1952	76.0	40.0	18.1	7.5
1956	69.4	53.2	28.1	11.9
1964	n.a.	48.5	n.a.	23.0
1968	63.5	58.3	35.1	32.5
1972	30.9	48.9	14.1	27.5

Sources: Adapted from Paul T. David, Ralph M. Goldman, and Richard C. Bain, *The Politics of National Party Conventions* (Brookings Institution, 1960), pp. 345, 347. Republican figures for 1964 and 1968 were obtained from the *Permanent Roll of Delegates and Alternate Delegates to Republican National Convention* for those years. Democratic figures for 1968 were supplied by Robert W. Nelson, staff director of his party's Commission on Party Structure and Delegate Selection, in a letter of March 10, 1971. Democratic figures for 1972 were supplied by the Democratic National Committee. Republican figures for 1972 are based on data compiled in early August by the National Republican Congressional Committee. Alternate delegates are not included in the table.

n.a. Not available.

publican.[9] Of both parties, a much smaller percentage are named delegates than under the ex officio procedure in Canada.

It might be thought that the higher proportion of federal legislative participants in Canadian conventions is a product of the more recent emergence of the convention system. If this proposition were valid, however, early national party conventions in the United States should include a higher percentage of federal legislators in the years shortly after 1832, when the convention replaced the caucus; such is not the case. In 1848, the earliest year for which David, Goldman, and Bain have the data, 27.3 percent of the Democratic senators were delegates (9 of out 33), and 4.5 percent of the Whig senators (1 out of 22). In the House, 13.0 percent of the Democrats (17 out of 131) and 7.7 percent of the Whigs (9 of 117) served as delegates to their respective party conventions.[10] The two house totals constitute a smaller percentage than in any of the modern conventions shown in Table 2. The 1848 figures indicate that from the beginning delegate apportionment reflected a distribution of power within American political parties in

9. This was not true, however, in 1972. See Table 2.
10. David, Goldman, and Bain, *Politics of Conventions*, pp. 345, 347

which state party organizations were the primary decision makers. In other words, the higher rate of federal legislative participation in Canada reflects differences in the strength of the legislative wing within the party structure. The data indicate both the greater strength of the legislative wing of the party organization, which one would expect in a parliamentary system, and the growing strength of the legislative wing of the party in the United States.[11]

Earmarked as youth and student delegates at the Liberal conventions in Canada were 264 constituency delegates, 130 university club delegates, and 54 delegates from the executives of youth and university organizations—448 in all, 18 percent of the eligible delegates. The Progressive Conservative party followed roughly similar guidelines for youth and student delegates.[12] In each case, the percentage was a minimum, and did not reflect the possibility that other delegate positions were occupied by participants under thirty years of age. One postconvention survey of Liberal delegates indicated that 20.8 percent were under thirty,[13] another indicated that 12 percent were under twenty-five and 19 percent between twenty-five and thirty-five.[14]

In the United States, representation of young party members continued to be at the discretion of the state party. Two mail questionnaire studies of the age distribution of delegates to the 1948 national conventions indicates that approximately 1 percent of the Democratic delegates and fewer than 2 percent of the Republican delegates were

11. It is too early to determine whether the 1972 delegate figures represent a temporary effect of attempts to increase the representativeness of state delegations or whether they reflect a longer-run decline in the strength of the legislative party.

12. The Progressive Conservatives designated 264 youth delegates at the constituency level, 116 student and 48 youth delegates-at-large, and 18 youths and students from the executives of their associations—a total of 446. See Vineberg, "Progressive Conservative Convention," p. 29.

13. From correspondence with Lawrence LeDuc, Jr. LeDuc's data were gathered from mail questionnaires sent to a random sample of 500 convention delegates (stratified by province) five days after the close of the convention. His response rate was 61 percent (305 delegates). Findings are reported in "Party Decision-Making: Some Empirical Observations on the Leadership Selection Process," *Canadian Journal of Political Science*, Vol. 4 (March 1971), pp. 97–118.

14. C. R. Santos, "Some Collective Characteristics of the Delegates to the 1968 Liberal Party Leadership Convention," *Canadian Journal of Political Science*, Vol. 3 (June 1970), p. 303. Santos' data were gathered from mail questionnaires sent to the 2,396 registered delegates at the convention. His response rate was 57 percent (1,383 delegates). The completed questionnaires were tested for representativeness only with reference to the sex distribution of respondents.

under thirty, while between 4 and 5 percent of the Democratic and 5 percent of the Republican delegates were between thirty and thirty-four years of age.[15] The limited data on the age distribution of delegates to the 1968 national conventions indicate little change over twenty years: the Democrats report that 4 percent of their delegates were under thirty, while the Republican National Committee reports that incomplete information indicates that twenty delegates (1.5 percent) were under thirty and seventy delegates (5.25 percent) were thirty to thirty-five years of age.[16]

By 1972, representation of the young had not been assured through the apportionment formula, but state delegations had been urged to consider the age distribution of convention delegates and to attempt to develop a representative delegation. As a result, 8.7 percent of the 1972 Republican and 21.4 percent of the Democratic delegates were under thirty.[17] It is important to remember, however, that this change was achieved by stressing the need to make state delegations more representative of party supporters within each state. The change was not achieved by adoption of the Canadian practice of providing direct representation for the organized youth and student segments of the party, nor by a national party policy requiring that local constituency organizations select a specified minimal number of delegates under thirty.

In the same way, women delegates to the Canadian conventions were selected through federal and provincial women's organizations, and through each of the 264 constituency organizations. The Liberal party thus ensured that at least 326 women, a minimum of 13 percent of the eligible delegates, would be chosen; the two surveys of Liberal convention delegates showed that almost 20 percent were women.[18] The Conservative party apportionment formula provided for an equivalent minimum. In the United States representation of women had been left totally to the discretion of the state delegation; at the

15. Reported in David, Goldman, and Bain, *Politics of Conventions*, p. 561.
16. For the Democratic data, see *Mandate for Reform: A Report of the Commission on Party Structure and Delegate Selection to the Democratic National Committee* (Washington: DNC, 1970), p. 28. Republican data were supplied by Josephine L. Good, convention director of the Republican National Committee, in a letter of April 23, 1971.
17. Figures taken from *Congressional Quarterly Weekly Report* (Aug. 12, 1972), p. 1998.
18. LeDuc, "Party Decision-Making"; Santos, "Characteristics of Delegates."

1968 conventions, 400 Democrats, or 12.9 percent of the delegates, and 223 Republicans, or 16.7 percent, were women.[19] In 1972, when state delegations were encouraged to be representative of party composition, the degree of representation increased considerably: 30.1 percent of the Republican and 39.9 percent of the Democratic delegates were women.[20] The increase was achieved through affirmative action, not through apportionment of delegates to units other than the state delegation.

In all four parties, convention representation for the most politically significant minorities—black Americans and French-speaking Canadians—was not assured through nationally established selection criteria. In the United States, the Republicans have traditionally had a greater number of black convention delegates than have the Democrats.[21] But in 1968, the Democratic convention, in part as a result of the credentials challenge of the Mississippi Freedom Democratic party in 1964, substantially increased its black representation: 170, or 5.5 percent, of its delegates were black, far more than the 26, or just under 2 percent, of the Republicans.[22] By 1972 the demand for affirmative action had resulted in 4 percent of the Republican and 15.2 percent of the Democratic delegates' being black.[23]

In Canada, French-speaking representation was facilitated but not assured by allocation of more than half the delegate positions to representatives from each federal constituency organization, to be selected by its members. Because of the geographical concentration of French-

19. Figures taken from *Congressional Quarterly Weekly Report* (Aug. 12, 1972), p. 1999.

20. The Democratic figure is from Robert W. Nelson (see sources for Table 2, above). The Republican figure is from Good (see note 16), who also indicated that there were 234 women delegates (17.9 percent) at the 1964 Republican convention. David, Goldman, and Bain, *Politics of Conventions*, p. 327, report the 1952 convention figures, based on compilation of the official delegate lists, as 12.5 percent for the Democrats and 10.5 percent for the Republicans.

21. David, Goldman, and Bain, *Politics of Conventions*, p. 329, report that in 1952 "Negro delegates seem to have held about 2.6% of the voting strength in the Republican national convention, and about 1.5% in the Democratic." In 1964, blacks held 65 of the 2,944 full delegate positions at the Democratic convention, or 2.2 percent, less than the Republican percentage in 1952. See *Congressional Quarterly Weekly Report* (June 7, 1968), p. 1341.

22. *Mandate for Reform*, p. 26.

23. Figures taken from *Congressional Quarterly Weekly Report* (July 8, 1972), p. 1642; (Aug. 12, 1972), pp. 1998–99.

speaking Canadians in the Quebec and New Brunswick constituencies, in each of which a majority is French-speaking, the apportionment formula encouraged their representation.

Survey data on Liberal delegates to the 1968 convention indicate that French Canadians were not significantly underrepresented:[24]

	Percentage of delegates	*Percentage of general population*
British	51	43.8
French	23	30.4
Other	26	25.8

If anything, the survey may have undercounted French-Canadian delegates.[25] While the French-Canadian delegate percentage is less than the French-Canadian share of the country's population, the delegate figure is high enough to support the conclusion that the failure to earmark delegate positions to French Canadians did not reduce their access to those positions, because French Canadians do not lack access to political power within the Liberal party. Penetration of the political elite has been achieved.

The Progressive Conservative party was the only one of the four to earmark representation for a segment of the academic community. A month before the Conservative party convention, a "thinkers' conference" was assembled to present and discuss policy issues that would come before the September convention. Eighty-six conference delegates were later accredited as delegates to the leadership convention, over the protest of one leadership candidate's supporters, who asked that not more than thirty be seated.[26] The weekend before the convention, the decision was affirmed by the twenty-five-member convention committee, which was apparently not in a position to overrule an earlier commitment to give a vote to those who had worked on developing party policy. Thus, still another interest group was given direct representation, in a manner that again showed how

24. Santos, "Characteristics of Delegates," pp. 304–05.

25. Note Santos' caveat (ibid., p. 305): "It is possible that there might be some reluctance on the part of French Canadian delegates to return the questionnaire, in spite of the fact that the questionnaire used in this study was bilingual."

26. See Vineberg, "Progressive Conservative Convention," pp. 41–43; *Toronto Daily Star*, Sept. 2, 1967.

delegate apportionment was centralized in the hands of a national party committee.[27]

The number of credentials challenges at the 1968 Democratic convention, a product in many cases of the decision to use national party machinery to increase minority representation on state convention delegations, is in sharp contrast to the Canadian convention practice. In neither Canadian leadership convention was any issue of delegate credentials brought to the floor. One explanation may be that Canadian provincial party organizations were given important roles in monitoring delegate selection at the constituency level, and in processing challenges to selection procedures. For example, all the eighty-eight Ontario Liberal constituency meetings, electing 528 delegates, "were supervised by a top official of either the Liberal party in Ontario or the Toronto and District Liberal Association."[28] Any challenge to the credentials of a delegate elected at a constituency meeting was directed first to the provincial party. The decision of the provincial organization could be appealed to the appropriate federal party committee.

Thus, while the national executives of the Progressive Conservative and Liberal parties had more power than the Democratic or Republican National Committee to define the composition of convention delegates, and to cut across provincial or state party boundaries, the Canadian parties delegate the monitoring of the selection process to provincial parties with less frequent appeal to the national convention than occurs in the United States. It may be that the smaller the degree of control a state or provincial party organization exercises over delegate selection, the greater the degree to which that state or provincial party organization can be used to monitor delegate selection and process challenges to selection procedures. By this argument, the number of challenges reaching the convention credentials committee will vary inversely with the degree of control the provincial or state party organization has over delegate selection. For example, there are fewer credentials challenges in states that select delegates through primaries over which the state party has less control.

27. The members of the original thinkers' conference attended by invitation; those invited were not required to be party members, and may have been members of one of the other political parties. For information on the accreditation of thinkers' conference members as delegates, the authors are indebted to T. L. Horswill, research officer, leader of the Opposition, House of Commons, Ottawa.

28. *Toronto Daily Star*, March 2, 1968.

While appeal to the national convention has increasingly been used to alter the racial composition of the Democratic convention, the extent to which the national party will intervene in state party affairs remains problematic.[29] In neither the Democratic nor the Republican party is there any indication that delegates will be apportioned to any constituent element other than the state party organization. If any one characteristic reflects the different ways in which power is distributed in Canadian and American parties, it is the primacy of state party organization in the United States and the secondary importance of provincial party organization in Canada in the process of leadership selection.

The provincial party associations were treated for apportionment purposes simply as another set of party associations, whose executive officers were awarded seats along with the leaders of the women's, youth, and student associations. The major portion of elected delegates in both parties came from the local constituency associations. The Conservative party, unlike the Liberals, apportioned delegates-at-large to each province (356 in all) and allowed these delegates to be chosen "by a committee consisting of the president, vice-president, and two national directors of each provincial party association."[30] Thus a large bloc of delegates could be named by a small group of provincial party executives; but even so, the great majority of delegates were apportioned in a manner that minimized the role of the provincial party apparatus.

If delegate apportionment in Canadian leadership conventions reflects the primacy of any element of the party, it is the parliamentary party, the very element which critics argue has been eclipsed by the advent of the leadership convention.[31] Unlike the American parties, the Canadian parties have closely articulated the convention structure

29. One precedent was established at the 1972 Democratic convention, when for the first time state delegations were divided during credentials challenges. In the past, no member of a challenged state delegation could vote on its own credentials. However, in no case did the national convention or its credentials committee designate which individual delegates could vote and which could not. Control over the designation of individual delegates remained within state party organizations.

30. *Toronto Daily Star*, Aug. 19, 1967.

31. See John C. Courtney, "Leadership Selection by Party Convention in a Parliamentary System: An Examination of the Canadian Experience" (paper presented at the Eighth World Congress, International Political Science Association, Sept. 3, 1970). For other examples, see Mary Southin, "Why Do We Need a Leadership Race?" *Vancouver Sun*, March 26, 1968; and J. R. Williams, *The Conservative Party of Canada, 1920–1949* (Duke University Press, 1956).

with the parliamentary party. Since the majority of Canadian convention delegates are elected from constituencies defined by parliamentary electoral boundaries, the individual federal member of Parliament is in a better position to influence delegate selection than he would be under any other system.[32] At the same time, no other organized segment of the party is given a greater element of control or a greater share of delegates. The apportionment of delegates among women's, youth, and university student organizations disperses influence among a number of groups, and prevents the provincial party organizations from exercising more substantial influence within the leadership convention.

The way in which the Liberal and Conservative conventions have tied the parliamentary party and members of Parliament to the apportionment of delegates shows an interesting tendency toward a synthesis of what Maurice Duverger termed "a basic distinction between two types of parties"—those based on the caucus and weak articulation, and those based on the branch system and strong articulation.[33] That is, the branches the two parties have developed, which can become the basis of a coherent system of organizational linkages characteristic of a strongly articulated party, coincide with parliamentary constituencies, and thus reinforce the connection between Parliament and party organization. While the two parties operate as cadre parties in much of their activity, the party convention provides an opportunity to develop a mass base, activate the party branches, and strengthen articulation of the diverse elements of the national party.[34] To the extent that the conventions mesh delegates with parliamentary

32. This proposition concerns the definition of the constituency, not the involvement reported by Smiley, "Leadership Convention," p. 377: "The late Senator C. G. Power wrote some years ago that it was normal for a sitting member of Parliament to choose and direct delegates from his constituency and that thus the convention system perpetuated the older tradition of leadership selection by caucus." John W. Lederle noted that the 1919 convention call "gave an overwhelming representation to the federal and provincial legislative groups." See his "The Liberal Convention of 1919 and the Selection of Mackenzie King," *Dalhousie Review*, Vol. 27 (April 1947), pp. 85–92.

33. Duverger, *Political Parties* (Wiley, 1963), pp. 46–47. The French edition was published in 1951.

34. Smiley, "Leadership Convention," makes a related point on p. 396. Note as well that in 1967 and 1968 the two leadership conventions were used to strengthen party organization at the constituency level, by requiring that constituency delegates be selected from newly redistributed ridings (that is, on the basis of the federal redistricting completed since the most recent federal election in 1965). Thus the process of selecting delegates to the national leadership conventions stimulated reorganization of constituency associations before the next federal election.

constituencies, they may evolve into institutions capable of supporting the role of Parliament, even though they were created in response
to the inability of parliamentary parties alone to deal with leadership
succession.[35]

If the apportionment of party convention delegates reflects and reinforces the parliamentary system, it also promotes the power of the
national party organization vis-à-vis the provincial parties, and thus
maintains a major operational distinction between Canadian and
American party conventions. Since the national party executive makes
decisions not yet delegated to the national committees of either major
party in the United States, it is the chief threat to parliamentary
power in Canadian parties, particularly when it is not controlled by
the party's leader in Parliament. Never was this more apparent than
in the unprecedented genesis of the Progressive Conservative leadership convention. The national party chairman, Dalton Camp, announced in 1966 that the party would hold a convention to decide
whether to hold a leadership convention. The decision was then made
by a party convention, over the opposition of the incumbent party
leader, to hold a leadership convention. The meeting in September
1967 in Toronto marked the first time in Canadian history that a
party leader's position was taken from him, not by his parliamentary
colleagues but by an extraparliamentary institution.

The Liberal leadership convention did not become a test of strength
between the party in Parliament and the national party committee.
But the independence of the convention from the caucus was illustrated by the only dispute to arise in the credentials committee. At
issue was the status of Ralph Cowan, a Liberal M.P. who was ex-
pelled from the Liberal caucus in Parliament. The committee spent
two days discussing whether to seat Cowan as a delegate to the leadership convention. A brief prepared for committee cochairman William
Godfrey concluded that there was no legal support for denying

35. The meshing of branches with parliamentary constituencies is also characteristic
of other Canadian parties. In Leo Zakuta's study of the way in which the Cooperative
Commonwealth Federation (CCF) changed from a movement to a party, one indicator of
that change was the federation's reorganization at the branch level, from clubs based on
location of party members to constituency groups coinciding with federal election boundaries. See *A Protest Movement Becalmed: A Study of Change in the CCF* (University of
Toronto Press, 1964). The use of federal electoral boundaries carried over to the New
Democratic party when that party emerged from an alliance of the CCF and the Canadian
Labour Congress.

Cowan's credentials, since he had been elected as a Liberal M.P. and had not voluntarily left the party. The committee sustained the conclusion and awarded the maverick legislator his credentials, giving him an opportunity to vote for a new leader—an opportunity that would have been denied him in a caucus system.[36]

In summary, delegate apportionment in both Canada and the United States can be explained in relation to party organization. American parties apportion convention delegates by states, reflecting the geographic decentralization of power within the Democratic and Republican parties. Canadian parties apportion convention delegates to a number of interests and associations at the national, provincial, and local constituency levels, reflecting the efforts of a national party to build a broadly based national organization in a parliamentary setting. Delegate apportionment in each country can also have its own impact on party organization: in the United States, by reinforcing the autonomy of state party organizations; in Canada, by preventing provincial party organizations from exerting more influence over one of the country's few extragovernmental political institutions—the national leadership convention.

Voting Rules

One of the simplest and most striking differences between Canadian and American national party conventions is the difference in voting rules. The Conservatives and Liberals both operated with two basic rules completely unknown to American national conventions: voting by individual secret ballot, and elimination of the candidate receiving the fewest votes on each successive ballot. These two rules—secret ballot and low-man-out—produce basic alterations in candidate strategy and in the probable outcome of convention voting. A unit rule is rendered impossible; constituency delegates are not bound by their association, in part because such action would have no meaning.

The effect of the Canadian voting rules can be seen in relation to one of the axioms of American convention literature: "An aspirant who leads in votes for the nomination must actually win nomination by a certain point in time, after which his chances of eventually winning decline precipitously, even though he remains in the lead for the

36. Information on the Cowan case is based on an interview with William Godfrey in Ottawa during the leadership convention.

time being."[37] Empirical data on American convention voting confirm this proposition. In ten Democratic conventions since abandonment of the two-thirds rule (1936–72), one convention has gone beyond the first ballot in nominating a president, and the early leader was defeated.[38] Of the nineteen Republican conventions in the twentieth century (1900–72), four have gone beyond the first ballot. In the two conventions that went to three ballots (1916 and 1948), the early leader won; in the two conventions that went beyond three ballots (1920 and 1940), the early leader lost. Of the ten Republican conventions in the nineteenth century (1860–96), the early leader lost four out of five times.[39] Of the nine Democratic conventions operating under the two-thirds rule in the twentieth century (1900–32), four went beyond one ballot and the early leader lost three out of four times.[40]

The Canadian convention system has worked in exactly the opposite way. The leader on the first ballot has always been elected to the party leadership. Of the four Liberal party conventions, two went beyond the first ballot: W. L. Mackenzie King, leading on the first ballot, won in three ballots in 1919, and Pierre Trudeau, leading on the first ballot, won in four ballots in 1968. Of the six Conservative party conventions, four went beyond the first ballot, the first-ballot leader winning each time: R. B. Bennett (1927), R. J. Manion (1938), and John Bracken (1942) each won on the second ballot, and Robert Stanfield won in 1967 on the fifth ballot.[41]

The working of the Canadian convention system in favor of the first-ballot leader is reinforced by voting behavior on the second

37. Nelson W. Polsby, "Decision-Making at the National Conventions," *Western Political Quarterly*, Vol. 13 (September 1960), p. 609.

38. In 1952, Stevenson, second to Kefauver on the first two ballots, was nominated on the third.

39. Lincoln started second, won in three ballots (1860); Hayes started fifth, won in seven ballots (1876); Garfield received no votes on the first ballot, won in thirty-six ballots (1880); Blaine led on first ballot, won in four ballots (1884); Harrison started fourth, won in eight ballots (1888).

40. The early leader lost in 1912, 1920, and 1924, and won in 1932, when Franklin Roosevelt was nominated. Roosevelt was the only early leader to win a majority of delegate votes on the first ballot. Data testing this proposition are from Bain and Parris, *Convention Decisions*, App. C.

41. The Canadian data are derived from tables in the appendix to Courtney, "Leadership Selection by Party Convention."

ballot. In five of the six leadership conventions that have gone beyond the first ballot, the first-ballot leader has registered a larger net gain than any of his opponents. The only exception occurred at the 1938 Conservative convention, when R. J. Manion achieved enough votes on the second ballot to win the leadership. On the other hand, in the nine Democratic and Republican party conventions in the twentieth century that went beyond the first ballot, the first-ballot leader achieved a larger net gain than his opponents on the second ballot in only four cases;[42] in five, the first-ballot leader lost ground.[43] The dynamics of the Canadian convention system clearly operate in favor of the early leader. One factor accounting for this difference appears to be the secret ballot, a procedural device characteristic of all Canadian leadership conventions, yet alien to the American system. The low-man-out rule, which may also operate to reinforce the strong position of the early leader, was first applied in the 1967 and 1968 leadership conventions.[44]

In 1971, the Democratic caucus in the U.S. House of Representatives for the first time used the secret ballot along with the low-man-out rule to elect a House majority leader. Five candidates were in the race; 128 votes were needed for election. The first-ballot leader was Representative Hale Boggs with 95 votes, short of the 100 votes his staff established as the minimum necessary to win on later ballots, but far more than Representative Morris Udall's 69. Although Udall hoped to combine his votes in a coalition with Representative James O'Hara after the first ballot, as happens in the Canadian system, the second ballot gave Boggs a larger net gain than any of his opponents, and the first-ballot leader was elected. This example suggests that it is the na-

42. Democratic conventions of 1920 and 1932; Republican conventions of 1916 and 1948.
43. Democratic conventions of 1912, 1924, and 1952; Republican conventions of 1920 and 1940.
44. The 1919 Liberal convention rules stipulated that "if no choice is made on the fourth balloting, the candidate receiving the lowest number of votes on the fifth and succeeding ballots shall drop from the contests." A leader was elected on the third ballot. See Lederle, "Liberal Convention," p. 90. The 1920 Tory convention provided for elimination of the low man on the third and succeeding ballots. "This precedent was adopted at the four subsequent conventions, but, in a desire to streamline the proceedings, the Convention Committee [in 1967] accepted Mr. Goodman's proposal that the low candidate on every ballot should be dropped." No Conservative convention before 1967 went beyond two ballots. See Vineberg, "Progressive Conservative Convention," pp. 36–37.

ture of the voting procedures rather than other variables that accounts for the greater success of first-ballot leaders in Canadian conventions than in American conventions.

It may be hypothesized that the secret ballot aids the early leader by limiting the variety of strategies available to other candidates, and by producing a perceptible tendency of delegates and candidates to throw their support to the first-ballot leader rather than to his major opponents. The formation of counter-blocs is inhibited by the secret ballot, since a candidate who wishes to withdraw and throw his support to an opponent of the first-ballot leader cannot exercise control over his supporters, who are neither clearly defined nor organized. His ability effectively to transfer support to another candidate is thus reduced.

Candidates in Democratic and Republican conventions are not in the same situation. The delegates supporting a given candidate are known, and the aggregate of delegates may be separated into a number of organized subgroups: the state delegations. The party leaders or the candidate's supporters in a state delegation are frequently in a position to exercise control over delegates—to organize their behavior. The higher degree of organization increases the likelihood that blocs of delegates can be effectively transferred from one candidate to another, especially to a major opponent of the first-ballot leader. Thus the lower degree of organization characterizing the Canadian convention system is associated with a greater willingness on the part of withdrawing candidates either to support the first-ballot leader or to refrain from supporting any of the remaining candidates. On the other hand, in American conventions there may be a greater willingness to declare for a candidate other than the front runner in an effort to create a blocking coalition.

Candidate behavior in the 1967 and 1968 Canadian conventions indicates that the early leader does accumulate the support of withdrawn and eliminated candidates more readily than his opponents. In the Conservative convention, Wallace McCutcheon, George Hees, and E. Davie Fulton all withdrew in favor of Stanfield; none of the other candidates supported runner-up Duff Roblin. In the Liberal convention, two candidates eliminated from the balloting (cabinet ministers J. J. Greene and Allan MacEachen) expressed support for Trudeau, and Paul Hellyer withdrew and threw his support to runner-up Robert Winters.

While the early leader obtains more support from withdrawn and eliminated candidates than do his leading opponents, the lack of control such candidates have over their delegate supporters may be one factor discouraging the endorsement of any candidate. Six candidates at the Conservative convention withdrew or were eliminated without supporting any remaining candidate. Supporters of runner-up Roblin had been particularly hopeful of obtaining support from former cabinet minister Alvin Hamilton, but he made no endorsement. Outgoing party leader John Diefenbaker withdrew after the third ballot without endorsing any candidate, although his opposition to Stanfield was well known. In the Liberal convention, four candidates withdrew or were eliminated but did not support another candidate; one of these was senior cabinet minister Paul Martin, from whom supporters of both Hellyer and Winters had hoped to gain endorsement. When candidates make no endorsement, their inaction is likely to reinforce the position of the early leader, since delegates have few other cues directing them to opponents of the early leader. A refusal to endorse leaves delegates without instructions, and perhaps more prone to follow the greater number of delegates and vote for the leader.

The effects of the secret ballot on delegate voting behavior and the impact of the strategic decisions of withdrawn or eliminated candidates are illuminated by the data on voting switches gathered by LeDuc in a survey of delegates to the 1968 Liberal leadership convention. The responses indicate that neither the candidates who endorsed Trudeau nor Hellyer, who endorsed runner-up Winters, could deliver their aggregates of delegate votes. In MacEachen's case, only 35 percent of his surveyed first-ballot votes went to Trudeau on the second ballot, while 45 percent went to Winters. More important than MacEachen's support of Trudeau in explaining the voting changes seemed to be the geographical base of MacEachen's first-ballot delegate strength, which came in great part from the maritime provinces, where Winters was born and raised. Greene's early supporters switched more frequently to Trudeau than to other candidates, but Greene's endorsement of Trudeau before the fourth ballot did not prevent his surveyed third-ballot votes from splitting between Trudeau and Winters. Hellyer was more successful than MacEachen or Greene in delivering a large number of votes to the candidate he endorsed. When Hellyer withdrew after the third ballot and endorsed Winters, 69 percent of his surveyed third-ballot support went to Winters.

However, the slippage was still sufficient—24.2 percent went to Trudeau—to forestall the effort to build a Hellyer-Winters counter-bloc.[45]

Two candidates, Eric Kierans and Paul Martin, withdrew after the first ballot without endorsing another candidate, and Trudeau received a higher number of delegate votes than any competing candidate from among their supporters who were surveyed: 57 percent from Kierans and 34.5 percent from Martin. One explanation was that both men had received first-ballot support from Quebec delegates who switched to Trudeau on the second ballot. At the same time, however, the lack of endorsement may itself have contributed to a tendency for delegates to support the first-ballot leader.

Also evident in the survey data is a tendency to vote-slippage in the direction of the early leader, Trudeau. Some of Hellyer's vote slipped to Trudeau on every ballot, the percentage increasing each time. On the final ballot, 8.3 percent of Winters' surveyed third-ballot votes slipped to Trudeau, even when the two men emerged as the major protagonists. Meanwhile, Trudeau lost only one surveyed vote on all three ballots; in the process, he held all 156 surveyed third-ballot votes on the fourth ballot. Delegate voting behavior thus contributes to a dynamic that helps propel the early leader to victory.[46]

What other elements of convention organization contribute to this dynamic? The low-man-out rule becomes important when a number of serious candidates enter the leadership race. The cabinet system of parliamentary government in Canada may encourage candidates who are in provincial politics to contest the party leadership as a means of gaining a federal cabinet position, and may encourage candidates who already hold federal posts to run as a means of increasing their influence in the cabinet. Since voting had gone beyond the first ballot in every leadership convention in which four or more candidates were entered, it is hypothesized that the low-man-out rule applied in the 1967 and 1968 conventions discouraged a strategy of delay through continued adherence to a political dark-horse candidate. If the low man had not been threatened with elimination at the Liberal convention, it would have been good strategy for a candidate such as Paul

45. LeDuc, "Party Decision-Making," p. 108.

46. The distribution of LeDuc's questionnaire responses shows slight variations from the distribution of convention votes. For example, on the first ballot, questionnaire responses overrepresent Turner's vote and underrepresent the Hellyer and Winters vote.

Martin to stay in the race rather than withdraw. While Martin was the first choice of few convention delegates, he was a senior leader in the party who could have been acceptable as a short-term leader if Trudeau had been deadlocked with Winters and Hellyer. But such a compromise candidacy requires a strategy of watching and waiting, and the rules make such a strategy difficult.

If dark-horse candidacies are so difficult, one would expect that candidates with less support would withdraw before the convention's voting day and throw their support behind the most preferable frontrunner. But of the twenty-one candidates at the 1967 and 1968 conventions only one did so: Liberal cabinet minister Mitchell Sharp withdrew forty-eight hours before the convention opened and endorsed Trudeau.[47] One of the forces maintaining the large number of candidates is the absence of a definitive technique for assessing individual candidate strength. There are no preconvention primaries. There are no test votes on the convention floor; by tradition the credentials report has not been contested, and in 1967 and 1968, no platform was passed at either convention.[48] Therefore, the candidate must rely on his private delegate polls and the public polls in the mass media. In these circumstances candidates seem more willing to stick it out through nomination and balloting.

Once the first-ballot leader is established, however, the room for maneuvering is limited. There is less need for bargaining on the part of the early leader, who can accumulate support without resort to bargaining with other candidates. And any bargain would have much less efficacy when made, because of the secret-ballot voting system. Furthermore, little time is available during the voting for candidates to engage in meaningful bargaining. As soon as the results of one ballot are announced, balloting begins again; thus, although each ballot takes time to process, bargaining is difficult because the candidates do not know what the pending vote announcement will reveal about the growth or erosion of their delegate support. In short, the whole convention apparatus tends to lock candidates into a limited range of strategies: they cannot measure their strength before voting

47. Upon Trudeau's election as prime minister, Sharp became minister of external affairs, one of the top cabinet portfolios.

48. The Conservatives postponed a vote on a draft platform; the Liberals postponed the construction of any platform until after the election of the new leader. The 1971 New Democratic party convention voted on party policy before the leadership vote, but none of the five candidates withdrew.

day, so they stay in the race; once in the race, they are not in a position to bargain with other candidates.[49]

The inability of leadership candidates to make deals and transfer support means that the Canadian conventions lack an instrument that defenders of the American convention system see as an essential and distinctive characteristic of the convention form of political organization. Aaron Wildavsky expresses the view most dramatically in his essay, "On the Superiority of National Conventions":

> Let us suppose that the smoke-filled room were abolished and with it all behind-the-scenes negotiations. All parleys would then be held in public, before the delegates and millions of television viewers. As a result, the participants would spend their time scoring points against each other in order to impress the folks back home. The claim that bargaining was going on would be a sham, since the participants would not really be communicating with each other. No compromises would be possible, lest the leaders be accused by their followers of selling out to the other side. Once a stalemate existed, it would be practically impossible to break and the party would probably disintegrate into warring factions.[50]

Thus the ability to make deals at a time of conflict and stalemate becomes a key argument for conventions as a way of doing political business.

Yet the Canadian conventions fulfill all the crucial needs that Wildavsky posits, with a set of rules and procedures that retard the use and effectively eliminate the role of the legendary smoke-filled room. The low-man-out rule reduces the efficacy of dark-horse candidacies, but it also assures the impossibility of convention deadlock: at some point in time, the convention will be presented with an unavoidable choice between two men. Wildavsky might argue in rebuttal that, although such a system produces a candidate, he may be a candidate of

49. Even when campaign organizations develop coalition plans, spatial and temporal arrangements, together with the convention communication structure, impede such plans. Hugh Thorburn commented in correspondence that his interview data point to an apparent arrangement among senior members of the Hellyer, Martin, and Winters campaign staffs before the convention. Fluctuations in the Hellyer and Winters vote between the first and second ballots created a situation in which neither would withdraw in favor of the other, and direct negotiation during the convention was too difficult to allow the nascent coalition to function.

50. In Donald G. Herzberg and Gerald M. Pomper (eds.), *American Party Politics: Essays and Readings* (Holt, Rinehart and Winston, 1966), pp. 310–11. Wildavsky's essay first appeared in *Review of Politics*, Vol. 24 (July 1962), pp. 307–19.

one party faction who would be rejected by a losing faction or factions. However, the convention practices that make it impossible to make deals at the time of the balloting—less time to make them, less ability to deliver them, and less need for them on the part of the front-runner—retard the organization of party factions. Factions may coalesce during the course of the balloting: the Liberal convention split to some extent between the Left and the Right, to some extent between French-speaking and English-speaking, and the Conservative convention split to some extent between East and West, between the supporters of former leader John Diefenbaker and those who worked to depose him. But these factions never had an opportunity to organize, either before the convention when multiple candidacies made coalition impossible, or during the balloting, when events moved too fast to convert delegate aggregates into party factions. Finally, the secret ballot ensures that no leader will be accused of selling out. It may be that the secret ballot was first devised by the Liberals in the 1919 convention to assure Quebec's continued presence in the Liberal party: had the Quebec delegates, whose members of Parliament dominated the parliamentary caucus, voted publicly in great numbers for the losing candidate, they might have been pressured to leave the party. Use of the secret ballot removed such a possibility.[51] Thus the Canadian conventions, lacking the attributes that Wildavsky and others admire in the American system, have developed an alternative set of procedures that are at least as effective in ensuring flexibility and party maintenance as the American national party convention.

In summary, the voting rules in Canadian party conventions affect the strategies of the candidates and, by retarding the organization of party factions, affect the party organization as well. In turn, the party organization, which lacks institutionalized factional subgroups, reinforces the continued use of the secret ballot and its related rules and practices. A well-organized group of party subleaders might recognize the value of changing the voting rules to enhance the opportunities for bargaining, but the convention system itself makes it difficult for those leaders to gain the power necessary to bring forth such a basic change in Canadian convention procedure.

51. Professor Paul Tennant of the University of British Columbia first suggested this to the authors as a possible explanation of the secret ballot. For another interpretation of the way in which voting rules retard factions, see Smiley, "Leadership Convention," p. 387.

Intermediate Leadership and Organization

In the Canadian convention system, delegate apportionment and voting procedures combine to produce an extremely weak system of intermediate leadership, and a lack of organized subgroups. In the American convention system, delegate apportionment and voting procedures combine to produce a strong system of intermediate leadership, based in state delegations.[52] Differences in the degree to which intermediate leadership is exercised through organized convention subgroups are not related to differences in convention rules and procedures alone, but to cross-national differences in the bases of party organization. In both Canadian parties, leadership conventions have been established within a parliamentary context, so that the national party organization defines a set of rules and procedures within which decisions can be made directly by the mass of delegates, without the intervention of an intermediate layer of organization. In both American parties, national conventions have functioned within confederated organizations and have been dominated by state delegations and their leaders. Thus out of the interaction of party organization and convention rules and procedures have arisen two distinct organizational types. Canadian leadership conventions follow a "mass-society" model in which each individual delegate operates within a commonly defined situation, with a common set of behavioral constraints and opportunities. National party conventions in the United States follow an intermediate leadership model, in which direction and control flow from the relations established among a number of autonomous sub-leaders of defined convention constituencies.[53] In Canada, the mass-society convention develops out of the dispersion of apportioned delegates among a large number of categories, the use of secret ballot, and the development of rules that reduce the need for and efficacy of voting blocs and party factions—all of which arose out of the construction of a political institution that could establish a national base for a parlia-

52. For examples of convention studies in which the state delegation is the focus of analysis, see Paul Tillett (ed.), *Inside Politics: The National Convention, 1960* (Rutgers University Press, 1962); and Paul T. David, Malcolm Moos, and Ralph M. Goldman, *Presidential Nominating Politics in 1952*, 5 vols. (Johns Hopkins Press, 1954).

53. See William Kornhauser, *The Politics of Mass Society* (Free Press, 1959); and Robert A. Dahl and Charles E. Lindblom, *Politics, Economics and Welfare* (Harper, 1953).

mentary party in a large and diverse federal polity.[54] In the United States, the intermediate leadership arises out of the apportionment of delegates to states, open voting by state delegations, and rules that facilitate and necessitate bargaining among subleaders to resolve conflict—all of which arose out of the construction of a political institution that could establish a national base for a confederated party with wide variations in appeal across geographical regions.

For example, the differences in the organization of Canadian and American conventions create different communication systems. In the United States, the communication structure takes the form of a wheel.[55] Intermediate leaders serve as relaymen linking members of state delegations to candidate and convention communication networks. Campaign organizations of the various candidates use designated state delegation leaders as relaymen between the delegation and the campaign. Relaymen are in the position to transmit information to and from state delegations, campaign organizations, and convention officials. The Canadian convention system lacks this kind of wheel communication structure; since there is a low degree of provincial delegation organization, provincial caucuses cannot be used as nodes within a communication structure linking convention officials, campaign organizations, and individual delegates. The absence of intermediate leadership produces an absence of well-defined relaymen. Because the structure of the convention does not define the communication structure, such a structure must be evolved.

The leadership candidates' campaign organizations thus sought to develop communication structures that would effectively gather information from and distribute it to individual delegates. In most instances, candidate organizations sought to develop wheel structures, in which members of the campaign organization served as relaymen. Candidate organizations differed in the ways in which they organized their communication structures. In some cases, persons were assigned

54. The New Democratic party, unlike the Liberals and Conservatives, was extra-parliamentary in origin and, unlike the two older parties, has a system of intermediate leadership through labor unions and through its newly organized Waffle group. The conflict between these two party factions played a central role in the NDP's 1971 leadership convention.

55. See Harold Guetzkow, "Differentiation of Roles in Task-oriented Groups," in Dorwin Cartwright and Alvin Zander (eds.), *Group Dynamics: Research and Theory* (2d ed., Row Peterson, 1960), pp. 683–704.

to relay information to and from delegates from the same province or geographical area, as in the characteristic American convention communication structure; in other cases, relaymen were assigned to youth or student delegates, reflecting the diverse bases by which delegates were defined.

Such strategies could have been effective during the week, but were impeded by spatial arrangements and election procedures for voting day at the end of both Conservative and Liberal conventions. Delegates did not have assigned seats on voting day, nor were they grouped together by province. The floor of the arena was cleared of seats used on previous days so that delegates could queue up in front of the voting machines strung out along one side of the floor. In both conventions, delegates were assigned particular machines at which to vote. At the Conservative convention, delegates were assigned to machines partly by apportionment categories, so that party officials congregated at certain machines, and delegates from provinces at others. This arrangement facilitated communication organized around geographical areas. The Liberal convention, however, assigned delegates in alphabetical order. As a result, delegates from given geographical areas and those with specific standings in the party were unlikely to be spatially concentrated, and might be dispersed across the entire convention floor. To compensate for this difficulty, some campaign organizations assigned relaymen to each voting machine. The relaymen were often unable, however, because of language, age, or status differences, to gather or transmit information successfully.

On election day there evolved a system whereby interested delegates could recognize the various candidates' relaymen by their badges, hats, or coats. While these relaymen could not define a specific constituency to link to their candidate's communication structure, they served as communication nodes on the floor, transmitting volunteer information to the campaign headquarters and quashing rumors about the candidate's withdrawal plans—in short, giving delegates a sense of the candidate's continued presence in the race.[56]

The difficulties encountered in the effort to evolve communication structures were brought home most vividly to the public watching on television and listening on the radio when Liberal candidate Allan

56. Joseph Wearing, in "The Liberal Choice," *Journal of Canadian Studies*, Vol. 3 (May 1968), p. 13, notes that "one key Trudeau organizer said afterwards that the purpose of communications is simply psychological—to impress the delegates."

MacEachen sought to withdraw after the first ballot. Since there were no microphones on the floor, the announcement had to be forwarded to the podium in writing. Although the withdrawal was known to the general public, the official notice thus reached the podium too late for the voting machines to be adjusted, and the withdrawal was not announced by the convention chairman before the beginning of the second ballot.[57] As a result, delegates were dependent on candidate communication structures to learn that MacEachen had in fact withdrawn and that he wished his delegates to support Pierre Trudeau. But MacEachen's name remained on the ballot, and he received eleven votes, which prompted an embarrassed chairman to pay tribute to MacEachen and explain why the vote was not a reflection on the candidate. The vote did, however, reflect the noise in the communication structures between and among delegates, candidates, and convention officials.

The difficulties of evolving effective communication structures gave an important role to the mass media. During the week, newspapers made continual delegate vote counts, which became important in the absence of test votes or other techniques for obtaining information on the voting strength of candidates. Endorsements of candidates, interpretations of convention events, and assessments of the effectiveness of candidates' presentations all took on increasing importance when alternative sources of information were not available.[58] The candidates themselves used such mass-media techniques as morning tabloid newspapers delivered daily to the hotel rooms of delegates, a technique also used in American conventions. What must be assessed is whether the mass media, considered by scholars to be important in American conventions,[59] influence delegate votes to a higher degree in a mass-society convention in which other communication structures operate with reduced effectiveness. Through such an inquiry, the convention communication networks, as an aspect of convention orga-

57. The Conservative convention also had no microphones on the floor during the entire proceedings.

58. For example, Robert Stanfield emerged as the potential first-ballot leader for the first time after his presentation to the party policy committee and the delegates early in the convention week. Toronto newspapers played up the policy speech and helped start the bandwagon. See Vineberg, "Progressive Conservative Convention," pp. 101–03.

59. For a recent example, see Karl O'Lessker, "The National Nominating Conventions," in Cornelius P. Cotter (ed.), *Practical Politics in the United States* (Allyn and Bacon, 1969), pp. 272–74.

nization, can be conceived of as a product of the interaction of party organization and convention rules and procedures.

Democratic Party Reforms and the Canadian Model

The different ways in which party and convention organization has been articulated in Canada and the United States provide a basis for analyzing both the changes in Democratic party organization adopted in 1972 and the proposed charter of the Democratic party.

In November 1969 the Commission on Party Structure and Delegate Selection, then chaired by Senator George McGovern, approved a set of regulations among whose requirements were that state parties take affirmative action to ensure minority-group participation in the delegate-selection process, eliminate discrimination by age and sex, remove all costs and fees in the selection process, prohibit proxy voting, develop written party rules, ensure that not more than 10 percent of a state delegation is made up of persons selected by state committees, and ensure that procedural standards will be applied to slate-making activity as well as to delegate selection.[60] In short, the commission's guidelines focused on limiting the discretion state party organizations may exercise in selecting delegates to Democratic national conventions. The assumption underlying the guidelines was that regulating state party procedures could produce a change in the composition of state delegations, which would in turn result in changes in the way the conventions were run. As this chapter has pointed out, these reforms certainly did change the composition of state delegations.

In November 1970 the Commission on Rules chaired by Representative James O'Hara recommended new mechanisms by which the convention credentials committee would screen state party delegations selected under the McGovern-Fraser Commission guidelines.[61] The draft recommendations call for a written notice of intent to challenge and a specific written answer. They authorize the appointment of a hearing officer, who may conduct public hearings with the aid of one

---

60. *Mandate for Reform*, pp. 33–48.

61. This was one of a number of issues considered by the O'Hara Commission. See "Issues and Alternatives: A Study Guide of Democratic National Convention Procedure and Practice" (prepared at the direction of the Rules Commission of the Democratic National Committee, October 1969; processed).

or more assistant hearing officers. The hearing officer's findings of fact are submitted to the full credentials committee for consideration, at which time all parties to a challenge are entitled to submit briefs and make oral argument.[62] In short, the Rules Commission has recommended the development of an administrative apparatus for the enforcement of the regulatory guidelines of the McGovern-Fraser Commission, a mechanism that was frequently used in 1972.

The reforms originally proposed by the two commissions did not question the assumption that the state party delegation is and should be the sole unit of convention organization.[63] As a result, the reforms did not lead to the redistribution of power at the convention to other constituent parts of the national party, but reinforced the intermediate leadership model of convention organization. In this way the purpose of the delegate selection guidelines was analogous to the original purpose of state primary elections. They sought to increase the degree of participation outside the convention in the delegate-selection process, but such changes did not affect the power of state delegations or their function as units of convention organization. Representatives of organized state delegations remained the key men linking delegates to the convention communication networks and decision-making processes, and the key-man role remained within the leadership of the state delegation.

By choosing to regulate the state party organizations rather than to redistribute their power to other constituent parts of the national party, the Democratic reform commissions developed procedural guidelines that were to be enforced by proceedings similar to those characterizing public administrative tribunals. The proposals have increased the degree of bureaucratization at the national party level, since they dictate an increase in written rules and the introduction of a professional staff to enforce the rules. But because the national parties continued to be a confederation of state parties, state parties continued to define the policies pursued through regulation. This will facilitate the capture of the regulatory mechanisms by the regulated groups, a

62. Rules Commission Memorandum No. 1 (November 1970), pp. 4–10.

63. The ruling that 120 California delegates whose credentials had not been challenged could vote on the credentials committee recommendations regarding seating of the contested delegates from California represented the first time that part of a delegation was permitted to participate while the other part was not. It thus challenged the assumption that the state delegation was the sole unit of convention organization.

phenomenon well documented in the literature of American political science.[64]

Although the two Democratic party commissions recommended changes in the Democratic national convention that did not challenge the traditional supremacy of the state party and the state delegation, the charter of the Democratic party, developed jointly by the two commissions, would considerably alter the role of the state party organization. Adoption of the charter should increase the similarity between the structure of the Democratic party and that of the Canadian parties. The attempts to define a national party membership independent of state parties, to assure the formal participation of Democratic officeholders, and to represent and stimulate organization within a broader cross-section of the party[65] are all reforms which would be likely to reduce the usefulness of the intermediate leadership model and increase the usefulness of the mass-society model.

The charter would no longer apportion all delegates to states. Delegates would be apportioned to congressional districts,[66] as are Canadian constituency delegates, to elected Democratic officials,[67] like delegates ex officio by virtue of public office, to regions,[68] and to other organized segments of the party such as the Young Democrats of America.[69] Thus the similarity between the Canadian and American systems in delegate apportionment, degree of state or provincial party organization, and the number and diversity of potential relaymen would be increased. Such changes in the organization of national policy conferences, the Democratic National Committee, and the National Executive Committee would undoubtedly produce changes in national convention organization. Thus, should the party charter be adopted, one could expect the Democratic party and its national convention to become more like Canadian parties and conventions. Perhaps through these changes a synthesis of parliamentary and presidential parties might evolve.

64. See Grant McConnell, *Private Power and American Democracy* (Knopf, 1966). For the distinction between regulation and redistribution, see Theodore J. Lowi, "American Business, Public Policy, Case-Studies and Political Theory," *World Politics*, Vol. 16 (July 1964).

65. These provisions are contained in Articles VI, II, and III of the Charter of the Democratic Party of the United States, as it is found in *Call to Order* (Democratic National Committee, June 1972), App. D.

66. Charter of the Democratic Party of the United States, Article II(d).

67. Ibid., Article II(e).

68. Ibid., Article III.2(e).

69. Ibid., Article III.2(g).

APPENDIX

The apportionment formulas applied at national party leadership conventions in Canada and the United States in 1967 and 1968 were as follows:

Liberal party[70]

Six voting delegates elected by each of the 264 Liberal constituency associations; one association for each federal riding; the six delegates must include one woman and one person under thirty.. 1,584
Members of Parliament.................................. 131
Defeated candidates for Parliament (November 1965 election).... 126
Newly nominated candidates for Parliament.................. 3
Privy councillors (members of federal Privy Council).......... 16
Senators (members of federal Senate)...................... 60
Retired senators....................................... 8
Members or defeated candidates for provincial legislatures (number of delegates equal to one-fourth of total membership of each provincial legislature)......................... 158
National party executive of:
Liberal Federation of Canada........................... 12
Women's Liberal Federation............................ 42
Young Liberal Federation............................... 13
Canadian Universities Liberal Federation................. 13
National Federation Standing Committee members:
Cochairmen.. 8
National representatives................................ 12
Provincial representatives.............................. 50
Provincial party leaders................................... 10
Provincial party senior executives.......................... 48
Provincial women's organization, members of executive......... 20
Provincial Young Liberal members of executive............... 18
University regional association executive..................... 10
Delegates from University Liberal Clubs..................... 130
Eligible voting delegates............................. 2,472

Progressive Conservative party[71]

Five voting delegates elected by the 264 Conservative constituency associations; one association for each riding; the five dele-

70. Jack Cahill, "Who'll pick our next PM?" *Toronto Daily Star*, Jan. 23, 1968.
71. Jack Cahill, "The Great Conservative Leadership Convention," *Toronto Daily Star*, Aug. 19, 1967.

gates must include one woman and one member of the Young
Progressive Conservative Association or person under thirty.   1,320
Delegates-at-large selected by committee of provincial party associ-
ation (roughly by population: Ontario, 90; Quebec, 90;
British Columbia, 30; Alberta, 25; Manitoba, 25; Sas-
katchewan, 25; New Brunswick, 20; Nova Scotia, 20;
Prince Edward Island, 10; Northwest Territories, 3; Yu-
kon, 3)..   356
Delegates-at-large selected by the president of the women's organi-
zation in each province (Ontario, 9; Quebec, 9; other eight
provinces and two territories, 3 each).................   48
Delegates-at-large selected by the president of the Young Progressive Conservative Association in each province (Ontario, 9;
Quebec, 9; other eight provinces and two territories, 3
each)...   48
Progressive Conservative Student Federation, 2 delegates from each
university recognized by the federation................   116
Ex officio delegates holding public and/or party office (47 privy
councillors; 30 senators; 95 members of Parliament; 190
members of provincial legislatures; newly nominated candidates; members of the national executives of the party association, women's association, Young Progressive Conservatives, and student federation: total, 552 minus 97 holding
two offices).....................................   455
Delegates to national Progressive Conservative "Thinkers' Conference" (August 1967) designated voting delegates ex
officio..   86
Eligible voting delegates............................   2,429

Democratic party[72]

Each state and the District of Columbia receives:
3 votes for each of the electors from that state in the electoral
college
1-vote bonus for each 100,000 popular votes, or major fraction
thereof, that were cast in the state in 1964 for presidential
electors pledged to the national Democratic nominees
10-vote bonus for each state that cast its electoral votes for the
1964 Democratic nominees

72. Adapted from *Congressional Quarterly Weekly Report* (June 7, 1968), p. 337. Note
that the Democratic party is the only one of the four parties that apportions votes rather
than delegates, allowing the appointment of delegates having fractional votes.

1 vote each for the Democratic national committeeman and committeewoman from the state

In addition, Puerto Rico was allotted 8 votes; Canal Zone, Guam, and the Virgin Islands, 5 votes each

Votes... 2,622

Republican party[73]

Each state receives:

4 delegates-at-large

2 delegates-at-large for each representative-at-large

6 additional delegates-at-large for each state that voted Republican for president in 1964 or elected a Republican U.S. senator or governor in 1964 or later

1 district delegate for each congressional district that cast 2,000 votes or more for the Republican presidential nominee in 1964 or a Republican candidate for U.S. representative in 1966

1 additional district delegate for each congressional district that cast 10,000 votes or more for the Republican presidential nominee in 1964 or for a Republican candidate for U.S. representative in 1966

Special allotments:

District of Columbia, 9; Puerto Rico, 5; Virgin Islands, 3

Eligible voting delegates.............................. 1,333

Apportionment Formulas, 1972

DEMOCRATIC PARTY

As in 1968, each state and the District of Columbia received three votes for each elector in the electoral college. Puerto Rico was allotted 7 instead of 8 votes, while the Canal Zone, Guam, and the Virgin Islands each received 3 votes rather than the 5 they were allotted in 1968. These provisions accounted for 1,630 votes, or 53 percent of the total. The remaining 1,386 votes were allocated to states "in direct ratio to each state's Democratic presidential vote in 1960, 1964 and 1968."[74] This formula eliminated the two types of bonuses provided in the 1968 apportionment formula. Although national committeemen and committeewomen elected in 1972 received voting privileges, additional votes were not allocated as they had been previously.

Votes... 3,016

73. Adapted from ibid., p. 1312.
74. *Call to Order*, p. 49.

REPUBLICAN PARTY

The Republican formula was changed in only minor ways from that of 1968. The election of a predominantly Republican (more than 50 percent) delegation to the House of Representatives was added as grounds for awarding bonus at-large delegates; the number of Republican votes for president or congressman required to earn one district delegate was increased from 2,000 to 4,000; a bonus district delegate required 12,500 Republican votes for president or congressman rather than 10,000; Guam was granted 3 delegates.[75]

Eligible voting delegates 1,347

75. Judith H. Parris, *The Convention Problem: Issues in Reform of Presidential Nominating Procedures* (Brookings Institution, 1972), pp. 21–22 and Table 2-1.

Chapter Four

The Selection of French Presidents

ELIJAH BEN-ZION KAMINSKY

OVER the last century and a half, Americans have developed an elaborate extraconstitutional process to identify significant presidential candidates and structure the presidential election. Candidates are *recruited* through procedures that encourage, if they do not guarantee, nomination of candidates able and willing to use presidential power. A nomination also usually requires a substantial *aggregation of support*; if a candidate without broad support survives the nominating process, he may well face disaster in the election. Things go easier for a candidate when the support that gains him the nomination is consistent with the support and personal image most likely to maximize his vote in the election. The *image* of the candidate as a potential president is first built up for purposes of nomination, but the process can so enhance the candidate's image that voters, even those of other parties, may consider him a realistic alternative. When a *meaningful choice* of candidates is presented to the voters, "power to the people" becomes a reality rather than an empty slogan.

This functional framework also describes the selection of contemporary French presidents. However different France may be from the United States, presidential candidates must be recruited, their support aggregated, and convincing presidential images created for the ordinary mortals who succeed a General Charles de Gaulle, and the voters given, if at all possible, a meaningful choice of candidates.[1] A nomi-

Note. Thanks are due the Arizona State University Research Committee for a faculty research grant that provided an opportunity to observe the French presidential elections of 1969.
1. This framework corresponds to five of the six Polsby-Wildavsky standards for presidential nominating processes; "preserving the two-party system" is the only standard not applicable to France. See Nelson W. Polsby and Aaron B. Wildavsky, *Presidential Elections: Strategies of American Electoral Politics* (2d ed., Scribner's, 1968), p. 229.

nating process is all the more essential in a multiparty country if the presidential election is to be more than a "sort of gaming like checkers or backgammon."[2]

It is true that the French presidential nominating process, unlike the American, cannot be delimited in time; no specific event denotes completion of nominations and the beginning of the main campaign. Although the French presidential nominating process has not yet been institutionalized through specific procedures, it is possible to determine when French politicians try to nominate presidential candidates rather than to disperse candidacies to get their favorite into the run-off.[3] How nominations are processed, and the implications of the French experience, will be discussed after a brief review of the institutional framework.

The Institutional Framework

The French president is elected for a personal term of seven years. No successor, interim or elected, serves out an unexpired term. In the event of presidential resignation, death, or disability, the president of the Senate serves as interim president of the Republic, with reduced powers, for the approximately fifty days needed to elect and inaugurate a new president. There is no limit to reelection.

The personal seven-year term originated in 1873 in a law designating Marshal MacMahon by name as president for seven years, during which time the monarchists were to decide which of two pretenders was to regain the French throne. MacMahon was followed by presidents rather than kings as the French Parliament continued to elect chiefs of state for personal seven-year terms. The "personal septennate" of weak presidents of the Third and Fourth Republics was continued by the 1958 constitution that created the powerful presidency of the Fifth Republic, and then specifically reaffirmed in the 1962 amendment providing for direct popular election of the chief executive.

Since the National Assembly is elected for a five-year term, parliamentary elections would normally take place once in some septen-

2. Democratic elections are so defined by Henry David Thoreau in his "Civil Disobedience," *The Portable Thoreau* (Viking, 1947), p. 115.

3. The classic description of the dispersal strategy is V. O. Key, *Southern Politics* (Knopf, 1959), pp. 417–18.

nates and twice in others. Irregular and unpredictable variations occur, however, whenever the president dies, resigns, is disabled, or dissolves the National Assembly; the appropriate election soon follows in each case. Lead time for the preparation of candidacies thus differs greatly from one election to another. Years of preparation preceded the 1965 presidential and 1967 legislative elections, while candidacies for the 1968 legislative and 1969 presidential elections had to be improvised within a few days.

An added complication is that French municipal elections are held simultaneously in all cities and towns every six years. The 1965 municipal election was directly related to the presidential election held a few months later; the 1971 municipals were not immediately connected with any national election. Finally, a referendum vote may be associated with the election of deputies, as in 1962, or with the election of a president, as in 1969. Under these conditions, the presidential nominating process is subject to the unsynchronized and unpredictable scheduling of potentially related elections.

The French presidential electoral law "manufactures" a majority president. First, to exclude frivolous candidates or those with purely local support, the law requires a candidate to obtain a total of at least one hundred signatures from eligible sponsors in ten of the ninety-nine departments into which France is territorially divided. The pool of sponsors includes the 487 deputies and 283 senators, the 200 members of the Economic and Social Council, the 3,331 members of departmental general councils (analogous to American county boards), and the 37,814 mayors.[4] The names, if not the number, of signers must be kept secret. Second, if no candidate wins an absolute majority on a first ballot, the second ballot two weeks later is confined to the top two candidates after withdrawals. A first- or second-place candidate who is unlikely to win on the second ballot can "desist" in favor of a third-place candidate thought to have a better chance.

In the 1965 presidential election, which was preceded by two years of preparation, six candidates qualified for the ballot; in the 1969 election, called at a moment's notice, seven candidates managed to qualify. Since no fewer than sixteen of the announced candidates in 1969 failed to obtain the required one hundred signatures, it is obvious

4. Claude Emeri and Jean-Louis Seurin, "Les suites du référendum et de l'élection présidentielle de 1969," *Revue du droit public*, Vol. 86 (May–June 1970), p. 639.

that the screening procedure is successful in reducing their number.[5] No purely local candidates qualified in 1965 or 1969, but in both elections unlikely candidates did slip through the screen: each election included one candidate who was not endorsed by any significant political force. There were thus four candidates in 1965 and five in 1969 whose exclusion would have deprived a regular political party, or a substantial sector of public opinion, of its own presidential candidate. Some French writers on presidential politics call for further reduction in number of candidates through joint endorsement of the same candidate by several parties or organizations. Whether this aggregation of support should be voluntary, or imposed through stiffer qualifications for candidacy, is in dispute.

The problem of opening up participation in presidential politics without excessive proliferation of candidates is common to France and the United States, but the American presidential primary makes it possible for a greater variety of interests, views, and groups to contribute to the president's nomination and election. Although selection of party candidates by dues-paying party members is conceivable in Europe, a primary open to voters unwilling to buy party membership cards is not likely. An interparty "primary" for competing candidates within the Gaullist coalition has been proposed by Valéry Giscard d'Estaing, leader of the Independent Republicans, a party allied with the UDR (Union des démocrates pour la République—that is, Gaullists) in the coalition that has governed France under the Fifth Republic. Instead of jointly endorsing the same candidate, Giscard suggests, parties in the coalition could run their own candidates on the first ballot, and then unite on the leading candidate for the second ballot.[6] This arrangement would seem much safer for the coalition in parliamentary elections than in the presidential contest; any candidate for deputy can remain for the second ballot if he polls at least 10 percent of the vote on the first, but since the second presidential ballot is lim-

5. Roger-Gérard Schwartzenberg, *La Guerre de succession* (Paris: Presses Universitaires de France, 1969), p. 99. Schwartzenberg is the Theodore White of French presidential elections; the above volume and his earlier study, *La Campagne présidentielle de 1965* (Presses Universitaires de France, 1967), are indispensable for students of French presidential politics.
6. See Marie-Christine Kessler, "M. Valéry Giscard d'Estaing et les Républicains Indépendants," *Revue française de science politique*, Vol. 16 (October 1966), p. 943; *Le Monde* (June 14, 1967), p. 8; *Le Nouvel Observateur*, No. 275 (Feb. 16–22, 1970), pp. 23–24; *L'Express*, No. 969 (Feb. 2–8, 1970), p. 28, and No. 980 (April 20–26, 1970), p. 17.

ited to the top two, dispersal of the vote among several coalition candidates might prevent any one of them from reaching that final vote.

To provide time for a campaign based on the candidates "nominated" on the first ballot, Giscard recommended that the period between ballots be considerably increased from the present one week for parliamentary and two weeks for presidential elections. This change, possible by statute for the National Assembly elections but requiring a constitutional amendment for the presidential contest, is highly unlikely. Neither the UDR in general nor President Georges Pompidou and Premier Jacques Chaban-Delmas in particular were likely to accept an arrangement that would assist Giscard d'Estaing in his repeated assaults against their dominance of the majority coalition. As for the Left, the fact that a Communist candidate might well lead in "primaries" among parties of the Left renders Giscard's proposal just as inadvisable for the opposition as it is for the UDR. It is not only that a Communist can hardly be elected president of the Republic; in a number of Assembly constituencies the Left is more likely to elect a deputy if a higher-placed Communist withdraws in favor of a Socialist, Radical, or other Leftist candidate with potentially broader support on the second ballot.

Although primaries are not yet in prospect for the French, national conventions are held very frequently, usually once a year, by almost all parties. In the aggregation of support, the French equivalent of the American nominating convention would seem to be a congress of several parties or major interest groups; such a meeting was proposed in 1963 but was never convened.[7] Allocating representation to different parties and groups would be difficult indeed, but a great assembly to confirm the nomination of a presidential candidate seems somewhat more consistent with French political tradition than a presidential primary.

In the United States, institutions specifically devoted to the process of nomination are supplemented or paralleled by contests for statewide public offices among would-be presidential candidates. To facilitate development projects and regional planning, reformers in France have proposed large regions with councils and presidents elected di-

7. Frank L. Wilson, *The French Democratic Left 1963–1969* (Stanford University Press, 1971) pp. 86–96. In *Ma part de vérité* (Fayard, 1969), p. 54, François Mitterrand suggested local "primary assemblies" of party members or even of ordinary voters.

rectly by the people of the region.[8] An elected regional president, or even a regional chairman chosen by an elected council, might have the political potential of an American governor. But the Gaullists were afraid that large regions would encourage integration of France into a supranational European community, and that regional democracy might prove a divisive influence threatening national unity. The government therefore set up twenty-two relatively small planning regions without democratic self-government. President Pompidou has been even more emphatic than his predecessor in rejecting all proposals that regional governments be chosen through popular election.[9]

This leaves only the parliamentary and municipal elections as preliminaries to presidential campaigns. Despite his contempt for parliamentarism, and his constitutional provision requiring legislators to give up their seats before serving in the government, President de Gaulle preferred that cabinet ministers run for seats in the National Assembly; if elected, they resign from the Assembly and are replaced by alternates elected on the same ticket with them for that purpose. Failure to win a seat diminishes a minister's prestige. It is not surprising, therefore, to find that among the first four prime ministers of the Fifth Republic, the two who have suffered defeats in legislative elections, Michel Debré and Maurice Couve de Murville, have received much less consideration for the presidency than Pompidou and Chaban-Delmas, both unbeaten in their home districts. This is not to say that election to the 487-member National Assembly confirms a presidential prospect any more than does election to the 435-member House of Representatives; election to either is merely a qualifying test.

In a by-election, when national attention is not dispersed among so many contests, could an ambitious national political figure build up his image and prestige? In 1970 the famous publisher, author, and political reformer Jean-Jacques Servan-Schreiber tried to do just that. He twice challenged the Gaullist coalition in campaigns aimed at rallying

8. See Club Jean Moulin, *Quelle réforme? Quelles régions?* (Seuil, 1969); and Michel Crozier, *La Société bloquée* (Seuil, 1970), pp. 217–19.

9. For Gaullist views, see Jean-Louis Quermonne, "Vers un régionalisme 'fonctionnel'?" *Revue française de science politique*, Vol. 13 (December 1963), pp. 849, 876, and the text of President de Gaulle's referendum on the regions in *Revue du droit public*, Vol. 85 (May–June 1969), pp. 460–73. For President Pompidou's attitude, see his Lyon city hall speech in *Le Monde*, No. 1149 (Oct. 29–Nov. 4, 1970) and his press conference on Jan. 21, 1971, published by Ambassade de France, Service de Presse et d'Information (New York), pp. 16–18.

to himself, as a symbol of authentic radical change, the support of voters regardless of their ideological or partisan predispositions. Servan-Schreiber did win a seat in Nancy, a Gaullist stronghold, but sustained a humiliating defeat in his challenge to Premier Chaban-Delmas in Bordeaux, where Chaban has long been a popular mayor. In both Nancy and Bordeaux the voters were more concerned with choosing a deputy who would gain benefits for the district than with national political and social change. In Nancy, where people were angry with the government for its alleged favoritism to the rival city of Metz and neglect of local interests, Servan-Schreiber impressed voters of diverse political horizons with his willingness to listen to their complaints and convinced them that he could accomplish more for their region than the Gaullist incumbent (who had provoked the by-election by his own resignation in protest against the government's neglect of Nancy). Bordeaux, in contrast, has manifestly prospered from the influence wielded by its mayor within the government; Servan-Schreiber could hardly claim that he could do more for both Bordeaux and Nancy, and his accusation that Chaban did *too much* for Bordeaux as premier was not what the local people wanted to hear. The inveterate parochialism of voters in the small French parliamentary constituencies, as well as a French republican tradition against "plebiscitary" exploitation of by-elections, eliminates these contests as possible trial heats for the presidential race.[10]

Premier Chaban-Delmas's continued service as mayor of Bordeaux is but one example of the enormous importance attached by French politicians to local government office. French mayors, who are definitely "strong" in the American sense, are elected for six-year terms by municipal councils immediately after the councilors are themselves elected by the people. Since councilors frequently run on slates pledged to elect or reelect a specific person as mayor, the mayor is often virtually chosen by the people. When Gaston Defferre, chairman of the Socialist group in the National Assembly, became the leading presidential candidate of the Left, the Gaullists were so anxious to block his reelection as mayor of Marseille, and thus perhaps deal his candidacy a fatal blow, that they revised the municipal election law to ensure his defeat.

Success in local government elections, like winning a seat in the

10. It is true that Servan-Schreiber pledged *not* to run for president, and he has indicated he would like to be premier, even under Pompidou. But this circumstance does not affect my conclusion about by-elections as presidential trial heats.

National Assembly, is good for one's political career, but does not necessarily build up a presidential candidacy. In spite of all that the Gaullists could do, Gaston Defferre was reelected mayor of Marseille in 1965, but that triumph did not save his candidacy from collapse a few months later. In 1969, when Defferre maintained his presidential candidacy to the bitter end, he polled only 37,830 votes out of the 440,394 cast for president in Marseille. Yet in the 1971 municipal elections Mayor Defferre was again easily reelected. It is apparent that the French, like many Americans, vote differently in local and national elections.[11]

In the absence of presidential primaries, nominating conventions, and relevant subpresidential elections, only the mass media, public opinion polls, and negotiation among politicians remain as channels for the creation of presidential candidates. How the French have selected presidents under these conditions will now be examined.

The October and November Elections of 1962

At the end of October 1962, the French people approved a constitutional amendment, accompanied by an implementing statute, providing for election of the president of the Republic by direct universal suffrage. Since the National Assembly had been dissolved by President de Gaulle because a censure motion had been carried against the Pompidou government in protest against the referendum, parliamentary elections followed in November. The result was confirmation of the referendum as President de Gaulle won a stronger and more reliable majority in the National Assembly.

All the non-Gaullist political parties, from extreme Left to far Right, opposed the referendum for direct election of the president. In the ensuing National Assembly election, the non-Gaullist and "antipresidential" Right lost almost all its seats, and was effectively replaced by Gaullists and their allies much better prepared to engage in presidential politics. On the Left, in contrast, most incumbent deputies were reelected, while many veteran politicans defeated in the 1958 landslide to the Right were returned to their seats.[12] Those ele-

11. The differences between French local and national politics are explained by Mark Kesselman in his fascinating study, *The Ambiguous Consensus* (Knopf, 1967). The Marseille election results are based on figures in *Le Monde* (Feb. 4, 1964), p. 2.

12. Mattéi Dogan, "Note sur le nouveau personnel parlementaire," in François Goguel (ed.), *Le Référendum d'octobre et les élections de novembre 1962* (Armand Colin, 1965), pp. 429–32.

ments in the Left most likely to find presidential politics distasteful were strengthened by the 1962 election.

In neither election campaign did the Left use the rather poor television facilities granted by the government to display fresh new political talent in preparation for the eventual presidential elections. The Left was thus associated with "old politics" while the Gaullists, by comparison, looked like progressive reformers. So far as presidential politics was concerned, the 1962 elections turned the Right toward the future and the Left toward the past. Yet the Left badly needed to develop a presidential nominating process to recruit a suitable candidate for the 1965 election. In President de Gaulle, the Right already had the best candidate of the century, while Premier Pompidou was already preparing for a future presidential bid through frequent and carefully planned appearances on television.[13] Handicapped both by its own traditional prejudice against dynamic personal leadership and by exclusion from the electronic media, the Left was far behind before the presidential competition ever started.

The Presidential Nomination Campaign of Gaston Defferre

The secretary-general of the Socialist party, Guy Mollet, a practitioner of traditional French politics, wanted the opposition to nominate an "honest republican," an "Albert Schweitzer," not necessarily a Socialist, to unite Frenchmen of all political backgrounds against de Gaulle's personal rule. For Mollet, the mission of the second president of the Fifth Republic was to repeat the achievement of Jules Grévy, second president of the Third Republic, who dismantled the presidency as an effective instrument for national political leadership. To this end, a common candidate would be selected through confidential negotiations among top leaders of the political groups concerned; the candidate would be bound by the joint program agreed upon by the contracting parties, which would supervise his campaign to prevent any deviation that might offend a component of the coalition. This procedure was intended to encourage inclusion of the Communist party in the electoral alliance, for the common minimum program would prevent the candidate from anti- or pro-communist gestures

13. See Pierre Rouanet's discussion of Pompidou's use of television in *Pompidou* (Grasset, 1969), pp. 153–56.

that might annoy the seemingly incompatible parties in the alliance. No party would have to deviate from its verbally orthodox ideology and yet a maximum aggregation of votes *against* de Gaulle, if not *for* anything in particular, could be achieved.

But Mollet did not act fast enough. By August 1963, still two and a half years before the scheduled presidential election, the rumor spread that President de Gaulle would take his manifestly unprepared opponents by surprise through sudden resignation and candidacy for re-election. A small group of professors, civil servants, and journalists who opposed de Gaulle, but favored presidential government for France, decided to anticipate any Gaullist maneuver by immediately initiating a presidential nomination campaign. They turned to Gaston Defferre as the candidate who could combine opposition to de Gaulle with a new "presidential sytle of politics." In addition to his achievements as mayor of a great French city, publisher of a major regional daily newspaper, and author of much-praised legislation for the decolonization of French Africa, Defferre was a leader of the reformist minority within the Socialist party that opposed Guy Mollet.[14]

In order to convince the reluctant Defferre to enter the race, and launch a boom to make him unstoppable, the nonsocialist weekly *L'Express* began on September 19, 1963, a series of articles describing "Monsieur X," ideal candidate for president, complete with interviews granted by this mythical personage. Even *Le Monde* reported speculation over the identity of "Monsieur X." After a month of this mystery campaign, before officially informing the leadership of his own party, Defferre revealed privately to leaders of the Club Jean Moulin, the most prestigious of French "political clubs," that he had decided to run for president. A few days later, *Paris-Match*, a French equivalent of *Life* and unimpeachably nonsocialist, declared that

---

14. In addition to the books by Schwartzenberg (*La Campagne présidentielle de 1965*) and Wilson (*French Democratic Left*), helpful material on the 1965 presidential campaign is found in William G. Andrews and Stanley Hoffmann, "France: The Search for Presidentialism," in William G. Andrews (ed.), *European Politics I* (Van Nostrand, 1966), pp. 77–138; Harvey G. Simmons, *French Socialists in Search of a Role 1956–1967* (Cornell University Press, 1970); George Suffert, *De Defferre à Mitterrand* (Seuil, 1966); Philip M. Williams, *French Politicians and Elections 1951–1969* (Cambridge University Press, 1970); David M. Wood and Sally Angela Shelton, "The Changing French Political Scene—The 1965 Presidential Election," *Business and Government Review* (University of Missouri), Vol. 7 (November–December 1966), pp. 5–16; Colette Ysmal, *Defferre parle* (Paris: Foundation nationale des sciences politiques, 1966); André Philip, *Les Socialistes* (Seuil, 1967), pp. 181–85.

"Monsieur X" was really Gaston Defferre. Only after this report did Defferre privately request Guy Mollet to put presidential candidacy on the agenda of the Socialist party steering committee. On December 11, *Le Monde* published a front-page article by Maurice Duverger exhorting "Monsieur X" to come out in the open. Two days later the caucus of Socialist deputies in the National Assembly voted a recommendation that their chairman, Gaston Defferre, be endorsed by the Socialist party for president. The next day *Le Monde* reported that the Socialist steering committee had agreed to discuss Defferre's candidacy. On December 17 an entire page of *Le Monde* was devoted to a manifesto drafted by Michel Crozier which expounded views identified with "Monsieur X," although Defferre was not mentioned by name. The manifesto was officially supported by a number of political clubs, and also signed by a few individual trade-union and farm-organization leaders. Finally, on December 18, Defferre emerged from the Socialist steering committee to announce briefly that he would run for president if authorized by the special Socialist party congress that was to meet at Clichy specifically to consider his candidacy.

But Defferre proceeded to kick off his campaign without waiting for party approval. On January 12, 1964, he gave a major address in Marseille to his own Socialist Federation of Bouches-du-Rhône, the biggest Socialist organization in France as a result of his leadership. Defferre made it clear that although he would not, as a loyal Socialist, run without party endorsement, he would refuse any dictation regarding his campaign or program from his own party or any combination of parties. And he demanded a prompt decision from the Socialist party, one way or another. This highly important speech, an official announcement of presidential candidacy by a top political leader, was not covered by either the Gaullist-controlled television network or the Socialist party's official organ, *Le Populaire*; since both these channels of communication were controlled by opponents of Defferre, they saw little need to report what he had to say.[15] But the "Monsieur X" boom proved strong enough to overcome these omissions. At the beginning of February 1964 the Socialist congress at Clichy unanimously endorsed Gaston Defferre for president. After indicating his objections to Defferre's candidacy and his preference for something quite

15. *Année Politique* (1964), p. 5; *Le Monde* (Jan. 14, 1964), p. 7.

different, an unhappy Guy Mollet had no choice but to join in the unanimous endorsement in order to maintain his own position in the party. It would, indeed, have made the Socialist party look ridiculous to reject at that point so outstanding a candidate as Gaston Defferre.

The investiture of Defferre by the Socialist party was only a beginning; Defferre knew perfectly well that he needed to gather a certain minimum of support outside the Socialist party if his candidacy was to be worthwhile—a minimum that is roughly the equivalent of the convention nomination for an American presidential candidate. To obtain this support Defferre embarked on three distinct but related strategies.

One strategy was to go directly to the great mass of people to build up the kind of popular support that would compel leaders of intermediary groups, including the political parties, to accept and support the candidacy of Gaston Defferre regardless of any ideological inhibitions or considerations of short-run tactical advantage. For this purpose Defferre held rallies all over France, spoke to large crowds, and even visited foreign countries to establish his standing as a statesman.

Defferre's second strategy was solicitation of direct support from both leaders and members of the so-called *forces vives*, the amateur political clubs on the one hand and the organized interest groups of labor, agriculture, and even business on the other. This strategy, like the first, emphasized trust and confidence in Gaston Defferre as a person rather than ideology or partisanship. Communist leaders were willing to commit their party's support only on the basis of a definite contract; Defferre, of course, refused to make any deals with Communist leaders, but expected to be able to attract the support of Communist voters once it became evident that their only effective choice was between Defferre and de Gaulle. In that way, Defferre hoped to avoid offending non-Left voters who might be eager to vote against de Gaulle but would never vote for any candidate contaminated by actual endorsement of the Communist party.

Neither of these strategies would shock an American, but they disturbed traditional French politicians, who felt Defferre was practicing a Gaullism of the Left. Then in the spring of 1965 Defferre added a third strategy that was not entirely consistent with his others, and which both French and American politicians might well agree was excessively bold. He called for nothing less than restructuring of the opposition to de Gaulle into a Democratic Socialist Federation that would organically merge the noncommunist Left (Socialists and Radicals) with the Center (Popular Republicans and diverse non-socialist liberals) as well as provide a place for political clubs, labor unions, and farm organizations. This "grand federation" was intended as a catch-all party on the Left (in a very broad sense) to balance the Gaullists and their allies, who already constituted a catch-all party on the Right. Such classical ideological conflicts as the church-state controversy and the clash between socialism and capitalism could then be the subject of dialogue *within* the two relatively flexible aggregations, rather than sources of conflict *between* parties relatively rigid in their ideological orthodoxy. Only after the formation of this "grand federation" would there be any discussion about the Communists, and certainly no concessions would be made to induce them to join; instead, it was hoped that a great noncommunist organization would act as a magnet for Communist voters, if not for their leaders. Gaston Defferre set the successful establishment of the "grand federation" as an indispensable condition for continuance of his candidacy.

All three strategies failed. When negotiations between the Socialists and Popular Republicans for the "grand federation" broke down on June 19, 1965, ostensibly on the church-state issue, Gaston Defferre dropped out of the presidential race even though he would have had no difficulty qualifying for the presidential ballot.[16] He had lost the "nomination" as defined by his three strategies. The failure should not be permitted to obscure the fact that these strategies were all justified in terms of their postelection effects. If they had worked, it seems likely that Defferre (1) would have eventually obtained a National Assembly he could live with as president; (2) would have offered the French a meaningful choice, making it possible to vote against de Gaulle without having to vote for weak and ineffective government; and (3) would have been accepted as a legitimate president because of election on his own merits rather than as a mere object of endorsements by leaders of incompatible parties. Defferre's aim was true, but he turned out to be incapable of firing the gun.

Defferre's recruitment as a candidate, quite innovative in France, was not lacking in features familiar to American presidential politics:

16. According to John Ambler, the "grand federation" failed because of "the reluctance of party leaders to give up the independence of their parties." *Government and Politics of France* (Houghton Mifflin, 1971), p. 101.

there was both a "draft" and a "boom," a candidate's attempt to snatch the endorsement of a key party organization from under its leader's nose, and a candidate who insisted on running his own campaign and explaining his own program regardless of platform. What was different about the Defferre candidacy was the inordinate impact on the nominating process of a relatively small sector of the mass media, working in cooperation with a few political amateurs. In effect, a weekly newsmagazine imposed upon one of the largest, oldest, most parochial and boss-ridden of French political parties a candidate for president against the wishes of the party's long-entrenched leadership. It was nonsocialists who produced the Socialist candidate. The recruitment process certainly produced a candidate quite different from what might have been expected from the French Left at the time; unfortunately, Defferre did not possess all the qualities needed to win nomination and election in the "presidential style" he himself thought appropriate.

On the positive side, it seems that Gaston Defferre, if elected, would have been a "real" president. Whatever he said, or will say, about the presidency for purposes of political campaigning or party negotiations, one can hardly imagine that Defferre would be content to "inaugurate chrysanthemums," as the French say, once he entered the Elysée. What made Defferre an unsuccessful candidate was a personality that is cool, reserved, and aloof rather than warm and re-assuring, together with a businesslike rather than inspirational style of oratory. He simply lacks that certain something—charisma, glamour, or sex appeal—that distinguishes a man who can move the masses from the highly competent executive who can manage a great enterprise or even lead a parliamentary delegation.[17] Excluded by Gaullist policy from television, where expert production might have presented him more appealingly, Defferre just could not be "sold."

Defferre's inability to move the masses, soon demonstrated in the public opinion polls, meant that he could not use popular support to exert pressure on party and interest-group leaders. However political they may be, noncommunist interest groups such as labor unions and

17. My own observation of Defferre in person and on television accords with these appraisals by French and American writers. Lowell Noonan adds that Defferre seemed too reticent during the campaign about revealing his true convictions about presidential government, and thus disappointed potential supporters. *France: The Politics of Continuity in Change* (Holt, Rinehart and Winston, 1970), p. 211.

farm organizations are expected by their rank-and-file to be non-partisan; in the absence of any mass enthusiasm for Defferre, interest-group leaders sympathetic to him had to soft-pedal their support. In Defferre's third and most daring strategy, the construction of a "grand federation," his lack of mass popular support compelled him to depend on old-fashioned negotiations among party leaders. And since Defferre had permitted Mollet to remain Socialist secretary-general because he had finally voted to endorse Defferre, Mollet could control negotiations with the Popular Republicans for formation of the "grand federation." It was hardly surprising that the Socialist and Popular Republican delegations agreed to disagree about a statement on church-state relations. But leaving Mollet in a position to do damage was much less fundamental than Defferre's failure to move the masses; if Defferre had captured the popular imagination, Guy Mollet, a political realist if ever there was one, would have supported his fellow Socialist just as he once found it opportune to support General de Gaulle.

Defferre might have had an opportunity to put his strategy to a test in the Marseille municipal election of spring 1965. But because of circumstances not entirely under his control, he ultimately won the election by attracting Gaullist votes against the Communists rather than the other way around, as his national strategy required. His re-election, necessary as it was for his political career, did not add to the credibility of his presidential candidacy.[18]

The Candidacy of François Mitterrand

With Defferre out of the picture, Guy Mollet resumed his search for an "honest republican," and expressed interest in Antoine Pinay, the patron saint of French conservatism. But before Pinay or any other "republican" could be committed, another leader of the Left seized the initiative. During the Fourth Republic, François Mitterrand led a small but well-placed catch-all parliamentary group that contributed a remarkably large share of the ministers of that period. During the Fifth Republic, Mitterrand put together a federation of political clubs, known as the CIR (Convention des Institutions Républicaines), which became his personal political base. Mitterrand's

18. This point is strongly made by Jean Daniel in "Des semaines décisives," *Le Nouvel Observateur* (March 25, 1965), p. 5.

refusal (until 1971) to join any of the traditional political parties, his collaboration with Pierre Mendès-France, his support of Defferre's attempted candidacy, and his open-minded view on presidential government, all combine to distinguish him from a traditional politician like Guy Mollet. But Mitterrand's obsession with the unity of the Left, which includes the Communists, and his personal evolution toward dogmatic socialism have probably encouraged tendencies within the Left toward reliance on ideological purity rather than on realistic programs as a means of gaining power.

In sharp contrast to Defferre, Mitterrand was capable of attracting popular support and used it to overcome the resistance of the entrenched party leaders of the Left. But Mitterrand's popular appeal has been uneven; after having improved during the years 1965–68, his prestige plummeted during the tumultuous events of May and June 1968, and yet he has recently made a remarkable political comeback.[19] Despite considerable popular approval on the Left, he tends to be especially disliked by conservatives, perhaps more so than other politicians of the democratic Left.

Like Defferre, Mitterrand announced his candidacy before getting permission from any political party; unlike Defferre, he did not explicitly grant any party the effective right to veto his candidacy by refusing endorsement. In that way he catered to the feeling of many French voters that the president should not be partisan, and he could scare off rival candidates waiting for him to drop out as Defferre had done.

In his strategy for building support, Mitterrand followed Defferre in demanding that groups and parties trust him as a person and not bind him to a detailed program agreed to by the party leaders. He insisted on announcing his own program and running his own campaign. But Mitterrand departed from Defferre's strategy by welcoming endorsements from party leaders, especially those of the Communist party, provided, of course, that they not try to supervise him. In turn, however, Mitterrand did not demand that the Left merge with the Center or that the parties of the Left immediately give up their iden-

19. The recent popular standing of Mitterrand and other French leaders is indicated in *Sondages,* Vol. 32, Nos. 1–2 (1970), pp. 27–33. For Mitterrand's comeback, see *L'Express,* No. 1011 (Nov. 23–29, 1970), pp. 14–15; No. 1017 (Jan. 4–10, 1971), p. 29; and No. 1041 (June 21–27, 1971), pp. 15–18. In June 1971 Mitterrand became first secretary of the Socialist party with Defferre's support and Mollet's opposition.

tities; instead, he gave the impression that, at least for the time being, his leadership would not fundamentally threaten the status quo within or between the parties. Defferre had been unable to bridge the gap between parties on such issues of the past as the church-state and socialism-capitalism controversies; Mitterrand was actually able to persuade the Communists and, with much more difficulty, the Unified Socialist party, to support him despite his quite different views on such contemporary issues as European integration and the existing constitutional regime. Indeed, the Communists went so far as to transform their opposition to the European Community into a demand for increased internal democracy in Community institutions, a position that left Mitterrand entirely free to blame General de Gaulle for obstructing the progress of European unity.[20]

It is hard to see how aggregation of the Left could have been pushed any further at the level of party leadership. But the very success at this level limited, as well as guaranteed, the vote Mitterrand could obtain from the electorate. Centrist voters who might have been attracted by the Defferrist strategy, as well as the most intensely anticommunist fringe of the Left, were turned away. Mitterrand received only 32 percent of the vote on the first ballot, as opposed to the more than 40 percent usually collected by the Left.

With Antoine Pinay, as well as Gaston Defferre, bowing out of the presidential race, the Center turned to the dynamic young president of the Popular Republicans, Jean Lecanuet, as a last-minute choice. It was his vigorous campaign, rather than Mitterrand's success in unifying the Left, that deprived General de Gaulle of his expected absolute majority on the first ballot and forced him into the runoff. The anti–de Gaulle majority was further swelled by more than 1.2 million votes cast for Jean-Louis Tixier-Vignancour, the ultra-Rightist candidate. In view of the traditional divisions of French public opinion and the novelty of presidential politics, the aggregation of support around these four candidates must be considered a remarkable achievement.

Indeed, the Lecanuet and Tixier candidacies can be said to have added substantially to the meaningful choice available to the French voters. The Centrist voters for Lecanuet were able to administer a stinging rebuke to General de Gaulle for his arrogance toward Parlia-

20. See Pierre Lethang, "La fin d'une croisade," *Le Nouvel Observateur* (Sept. 22, 1965), p. 6; and an interview with the Communist leader Waldeck-Rochet in *Le Nouvel Observateur* (Oct. 13, 1965), pp. 10–12.

ment, his policies regarding European integration, and above all his alleged neglect of the farmer; after having effectively made their point, they could elect de Gaulle on the second ballot. To these voters, to whom Mitterrand may have seemed an intransigent Socialist who had sold out to the Communists, Lecanuet's candidacy provided a way to participate in the election. Tixier-Vignancour gave Frenchmen who were bitter about de Gaulle's Algerian policy a chance to protest "within the system." Although Tixier endorsed Mitterrand as the lesser of two evils for the second ballot, the endorsement did not overcome Mitterrand's inability to attract Centrists who had voted against de Gaulle on the first ballot. Failure to aggregate the Center with the Left before the first ballot could not be offset by the brief campaign between the ballots.

Although Defferre, Mitterrand, and Lecanuet tried to build up a presidential image that could transcend party and ideology, none of the candidates on the ballot against de Gaulle was able to develop real appeal outside the normal clientele of his party or movement. Only General de Gaulle possessed a sufficiently national image to draw support from all classes and ideological predispositions. If it is compared with the normal distribution of votes in French elections when they are vigorously contested by candidates rather than by propositions on a referendum, de Gaulle's 43 percent on the first ballot was a stunning performance. But de Gaulle, unaccustomed to being judged as an elected officeholder rather than a republican monarch, was taken aback by the results of the first ballot, and it took considerable persuasion by Premier Pompidou to encourage him to come back fighting, as he did, for the second ballot.[21] If the election reduced de Gaulle's authority, it is only because his authority was so awesome to begin with. His triumph on the second ballot surely increased his democratic, if not his "historical," legitimacy, precisely because he was faced by a reasonably capable opponent. No one could say that de Gaulle was elected by default; the French people really made a choice.

Between Presidential Elections: 1965–69

During and immediately after his 1965 presidential campaign, François Mitterrand led in the formation of a "little federation" of the Left, which included the Socialists, Radicals, and the CIR. Unlike

21. On this curious episode, see Rouanet, *Pompidou*, pp. 121–53.

Defferre's projected "grand federation," this Federation of the Democratic and Socialist Left (FGDS) shunned any alliance with the Center but treated the Communist party as a "privileged ally." Merger of the components making up the FGDS into a new "Socialist party" (as distinguished from the Socialist party long known by its initials SFIO) was planned for the future but was hardly a goal unanimously desired by all participants in the new federation. For purposes of traditional parliamentary politics, the FGDS proved very useful. In the National Assembly the FGDS formed a parliamentary group much larger than would any of its component parties, with attendant advantages in committee representation, floor procedures, and publicity. In the 1967 parliamentary elections, it was able to increase both the total number of seats for the noncommunist Left and the proportion of those endorsed as authentic Leftists by the federation, even though the popular vote share of the noncommunist Left increased only slightly. As the Communists gained much from cooperation with the FGDS, the gain for the entire Left in Assembly seats endangered the government's majority. At the parliamentary level, the FGDS enabled the Left to derive a greater advantage from an electoral base that had shrunk greatly since the Fourth Republic, but whether the FGDS was itself evolving toward an alternative "party of government" capable of replacing the Gaullist coalition is, of course, highly debatable.

In presidential politics, the inadequacy of the FGDS as a device for gathering support was obvious enough; Mitterrand polled only 32 percent in 1965, despite endorsements by the Communist party as well as by the parties and groups that soon afterward formed the federation. The federation did, however, furnish a vehicle for the development of recognized personal leadership, indispensable for presidential politics but contrary to the tradition of the French Left. Mitterrand emerged as the leader of the noncommunist Left; the mass media and public opinion polls treated him as its personal symbol, and in general public esteem, as measured by the polls, he threatened to overtake Premier Pompidou. His position as formal head of the FGDS could not, of course, have elevated Mitterrand to such a strong leadership role if he had not already been the much-publicized presidential candidate of the entire Left. But he was better able to maintain the momentum generated by his candidacy because he did not have a rival for attention as head of the FGDS, and was independent of the peer-group resistance that a long-time member of a major party, such as Gaston Defferre, encounters when he engages in personality politics inconsistent with Leftist tradition (if not always with Leftist practice).

The trend toward personalism pervaded the other political groupings of the Center and Right. In the 1967 parliamentary elections Jean Lecanuet for the Center and, to a surprising extent, Premier Pompidou for the Gaullists became personal symbols of their electoral alliances. The reverses suffered by the Center therefore hurt Lecanuet very seriously, just as the gains of the Left enhanced Mitterrand's prestige. Lecanuet's eclipse and the Center's inability to replace him with anyone whose image was as "modern" and yet as anti-Gaullist demonstrates the disdavantage for presidential politics of the British type of standby leader. The very existence of the permanent, British-type Leader (with a capital "L") hinders the recruitment of other potential presidential candidates. If a mishap, whether physical or political, should befall the Leader, his organization might be caught without a candidate just when one was most needed.

That is precisely what happened to the Left after the general strike and student revolt known in current French history as the Events of May–June 1968. For reasons that need not be discussed here, Mitterrand came out of those events thoroughly discredited, at least temporarily, with virtually all sectors of opinion except his own CIR.[22] Pierre Mendès-France, his potential replacement, came out somewhat better, but Mendès had so alienated the Communist party that he could never hope to lead a united Left.

Mitterrand not only had to step down from his leadership of the FGDS after the parliamentary defeat of the noncommunist Left in the 1968 elections, but he was even excluded from television during the campaign over the 1969 referendum called by President de Gaulle. Jean Lecanuet had similarly been kept off television during the 1968 election campaign.[23] Once the Leader is overthrown, his enemies within the party try to make sure he does not revive. With these well-

22. Reasons for Mitterrand's eclipse (which has turned out to be temporary) are given by Frank L. Wilson in "The French Left and the Elections of 1968," *World Politics*, Vol. 21 (July 1969), pp. 539–74.

23. Lecanuet's exclusion is noted in Colette Ysmal, "Unité ou pluralité du centrisme?" *Revue française de science politique*, Vol. 19 (February 1969), pp. 171–72, and Mitterrand's in *Année Politique* (1969), p. 32.

televised figures now shoved into the background, where could the opposition recruit a candidate sufficiently well known to be able to compete with a Pompidou, whose successful television performances had become almost a regular feature since 1962?

If Mitterrand was brought down by the events of May–June 1968, Georges Pompidou was virtually apotheosized. It was obviously Pompidou, not de Gaulle, who had saved the regime, or at least had prevented bloodshed and greater losses to the economy. After leading the Gaullist coalition to an unprecedented election triumph, Pompidou was replaced as premier by the austere diplomat Maurice Couve de Murville. When he released Pompidou, President de Gaulle implied that the former premier might some day be called to an even higher office, which obviously could only mean the presidency. Pompidou, who had expected to remain premier, reentered the National Assembly and made it clear he would run for president whenever that post became vacant. This announced intention annoyed de Gaulle, who insisted he would serve out his term (which ended in 1972), but he neither ruled Pompidou out as a possible successor nor supported the candidacy of Pompidou's rivals.

During the Events of May–June 1968, de Gaulle had wanted to hold a referendum, but Pompidou managed to talk the president into dissolving the National Assembly, a move that was spectacularly successful. With Pompidou no longer in a position to discourage it, de Gaulle went ahead in April 1969 with a referendum combining (1) a reorganization and reduction in authority of the Senate, (2) new, but nondemocratic, governing bodies for the regions, and (3) designation of the premier, rather than the president of the Senate, as interim president of the Republic. By requiring the voters to accept or reject this miscellany as a package, de Gaulle made it obvious that the referendum was nothing more than a vote of confidence.[24]

Pompidou could hardly be excluded from the referendum campaign, lest his absence be construed as a reflection upon six years of Gaullist government or, worse yet, as an indication that Pompidou had some doubts about the referendum. On television and in person Pompidou defended its dubious propositions, but each time he appeared his very existence reminded his audience that the man who saved the regime in

24. The 1969 referendum falls squarely within the model of Gaullist plebiscites described six years earlier by Henry W. Ehrmann in "Direct Democracy in France," *American Political Science Review*, Vol. 57 (December 1963), pp. 883–901.

1968 was ready to step forward and save it again should the founder of the Fifth Republic feel unable to carry on.[25]

The Presidential Election of 1969

By resigning promptly after the defeat of his referendum, President de Gaulle caught the opposition unprepared to fight a presidential election, just as it had feared would happen in 1963. Georges Pompidou, however, was fully prepared. Waiting only one day after de Gaulle's departure, Pompidou followed the Defferre-Mitterrand precedent of initiating his own candidacy before he had party endorsement, refusing to be bound by any party program, and insisting on running his own campaign. Like Mitterrand, Pompidou made it clear that he would run whether or not the parties chose to endorse him, that he would welcome endorsements by party leaders and committees, and yet he refused to negotiate with anyone for endorsement.

In a sense, Pompidou had been recruited for the presidency when de Gaulle made him the second premier of the Fifth Republic, a position Pompidou exploited for television and press exposure as well as to build up a strong personal following within the UDR. Although his earlier experience and training had been in belles-lettres, bureaucracy, and banking, Pompidou became a master politician, able and willing to wield presidential powers. With the two previous premiers of the Fifth Republic unable to carry an Assembly constituency in metropolitan France, with the ever-popular Antoine Pinay as unwilling to run in 1969 as in 1965, and in the absence of any specific designation by de Gaulle of a successor, Georges Pompidou was the obvious choice.

Pompidou's strategy, the so-called policy of *ouverture*, included the reestablishment of an alliance between the UDR and the Independent Republicans of Giscard d'Estaing, and the inclusion of key Centrist leaders in the Gaullist coalition. Since the defection of the Independent Republicans and the opposition of the Centrists had provided the margin that defeated de Gaulle's referendum and led to his resignation, many loyal Gaullists were shocked by Pompidou's willingness to "pass the sponge" over what they thought was virtual treason. Although Pompidou himself had clashed bitterly with Giscard d'Estaing

25. Schwartzenberg, *La Guerre de succession*, pp. 32–33.

and other Independent Republicans and Centrists, he knew, as a political realist, that if a de Gaulle could not survive without the support of these "traitors," a Pompidou could hardly dispense with their support. An additional, and very substantial, benefit of *ouverture* was that Pompidou became less dependent on the UDR as a whole, for he could play its internal factions and outside groups against each other both before and after his election.

The mechanics of nomination moved swiftly. News of Pompidou's candidacy was released at 9:30 A.M., April 29; at 10 A.M., Pompidou proceeded with a press conference. On that same day he was endorsed by the steering committee of the UDR parliamentary group, then by the caucus of UDR deputies, and finally, at 6 P.M., by the organization's national executive committee. An hour before that meeting, Pompidou appeared before the caucus of Independent Republican deputies. Giscard d'Estaing managed to delay an endorsement for one day to see if he could round up support for another candidacy, but his group, too eager to join the Pompidou bandwagon, voted on April 30 to endorse the former premier; Giscard had no choice but to lead his followers where they wanted to go.[26] Pompidou was thus "nominated" in just two days. He subsequently broadened his support by obtaining the endorsement of no fewer than twelve of the thirty-three Centrist deputies in the National Assembly.

With their previous presidential candidates too politically "used up" for a rerun, and under pressure of time to make a quick decision, the opposition parties eventually accepted as their leading candidate one prepared for that nomination by a curious combination of television exposure during the referendum campaign, results of public opinion polls, and a provision of the 1958 constitution that the 1969 referendum was intended to repeal:

> In the Center there emerged, almost by constitutional prestidigitation, Alain Poher, a politician previously almost unknown to the public. He had been elected as speaker of the Senate a few months earlier. Quite naturally he moved into the foreground of the fight against the referendum which sought to transform thoroughly the traditional upper house

26. According to a biography of Giscard published in 1968, the Independent Republican leader set "the beginning of the next decade" as the date on which he would run for president against Pompidou. Michel Bassi, *Valéry Giscard d'Estaing* (Grasset, 1968), p. 136. Was April 1969 too early?

over which he presided. According to . . . the constitution, General De Gaulle's resignation made him the interim President.

M. Poher's elevated position exposed him to public scrutiny, and for a moment it appeared that Frenchmen liked what they saw, were it only because he seemed to represent the very opposite of the leader who had disowned them. According to the first public opinion poll organized after the interim President had announced his candidacy, it seemed likely that Pompidou would be ahead in the first ballot without however winning the required majority (43 percent for Pompidou, 35 percent for Poher), but that in the second ballot when presumably all non-Gaullist forces would unite behind Poher, the latter would beat the Gaullist candidate with 55 percent as against 45 percent for Pompidou.[27]

Here at last was the "honest republican" for whom Guy Mollet had been searching for so long. For traditionalist politicians of the Left and Center, Alain Poher was nothing less than the candidate of their dreams. At first, however, Poher was reluctant to run. He was not sure that it was proper for the interim president to run for president, and, in any event, he definitely did not want to repeat Lecanuet's experience of running as a Centrist while the Left united around another candidate.

Before making his decision to run, Poher consulted experts from the Société Française d'Etudes par Sondages (SOFRES) about their firm's poll of May 5–6. From his discussion with these experts, who explained the results in detail, Poher formed the conclusion that if he did not run against Pompidou, the former premier would be elected on the first ballot. This consideration was an important element in Poher's eventual decision to run for president.[28]

Although assured that such possible conservative candidates as Antoine Pinay and General Pierre Koenig would definitely stay out if he entered, Poher was afraid that François Mitterrand could still make a comeback as candidate of a united Left with Communists included. Mitterrand had been able to reestablish contacts with Communist leaders, and was attracting favorable crowds in a swing around the country. To forestall any "united Left" candidacy and reassure Poher, Guy Mollet decided to have the Socialist party endorse a purely token candidate, surely an egregious example of nonaggregation of support.

27. Henry W. Ehrmann, *Politics in France* (2d ed., Little, Brown, 1971), p. 117.
28. Jean and Monica Charlot, "Les campagnes de Georges Pompidou et Alain Poher," *Revue française de science politique*, Vol. 20 (April 1970), pp. 227–29.

Once again Mollet did not move fast enough to head off Gaston Defferre, and once again Mollet got his own way in the end regardless of Defferre. The mayor of Marseille announced his candidacy only a few hours after Pompidou's announcement on April 29. This time Defferre did not try to realign the parties but assumed, instead, that there was already a de facto alignment of the parties and voters constituting the majority that had voted *non* in the referendum. He expected to scare off the hesitating Poher by announcing his candidacy early; and by shunning the Communists, as in 1965, he would attract enough Centrist votes to reach the second ballot. Confronted with a choice between the Socialist Defferre and the Gaullist Pompidou, the Communist voters would then presumably be willing to vote for Defferre regardless of the wishes of their leaders, with whom Defferre would make no deals lest he alienate the equally essential Centrist vote.

Guy Mollet was unhappy with Defferre's initiative, just as he had been in 1963, but it turned out that Defferre, in spite of himself, served the purpose of token Socialist candidate just as efficiently as Mollet's own choice for that menial task, Christian Pineau. Many of Defferre's supporters within the Socialist party agreed with Mollet that Poher was the best available candidate at the time, and it was one of Defferre's leading supporters who pulled the rug from under his candidacy by moving a resolution at the Socialist party congress to the effect that Defferre should withdraw whenever another "republican candidate" seemed more likely to beat Pompidou. This motion passed by a unanimous voice vote, and many Socialist militants (including Guy Mollet, needless to say) were to behave as if Defferre were not the official Socialist presidential candidate.

Defferre found himself deserted not only by Socialist organization regulars, friends as well as foes, but also by groups both within and outside the Socialist party that supposedly favored a renewal and modernization of the Left, a cause for which Defferre had fought hard and long. His acceptance of the Socialist party endorsement under conditions apparently dictated by Guy Mollet gave the impression, to those who were eager to believe the worst, that Defferre had become a mere errand-boy for the Socialist party secretary. Pierre Mendès-France, appalled by the prospect that the noncommunist Left would be utterly overwhelmed, tried to rescue Defferre by agreeing to "run" on the same ticket as Defferre's premier-designate. In spite of the fact that not even the worst enemies of Mendès-France could really accuse him of selling out to Guy Mollet, this laudable effort, particularly difficult for Mendès because of his conscientious objection to presidential politics, neither brought to Defferre the necessary campaign workers nor dissuaded other Left-wingers from entering the presidential race. No less than four candidates, including a Communist, finally represented the Left. Yet in total percentage of votes cast, these four candidates did just about as well as Mitterrand in 1965, a remarkable performance in view of the drain of Socialist votes to Poher on the first ballot.

When it became apparent that Poher was a far more popular candidate than Defferre, at least for the first ballot, the strategy of the Defferre–Mendès-France "tandem" changed to a drive for third place; Defferre declared that if he got one more vote than Jacques Duclos, the Communist candidate, he would be content. Such a result would not only maintain the position of the noncommunist Left, but might even induce Poher to withdraw from the second ballot in favor of Defferre, under the assumption that Defferre could pull more votes from the Left, including Communists, than the Centrist candidate. Curiously enough, this strategy, and any remaining hope of stopping Pompidou, required that Poher increase or at least maintain his strength.

But this is precisely what did not happen. In Poher's downfall, the significance of the polls published in newspapers during the campaign was not their accuracy or consistency, but the cumulative impact they may have had on the voters who read them.[29] What voters saw in the press was Poher on the rise during the first half of May and then on the decline during the rest of the month until the election. When they looked at the score for Jacques Duclos, the Communist candidate was pulling only 10 percent of the vote early in May, one-half the normal Communist poll. But as the Communist machine went into action and Duclos waged a brilliant campaign on television, Communist voters who might have been tempted to support Poher went back home to their party. By May 29, the voters could have read that Poher had declined to 25 percent from his peak of 39 percent, while Duclos had arrived at 18 percent. The actual vote on June 1 was 23.42 percent for

29. The polls are very conveniently listed in order of their publication by David B. Goldey in "The French Presidential Election of 1st and 15th June 1969," *Parliamentary Affairs*, Vol. 23 (Autumn 1969), p. 331.

Poher and 21.52 percent for Duclos, who missed the second ballot by only 420,000 votes. Defferre arrived a very poor third with 5.0 percent, not much ahead of Michel Rocard, Unified Socialist, at 3.66 percent. Defferre's exhortations to keep the Communist off the second ballot obviously backfired; the weaker Poher seemed to the voters, the more imperative it was for the more anticommunist among them to abandon Defferre and support the only candidate who could beat Duclos. The picture presented by the public opinion polls thus deprived voters of their freedom of choice.

In terms of sheer talent, the recruitment of presidential candidates for the first ballot in 1969 must be considered successful. Pompidou, Defferre, and Michel Rocard might well be capable presidents. But with the breakdown of the aggregation process on the part of the opposition, the candidate who ended up as apparent leader was the one least likely to impress the people as able and willing to exercise presidential power. Between a Poher and Pompidou, the people were not given a meaningful choice.

Poher's apparent weakness gave the Communist party an opportunity to stage a rare and frightening demonstration of its power: Communist voters were ordered not to vote, and two-thirds of them apparently followed this unusual directive.[30] After the election, the Communist leaders made it clear that any candidate who wants Communist votes will have to come to terms with Communist party leadership. Since a substantial minority of French voters prefer to vote Gaullist, even with reluctance, rather than support a candidate who has capitulated to Communist pressure, Communist policy helps to perpetuate the Gaullist grip on the presidency.[31]

Against an inept campaigner deserted by important allies, Pompidou obtained only 57.6 percent of the vote on the second ballot, a result that does not compare favorably with the 54.5 percent received by de Gaulle against much more formidable opposition. But even if Pompidou had been approved by a much greater majority, the fact would remain that he was put to the kind of obvious, difficult, and meaningful test that enhances presidential legitimacy and authority.

30. Alain Lancelot and Pierre Weill, "L'Evolution politique des électeurs français de février à juin 1969," *Revue française de science politique*, Vol. 20 (April 1970), pp. 278–79.

31. For a careful consideration of solutions to the Centrist-Communist dilemma of the opposition, see Charles A. Micaud, "Gaullism after de Gaulle," *Orbis*, Vol. 14 (Fall 1970), pp. 657–72.

Some Conclusions and Implications

This review of France's short experience with the popular election of presidents suggests a number of general conclusions about the process of selecting chief executives. Some of these seem to be of particular relevance to Americans at a time when their selection process is under considerable attack, and there is a real possibility of significant changes in the traditional way of choosing presidents.

Drawing conclusions of general applicability from the experience of a single nation is always hazardous; to attempt to apply these findings to the political life of another country would seem, to some scholars, to verge on the foolhardy. Perhaps, in view of the state of political knowledge, it is. But it would be irresponsible not to at least attempt to draw inferences from French experience that would illuminate issues of presidential politics in the United States. For what other reason should an American audience be concerned about the selection of French presidents?

The conclusions to this chapter therefore consist of ten rather general arguments, or hypotheses, drawn from the brief French experience outlined above. Each offers a moral for Americans seeking to evaluate or to change the way U.S. presidents are chosen.

1. Popular election of a president without an institutionalized nominating process leads to unpredictable and, in a sense, random intervention by the mass media, public opinion polls, and small groups of amateurs who are all too likely to start something they cannot finish. Although frequently unrepresentative of significant political forces, these elements may be able to impose on political parties a candidate who does not belong in the presidential race. The futile Defferre and Poher candidacies, if initiated at all, should have been eliminated early in the campaign. Defferre and Poher were innocent victims of a lack of system that wasted their time, energy, and political credit to no useful purpose.

In the United States, unlike France, the nominating process was well institutionalized before the advent of television and the public opinion polls, and indeed was in many respects established before the rise of the mass-circulation press. As a result, the impact of the channels of mass communication is resisted and checked by various institutions. The capability of a candidate to win can be verified, for example, through contests for high office or presidential primaries; it is not exclusively dependent on public opinion polls. It is not that there is anything sinister about the mass media or the public opinion polls; but when they are allowed to dominate presidential nomination, as can happen in France, the results are likely to be undesirable. American nominating institutions provide an essential element of coordination, discipline, and planning in the nominating process that is conspicuously lacking in France.

It follows that any reform of the American presidential nominating process should avoid weakening the net effect of formal nominating institutions, in the broad sense, on the total nominating process. The influence of the media and the public opinion polls must be kept within bounds, but this limitation should be accomplished through strong countervailing institutions rather than by restrictive government regulation.

2. Maneuvers that dissipate support in an underinstitutionalized environment may actually facilitate the final aggregation of support when practiced in the framework of a highly structured nominating process. Thus, for example, Guy Mollet's device of using a token Socialist candidate to run interference for his real candidate, Alain Poher, is a maneuver quite familiar to observers of American presidential nominating politics. It may take the form, for example, of a "favorite son" who freezes his delegation's votes so that they are withheld from a leading candidate long enough for a competitor to overtake him. The difference between the French and American situations is that manipulative behavior of this type in France is likely to lead to the proliferation of candidacies, while in the United States a single candidate ultimately emerges.

American presidential nominating institutions, including the national nominating conventions, are characterized by all sorts of complexities, loose ends, vagueness, and room for maneuver, so that it is possible to accommodate diverse political maneuvers and still come out with a single candidate. It is important to maintain and, if possible, to strengthen the capacity of the process to transform divisive behavior into manipulations that lead to an aggregation around a single candidate. This transformation does not occur in France because there are no structures to induce it. In the United States, the existing structures should not be eliminated, simplified, or rationalized to such an extent that the impact of divisive moves will be transmitted, by way of multiple candidacies, to the presidential election.

3. French experience strongly supports the view that short campaigns and presidential politics are incompatible. Cutting short the time available for nominating processes heavily favors (a) incumbents in high office, (b) former presidential candidates, (c) persons with access to broadcast time under their production control, (d) persons whom the mass media have selected for attention and buildup, and (e) national political machines (in contemporary France, the Communist and Gaullist organizations).

French experience with a two-week period between the ballots of a two-round election suggests that two weeks is insufficient for the reaggregation of support required by the elimination of lower-placed candidates, and yet long enough to tempt politicians into thinking that they can make up between ballots for deficiencies in their campaigns before the first ballot.

The total time consumed by presidential nominating politics in the United States should not be drastically reduced. The only way to shorten preparations for presidential campaigns is to cut the president's term of office or to let the president call elections at his pleasure without notice. French experience suggests that the latter practice favors the "ins" over the "outs."

In the unlikely event that the United States should adopt a two-ballot arrangement for direct election of the president, the second ballot either should take place a week after the first, in order to encourage completion of the nominating process before the election, or should be scheduled at least six weeks later to permit a campaign based on the results of the first ballot.

4. Whether presidential, legislative, or other elections should be held simultaneously or separately is not as crucial as the predictability of election dates and their relation to each other. The device of a leader with a shadow cabinet, which provides a standby candidate ready for any sudden election, may be more appropriate for a purely parliamentary system than for presidential politics. If the leader is subject to vicissitudes that can bring him down, he may not be available for presidential candidacy just when he is most needed; the submergence of Mitterrand and Lecanuet exemplifies this outcome. But if the leader achieves firm stability of tenure, as in Britain (particularly in the Labour party), the recruitment of fresh presidential talent and the aggregation of support as the result of shifts in public opinion and party disposition may be hampered. Needless to say, a strong

presidency could hardly be maintained if the "strong man" of a party or coalition, if there is one, nominates a hand-picked candidate subject to his orders rather than running for the office himself.

If the strong, permanent leader is rejected as a solution, then it seems imperative that elections be held on a schedule that provides the nominating process with sufficient time, and a sufficiently definite deadline, to produce candidates when needed. The American system of elections by the calendar offers this advantage.

5. Nothing in French experience supports the desirability of a long presidential term. The seven-year term simply lengthens the time for intrigue over presidential candidacy; consideration of candidates for the 1976 presidential election started no later than 1970.[32] A long term also increases the probability of the president's resignation, disability, or death. Whether vacancies are filled by election of a new president or by a vice-president completing the unexpired term, the result is that the president is less likely to be chosen through a nominating process that gives the people a meaningful choice of authentic candidates. The lesson for the United States is that the term of the president should remain at four years.

6. To assure a meaningful choice of candidates, so that the victor is thought of as the "people's choice," not merely as president by default, the major candidates must (a) have the will and desire to win, (b) make the presidency their main objective, and (c) respond to popular expectations of the effective use of presidential power.[33] The election is falsified when a major candidate is primarily concerned with creating a new political style, reforming and realigning the political parties, restoring ideological purity and distinctiveness, winning control of legislative bodies and local governments, or "running for exercise." Although in 1965 both Defferre and Mitterrand turned out to be insufficiently single-minded about the presidency, the nominating process failed to eliminate Defferre early enough and permitted Mitterrand to become a major candidate. French experience suggests that if nomination comes too easily, if it depends more on chance or a "fast draw" than on hard work and a zest for political combat, nomi-

32. See *L'Express*, No. 1004 (Oct. 5–11, 1970), p. 11, and No. 1015 (Dec. 21–27, 1970), p. 12.

33. Roy Pierce pointed out in 1968 that a candidate who can win the French presidency would not "willingly confine himself to a placid role as ceremonial chief of state." *French Politics and Political Institutions* (Harper and Row, 1968), p. 223. This prediction was certainly borne out by the 1969 election of Pompidou rather than of Poher.

nees may lack not only the will but also the energy, the aggressiveness, and the toughness to compete for the presidency. In such cases the loss to the people of a real choice among effectively competing candidates is a much more serious matter than the loss of an election by a particular candidate.

Of the French presidential candidates, only Georges Pompidou resembles Franklin D. Roosevelt, John F. Kennedy, or Richard M. Nixon in that he aimed at the presidency early in his political career, never lost sight of the objective, and created an image of the ability to use presidential power if he was elected. If General de Gaulle is omitted as being unique, the fact that few, if any, of the other nine persons who have qualified for the French presidential ballot come close to fitting the pattern of a highly motivated candidate is evidence of a certain deficiency in the nomination process, especially on the part of the opposition. On the other hand, the emergence within the Gaullist coalition of personalities with manifest presidential ambitions, of which Giscard d'Estaing is but one example, could mean trouble for the present majority if suitable nominating processes are not available to decide on one candidate and eliminate his rivals from the competition.

It may be true that the financial and physical demands on American presidential candidates are excessive. But measures to relieve candidates of these burdens should not allow the nomination of candidates who lack the desire and the will to win and use the presidency. Major candidates with nonpresidential objectives, however worthy, should be eliminated as early in the nominating campaign as possible.

Gerald M. Pomper has pointed out that in 1964 the American nominating process failed, in that the Republicans and their candidate were more concerned with ideology than with beating Lyndon Johnson.[34] President Johnson derived less authority, in the long run, from his lopsided majority than his predecessor obtained from the narrowest of victory margins. Although there is no way to guarantee that a candidate will really compete, the nominating process should be tough and competitive enough to eliminate the less motivated as well as the less vigorous.

7. "Third-party" candidates who are unlikely to win the presidency are dysfunctional under some circumstances, but not always.

34. *Nominating the President* (Norton, 1966), pp. 273–75.

Minor candidates who emerge directly from the failure to gather support for a major candidacy are highly undesirable. In 1969 either Defferre or Poher could conceivably have been the major opposition candidate, but not both: it was as if the Democrats in 1972 had nominated both McGovern and Humphrey because they could not make up their minds.

Another dysfunctional minor candidacy is one put up by a national political machine with a controllable and deliverable block vote. In 1969 the French Communist party demonstrated once again that it does, in fact, control approximately one-sixth to one-fifth of the votes cast, and that the great majority of its voters will follow its directives, however unconventional, with a regularity that any nineteenth-century American political boss would envy. The fact that this power is exercised by Communists, or that it was used to keep voters away from the polls, is not the main point. When voters protest against an inadequate choice of candidates by abstention or by casting invalid ballots, they may contribute to the eventual effectiveness of presidential politics. But if a block of votes becomes the property of any specific clique of leaders, however nonrevolutionary and conformist they may be, it is much more difficult to provide a meaningful choice of candidates to the majority of people who presumably want to make a choice of their own without dictation.

The entry of minor candidates who represent, rather than control, voters who feel ignored by the major candidates may well contribute to the effectiveness of presidential politics. In 1965 the campaigns of Jean Lecanuet and Jean-Louis Tixier-Vignancour gave millions of voters who could not have voted for Mitterrand (at least on the first ballot) a chance to make their weight effectively felt in the election. Once they had made their point by forcing General de Gaulle into a second ballot, some of these voters proceeded to elect him. In 1969 Pompidou took over much of the Center and received the endorsement of none other than Tixier-Vignancour as the extreme Right evaporated as an electoral force. Thus the protest candidacies of the Center and far Right were followed by integration and reconciliation rather than alienation and fragmentation.

It is too soon to tell whether the extreme-Left candidacies of Michel Rocard and Alain Krivine will be followed by similar effects, but in the short run these candidacies surely did no damage of their own, and they gave some people a chance to relieve their frustrations at the polls rather than at the barricades. The smallness of their vote in an election in which Leftist voters had every incentive to cast a protest vote for a splinter party is an indicator that may prove useful in future political planning.

There is a legitimate place in the United States for the "no-win" third-party candidate who represents a significant sector of public opinion neglected by the major candidates. Although such a force is undesirable under the current electoral college system, in which a third-party candidate like George Wallace might be able to "arbitrate" if no candidate won a majority of the presidential electors, direct popular election of the president would make such undemocratic arbitration possible only if the minor candidate controlled a block vote. In the opinion of this writer, the intervention of George Wallace or a hypothetical "peace candidate" (such as Eugene McCarthy) in a two-ballot election would be more like the candidacies of Lecanuet, Tixier-Vignancour, Rocard, and Krivine than like that of Jacques Duclos, the mouthpiece of a national political machine that controlled a block vote. It is quite possible, then, that a two-round arrangement for direct election of the president might work better in the United States than in France.

8. In French presidential nominating processes there are no elections below the presidential level that can effectively recruit and test presidential talent. This deficiency is a great handicap to the opposition.

In the United States, such subpresidential elections and offices have become testing grounds for presidential talent. The willingness of certain senators, governors, and even mayors to be distracted from their important jobs by presidential politicking may reduce the effectiveness of local government or of the Senate, but French experience suggests that this is a price well worth paying for the recruitment of superior presidential talent.

9. Joe McGinniss's *The Selling of the President* may have been a shocker to many who were unaware of political realities, but French experience suggests that when a candidate cannot be sold at all, the situation is even worse. It is not only a question of fair and equal treatment in the media, important as that surely is. Debates over issues, policies, or ideologies, however educational or well balanced, are no substitute for exposure to the person who may be running for president. In addition to the exhibition of candidates under conditions set by the media, it is essential that candidates also be able to present for

mass exposure *any image of themselves they may want to create.* That is the only way to prevent the mass media, the public opinion polls, and possibly the government from determining a candidate's image for him.

Care should be taken that restrictions on campaign spending, access to television, or exploitation of public opinion polls do not put candidates, especially those of the out-party, at the mercy of the mass media. A presidential candidate must have a fair chance to present himself before the people even if he is not a favorite of broadcasters, publishers, journalists, professors, or literary pundits.

10. The weak French presidents of the past were elected by Parliament, in a "house without windows," without reference to public opinion. Only popular election can make possible, although it cannot guarantee, a strong president. But the approval of Gaston Defferre by the Socialist parliamentary caucus in 1965, and of Georges Pompidou by the UDR caucus in 1969, suggests that parliamentary participation in the process of nomination is not necessarily biased toward the selection of manifestly weak presidents. Perhaps the time has come to rethink the role of the Congress in presidential nominating politics.

☆

Chapter Five

☆

A Theory of Presidential Nominations, with a 1968 Illustration

JAMES P. ZAIS *and* JOHN H. KESSEL

"I'm going to Atlanta, Teddy, I'm going to wrap up the whole campaign there. Come along with us."

Richard M. Nixon, May 28, 1968

So SPOKE the experienced politician to the journalist just after the results of the Oregon primary had been announced. Theodore White tells us of the professional skill shown by Nixon's analysis: "More important to him was Reagan's poor showing; Reagan had made a massive TV effort; defeat had now eliminated him as a viable national candidate to be put forward by the South" and describes "the quick anticipation of mind" with which Nixon spoke of the opportunity now open to him.[1] But what does this comment suggest about the nomination process? Why did Richard Nixon sense that this was the time, and the South was the area, in which to make a move to wrap up the nomination? Why had Nixon felt it important to reach Maryland's Spiro T. Agnew quickly after this proud man had been affronted by Governor Nelson Rockefeller's failure to let him know he was not going to announce his candidacy on March 21? Still earlier, why had the Nixon strategists decided it would be important to break into the strength of some favorite sons and begin to seek support in the New Jersey delegation?

1. Theodore H. White, *The Making of the President 1968* (Atheneum, 1969), p. 137.

The literature on nomination politics gives one little theoretical purchase on such questions. Two descriptive books, one by Gerald M. Pomper,[2] the other by James W. Davis,[3] tell what has happened and what the rules have been. The five-volume 1952 study edited by Paul T. David, Malcolm Moos, and Ralph M. Goldman[4] is a model of comprehensive detail. There are some excellent case studies on such aspects of nomination politics as leadership, communication, decision making, and the organization of state delegations.[5] But the closest thing to theory is the identification of historical patterns—confirmation, inheritance, inner-group selection, compromise, factional victory—by David, Goldman, and Bain,[6] and the Polsby-Wildavsky view that "the patterns of events at national conventions are largely a product of three factors: the goals of the politicians who do their business there; the disparity between the information these politicians need in order to pursue their goals and the information at their disposal; and their power relationships."[7]

Why is it that more is known about aspects of nomination politics than about the nature of the process itself? One reason lies in the complexity and indeterminacy of the nomination process. Consider some of its characteristics. Thousands of actors residing in all parts of the country are engaged for at least a year before the convention meets. No single group is large enough to act decisively without considerable help from other groups. In the party out of power, there are no party leaders who can dominate the process or compel it to take a given course. The rate of turnover among delegates, leaders, and aspirants themselves is likely to be high enough to inhibit their developing much mutual understanding. The process is not one whose mysteries are likely to be instantly comprehended.

Yet the same features that inhibit intuitive understanding of nomination politics facilitate its analysis in terms of coalition formation. William A. Gamson, one of the most perceptive students of nominat-

2. *Nominating the President* (Norton, 1966).

3. *Presidential Primaries: Road to the White House* (Crowell, 1967).

4. *Presidential Nominating Politics in 1952* (Johns Hopkins Press, 1954).

5. Many of these were published in Paul Tillett (ed.), *Inside Politics: The National Conventions, 1960* (Oceana Press, 1962).

6. Paul T. David, Ralph M. Goldman, and Richard C. Bain, *The Politics of National Party Conventions* (Brookings Institution, 1960), Chap. 5.

7. Nelson W. Polsby and Aaron B. Wildavsky, *Presidential Elections: Strategies of American Electoral Politics* (2d ed., Scribner's, 1968), p. 69.

ing conventions, points out that there are certain conditions that constitute a full-fledged coalition situation.

1. There is a decision to be made and there are more than two social units attempting to maximize their share of the payoffs.

2. No single alternative will maximize the payoff to all participants.

3. No participant has dictatorial powers, i.e., no one has initial resources sufficient to control the decision by himself.

4. No participant has veto power, i.e., no member *must* be included in every winning coalition.[8]

The application of this definition led Gamson to analyze national convention voting as an instance of coalition formation. Central to his theory is the proposition that there is a mutual expectation among the actors that each will demand a share of the payoff proportional to the amount of resources contributed to the coalition. His operational definition of resources contributed is the number of votes cast by a state for a given candidate. Unfortunately, this requires that there be more than one ballot during any convention in order to establish the existence of coalition groups, which limits the applicability of his theory to only eight of the thirty-six major party conventions in this century.[9] Still, Gamson must be credited with moving one closer to an understanding of the nomination process.

A Theory

The particular line of argument we want to follow here was developed by one of us, John Kessel, who said: "The bare bones of coalition formation can be thought of as a stochastic process. . . . Here one is concerned with state probabilities, the likelihood that a phenomenon will be in a given state at a given time, and transition probabilities, the chances that the phenomenon will change from one state to another between successive intervals."[10]

In the process we are about to describe, "the transition probabilities depend on the overlap in attitudes and a step function which reflects selection characteristics of the coalition."[11] These terms will be

8. Gamson, "A Theory of Coalition Formation," *American Sociological Review* (June 1961), p. 374.

9. William A. Gamson, "Coalition Formation at Presidential Nominating Conventions," *American Journal of Sociology* (September 1962), pp. 157–81.

10. *The Goldwater Coalition* (Bobbs-Merrill, 1968), p. 33.

11. Ibid., p. 34.

defined below. It will then be clear, as is suggested by the diagram below, that in our application each "actor" has a choice between joining one of the coalitions in the 1968 Republican nomination contest and remaining uncommitted. The degree to which he is persuaded to take any action will of course change over time.

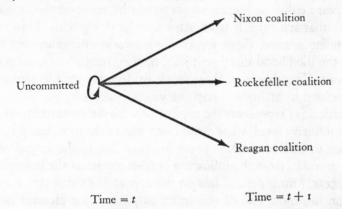

Before spelling out exactly how we have made the theory for the 1968 case operational, we will consider the reasoning behind our application in its most general form. By so doing, our reasoning may be found applicable to other coalition situations; at least it may have potential in other areas.

Imagine any actor at a particular point in time desiring to join a coalition that is located at some ideological distance from him. The strength of this desire can be thought of as the likelihood that actor i will join coalition j and can be written (without time subscripts) as follows:

$$(1) \quad \text{Likelihood}_{ij} = \left(\frac{\text{Size of coalition}_j}{\text{Size needed to win}} \right)$$
$$\times \left(\frac{\text{Maximum distance} - \text{distance}_{ij}}{\text{Maximum distance}} \right)$$

Here the likelihood that actor i will join coalition j is equal to the product of two ratios: the size of the coalition relative to the size needed to win, times the relative distance of the actor from the attitudinal position of the coalition over the maximum distance that the actor could be located from the coalition. Note the two simple features of this equation: (1) the likelihood of joining (other things being equal) will increase as the coalition reaches the winning size—as the first ratio approaches one—and (2) the likelihood of joining (other things being equal) will increase as the attitudinal position of the actor moves toward that of the coalition. The overall likelihood, then, is the interplay between these two forces over time. Coalition j can attract actor i either by increasing its size or by reducing the attitudinal distance that separates it from actor i, or by doing both. Thus at any given point in time, these forces might work simultaneously to increase the likelihood that i will join, or they might work in opposite directions. The direction they work in depends on the size of the coalition and its attitudinal position vis-à-vis actor i.

Equation (1) represents the type of process we want to investigate. On the intuitive level, what would one expect the membership of any coalition to be like at some point in time? Surely the appeal of this equation comes from the following characteristic: at the beginning of the process, j must depend less on the appeal of its size (the first element on the right side of the equation), since that element is very small. Thus coalition j must move in the direction of its "natural" friends, in an ideological sense. As time goes on, the coalition can rely more and more on its size to make its appeal. The process is thus movement outward from one's natural friends toward those farther down the line on the political spectrum; as a result, the character of the appeal changes from ideological similarity to political power.

The elements necessary to test such a theory are:

1. *Attitudinal position of actor* i—some indicator as to where in a relevant ideological space i can be located.
2. *Attitudinal position of coalition* j—a comparable locational value (on the same scale as 1 for the coalition j). This should represent some "center of gravity" of the coalition. Thus the location should be some weighted function of the attitudinal position of the various members in the coalition.
3. *Distance*—the absolute value of the difference between 1 and 2.
4. *Maximum distance*—the highest value that 3 can take.
5. *Size of the coalition*—the amount of resources in the group brought to it by its membership; in this case, the resources and the size are used interchangeably: they are convention votes.
6. *Size needed to win*—specified by convention rules.

These six components could be descriptive of any number of coalition-building situations in which the ideological positions of the actors as well as the resources they command are thought to be the prime variables. In the case of the presidential nomination, one other factor is important—the candidates themselves; since they are at the centers of the coalitions, we must also allow for their personal influence. It is an easy matter to extend the foregoing to include a seventh factor:

7. *Attitudinal position of the candidate* j—the candidate of coalition *j* having some location in the same space as defined in 1 and 2.

The influence of the candidate's attitudinal position on the coalition must also be weighted, since some candidates are ideologically more rigid than others. The eighth element, then, is:

8. *Weight of the candidate*—an estimate of the flexibility of the candidate. Is he ideologically accommodative (his weight will be small) or is he ideologically rigid, insisting that the members of his coalition come around to his position (his weight will be large)?

Thus far, the leaning of any actor toward any coalition has been referred to as the "likelihood" of his joining the coalition, since the theory has not yet been formalized to the extent that treating these fractions as probabilities would allow the use of theorems of more formal stochastic processes. For the present, the process will be considered in terms of a computer simulation; manipulation of the "likelihoods" will thus be somewhat crude. Only after they have been assigned mathematical properties can formal probability models be used.

The basic flow chart for the computer program is given in Figure 1. While this flow chart should be easy to follow, the following description may be useful.

Step 1. Input the data that will constitute the eight necessary components outlined above: attitude measures, size, candidate weightings, and so forth; initial time is one.

Steps 2 and 3. Calculate summary measures of attitude to arrive at an ideological location for both actors and candidates. For the present, consider the ideological position index to be a simple summary measure over eight items. (See below.) The same indexing rule is used for both candidates and actors.

Step 4. Assign an initial value to each coalition (see below) and calculate its size. This will be the number of votes the coalition has at any point in time.

FIGURE I. *Basic Flow Chart for the Coalition-building Process*

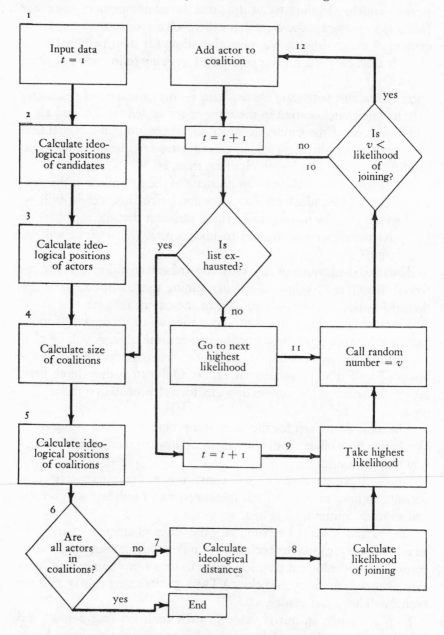

Step 5. Calculate the ideological locations of the coalitions. The following reasoning will be used initially.

The ideological position of a coalition is a function of the influence of the actors in the coalition and the candidate of that coalition.

$$\Theta_j = f(A_j, C_j).$$

Specifically, this function will be the result of the relative influence of each member, and the position will be normalized to keep the ideological positions of candidates, actors, and coalitions comparable. Call this normalization factor λ; then,

$$\Theta_j = \frac{1}{\lambda}(A_j + C_j),$$

where A_j is the influence of the actors in the coalition and is a function of their own positions and the resources they bring to the group. In other words, the more resources an actor has, the more he contributes to the "center of gravity" of the group. In this formulation, the relationship will be a simple product. Then for all N actors in the coalition, the influence is the following:

$$A_j = g(R_i, \Theta_i) = \sum_{i=1}^{N}(R_i, \Theta_i),$$

and C_j is the influence of the candidate in determining the position of coalition j. It is the simple weighting of the candidate's position by his flexibility (8 above):

$$C_j = h(CW_j, C\Theta_j) = (CW_j \cdot C\Theta_j).$$

It therefore follows that the positioning of coalition j is determined by:

$$\Theta_j = \left[\left(\sum_{i=1}^{N} R_i \Theta_i\right) + (CW_j - C\Theta_j)\right],$$

where

$$\lambda = \left(\sum_{i=1}^{N} R_i + CW_j\right) N_j.$$

Step 6. If all actors are in coalitions, the program ends.

Step 7. Ideological distances between each actor and the various coalitions are determined by a distance formula appropriate to the dimensionality of the ideological space. (See below.)

Step 8. The likelihood of each actor's jo ning each coalition is determined through the use of equation (1), above.

Steps 9, 10, and 11. Start with the highest likelihoods and compare them to random numbers to judge whether particular actors join the coalition. If so, update time and add the actors to that coalition (step 12). Otherwise, go to the next highest likelihood and apply a similar test.

As any group takes on a new member, its size and ideological position change; therefore start the process again at step 4.

Problems in Evaluating the Theory

To evaluate this theory, attention should be given to at least two questions: the degree to which it approximates real-world nomination politics, and the availability of data that will give operational meaning to our variables. Many theories of coalition formation concern themselves with the size of the coalitions and the groups joining them. The best-known dynamic theory, that devised by William H. Riker, depends entirely on the size of the proto-coalitions.[12] The theory being tested here gives equal weight to the attitudes of the actors and the size of the proto-coalitions.[13] In 1968, James W. Clarke and John W. Soule conducted a survey of a random sample of national convention delegates, interviewing 187 Democrats and 171 Republicans. One of their questions concerned "the most important attribute a candidate should have." Clarke and Soule's data, presented in the following table,[14] clearly indicate that ideological agreement between the delegates and the candidate should be taken into consideration; nine out of ten of the 1968 delegates mentioned the point, while few made reference to indicators of their candidate's chances of winning:

12. *Theory of Political Coalitions* (Yale University Press, 1962).

13. We regard the relative importance of coalition size and attitudinal proximity as questions for empirical determination. The simulation program contains provision for adjusting these weights. In this initial work with the program, however, we have adopted the simple expedient of equal weighting for both factors.

14. Personal communication from James W. Clarke. See J. W. Clarke and J. W. Soule, "Amateurs and Professionals: A Study of Delegates to the 1968 Democratic Convention," *American Political Science Review*, Vol. 64 (September 1970), pp. 888–98.

Most important attribute	Democrats *(percent)*	Republicans *(percent)*
Agreement in principle (between delegate and candidate)	85	90
Understanding of local and regional issues	12	6
Strength in the polls	1	4
Success in the primaries	2	0
Number of delegates responding	170	141

The next real-world consideration is how to handle the legal and structural constraints on nomination politics. What does one do with the myriad procedures for selecting delegates to national conventions, for example? Where in time does the actual selection of delegates overlap considerations of the preferences of the delegates chosen? What does one do with primary election results in this theory? For the present, a number of simplifying assumptions about these structural and legal aspects will be made: (1) each presidential candidate will be given his home state delegation as an assumed base on which to begin his coalition building; (2) each candidate who entered and won primaries will be given the votes of those state delegations; (3) all other legal and structural elements will be assumed to be equally open and flexible to the coalition politics that follow from the establishment of these bases of power.

A related problem involves denoting the "actors." This is not an easy question since one may work on many levels—individual delegates, groups of delegates, state delegations, or regions—depending on whether one wishes to capture more real-world detail or to simplify the process in the interest of parsimony. Thirty-five of the fifty-three states and territories split their votes at the 1968 Republican national convention. A survey of the delegates in one state suggests that in split-vote situations delegates supporting candidate A or candidate B may be considered as true groups on the basis of shared attitudes.[15] In this simulation, however, we have assumed that the actors are state delegations acting in unison. In part, this can be defended as a necessary simplification; even with this assumption, we are working with

15. Forty-six percent of the Pennsylvania delegates who could be classified as liberal (rather than as neutral or conservative) voted for Governor Rockefeller; 63 percent of those who could be classified as conservative voted for Richard Nixon. John H. Aldrich, "An Analysis of the Pennsylvania Republican Delegation, 1968" (senior project, Allegheny College, 1969).

fifty-three actors. More practically, problems of disaggregation would arise if we worked with smaller units of analysis. Convention balloting is reported only by states, and individual delegate votes are retrievable from convention records only if a delegate from that state demands that the delegation be polled at the time the vote is taken.

What data could be used to give operational meaning to our variables? "Resources" do not constitute a problem in specification, since the number of votes each state has is allocated by convention rules. The data necessary to position the states in attitudinal space are another story. Ideally, one might wish for attitudinal measures for each of the delegates, hard data that would permit a reasonably certain test of the theory. Since these were not available, one of us (John Kessel) made estimates of where each state's Republican delegation would rank on eight seven-point scales. The scales concerned the relative desire for a national election victory, the liberalism or conservatism of the state (which bore on whether a liberal or conservative nominee would be more likely to aid Republican prospects within the state), the state's political memory as reflected in the Munger-Blackhurst analysis of past convention voting,[16] and attitudes toward the power of the federal government, spending and welfare policies, cities and civil rights, general foreign affairs (nationalism versus internationalism), and Vietnam.[17] To test the reliability of the estimates, two other knowledgeable Republicans were asked to make separate ones.[18]

16. Frank J. Munger and James Blackhurst, "Factionalism in the National Conventions, 1940–1964: An Analysis of Ideological Consistency in State Delegation Voting," *Journal of Politics*, Vol. 27 (May 1965), pp. 375–94. Since this analysis had discerned five voting blocs, the states were assigned to five magnitudes (2 through 6) on this particular scale.

17. Note that only the last five of these attitudes concerned public policy. Hence the attitudinal space within which one envisions proximity between actors and coalitions assumes a broader definition of political culture, including party goals and norms as well as questions of ideology.

18. Besides Kessel, the other two professors who made estimates were George Grassmuck and M. Kent Jennings of the University of Michigan. Each had a slightly different experience. Grassmuck had done some work on the sectional basis of foreign policy, but was also Vice-President Nixon's research director in 1960, and has since become a member of the White House staff in the office of Robert Finch. Jennings was a National Convention Fellow in 1964, but had also directed two nationwide surveys, one on political socialization and one on school politics. Kessel was a National Convention Fellow in 1960 and a National Committee Fellow in 1963–64, and had done some secondary analysis of national survey data. Interjudge reliability was estimated by computing Pearson in r's for each scale (other than that derived from the Munger-Blackhurst analysis). As between Grassmuck and Jennings, the mean was 0.48 and the range from 0.05 to 0.77; between Grassmuck and Kessel, the mean was 0.52 and the range from 0.26 to 0.72; between

Their judgments were sufficiently similar to encourage us to proceed. Although our general position is that the data are being used as preliminary estimates, our success in using them suggests that political scientists might consider giving such formal expression to their own expertise, and recognize that this constitutes a legitimate form of data.[19]

Candidate weightings were not determined by a priori estimation for the present simulation; instead, it was assumed that each candidate would be in a controlling position at the outset. Therefore the candidate-weighting parameter was set at a value that caused the initial coalition to be located at the attitudinal position of the candidate in whose support they were forming.

Simulating the 1968 Republican Nomination

We turn now to the simulation. Since the theory is stochastic, the results of any single run are not, in themselves, important. Instead of analyzing a particular run in detail, we ran the model a number of times to get a distribution of outcomes. The average outcome of twenty-five runs of the first version of the model is compared to the actual convention outcome in Figure 2.

The figure shows a reasonable congruence between the predictions of the model and the actual delegate count at the convention. Note that the model assumes the existence of only three coalitions: those of Rockefeller, Reagan, and Nixon. It does not, therefore, predict when a coalition will arise, and who will lead it; nor does it designate different times at which the three candidates "threw their hats into the ring"—that is, the competition modeled gives an "equal chance" to each of the candidates to win all uncommitted states. In determining the decision of each state, the model assigns the 182 votes that actually went to "others" to one of the three candidates. (Later, we shall change the model by excluding all "favorite son" states.)

Jennings and Kessel the mean was 0.76 and the range from 0.72 to 0.84. In each case the highest interjudge correlation was on the general liberalism-conservatism scale, and the lowest was on the nationalism-internationalism scale.

19. The only cases in which our estimates handicapped the simulation were those of Puerto Rico and the Virgin Islands. Since we lacked knowledge, we tended to place these delegations in the middle of the scales, which meant that they became early recruits to the centrist Nixon coalition. However, this only involved a total of eight votes. It is clear that our assumption that each state delegation should be regarded as a single actor was a much more serious constraint than our use of estimates of the states' attitudes.

FIGURE 2. *Model Predictions and Actual Convention Delegate Count, Republican Convention, 1968*

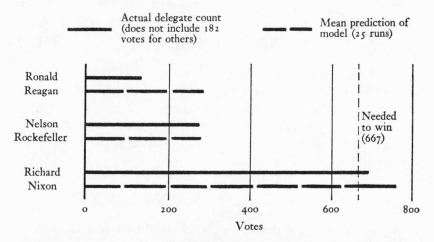

A second systematic source of error in prediction is that stemming from the assumption of unison voting. However, the actual votes in split delegations going to candidates favored by a minority in those delegations (a total of 142 votes) are spread quite evenly over the three coalitions, so that they do not introduce systematic bias in one direction; at worst, they inflate the predictions by the model.

In view of Nixon's close win in actual convention balloting (he had just twenty-five more votes than the number needed to win), should one expect a prediction of Nixon's winning on each run of a stochastic model? We did not. And our prediction was supported by the actual workings of the simulation program. Of the twenty-five runs of the model, Nixon won sixteen, and the nomination was blocked on the remaining nine. In no case did either Rockefeller or Reagan win the nomination in our simulated runs. Thus, in the precarious undertaking of "predicting" from the model, Nixon had a 64 percent chance of winning the nomination, there being a 36 percent chance of the nomination's being blocked.

The blocked-nomination runs, understandably, required runs of the program longer than those in which Nixon won. Because of the particular configurations of the "likelihood-to-join" indices for the uncommitted states, the time required to change these states to a committed status exceeded the average time for the runs that resulted in a win. This clear relationship is shown in Figure 3.

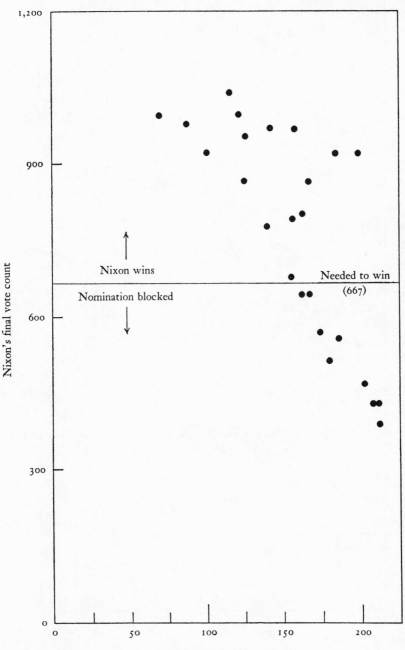

FIGURE 3. *Relation between Computer Time and Nixon's Final Vote Count*

FIGURE 4. *Typical Computer Run, Republican Nomination, 1968, Version 1*

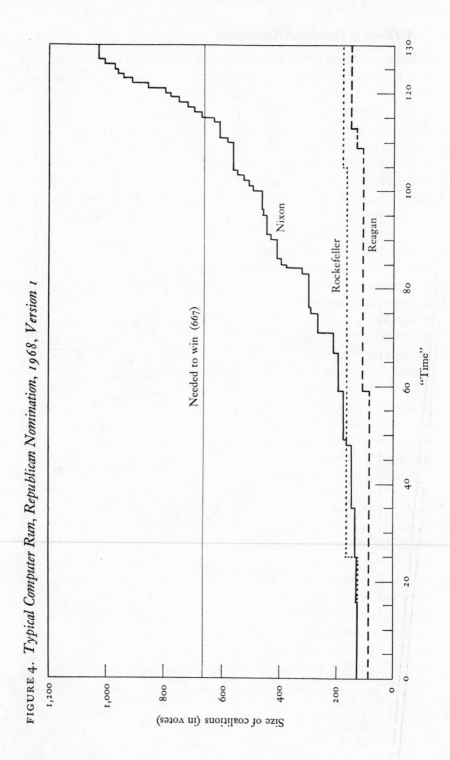

Some idea of the reason for this may be had by examining the pattern of a "typical run" in Figure 4. For roughly the first half of the run, all three coalitions are growing quite slowly. If one were to plot slopes through "time" 65 (actually, the number of iterations), the projection would indicate that Nixon would have the largest coalition but not one reaching winning size for a long time. Once the Nixon coalition achieved a superior position (slightly after "time" 55), the Nixon slope became exponential. The reason for this lies in what was happening to the first expression on the right-hand side of equation (1). As the size of the proto-coalition increased, the "likelihood-to-join" indices became larger. New recruits then swelled the coalition, which again increased the quasi probabilities, producing a bandwagon effect. The Rockefeller and Reagan coalitions were recruiting some new states late in the run, but these were still "natural allies" (Connecticut for Rockefeller and Alabama and South Carolina for Reagan on this run), while the Nixon coalition was able to gain new support over a greater attitudinal range. This may be seen most clearly if one looks at the last states to join the Nixon coalition on this run (after the Nixon coalition had attained winning size). These were Maine, Pennsylvania, Washington, D.C., and Rhode Island, states attitudinally proximate to the Rockefeller coalition, and Texas, Arizona, Georgia, and Louisiana, "natural allies" of Governor Reagan. This corresponds to the real-world situation in which vote-switching to the winner occurs after a nomination has been made.

Another aspect of this mode of analysis is the spatial interpretation of the "arena of competition." The model was constituted in such a way that the competition between coalitions would take place in n-dimensional attitudinal space. Each scale potentially provides an additional dimension along which distance may be measured. As things turned out, the dimensions reduced to what may be considered a single summary index. This took place because the attitudes of the three candidates happened to be in the same order (Reagan, Nixon, Rockefeller) on all of these scales. In this special case where order is maintained between the candidates, a state's attitudinal distance from any one candidate determines its distance from the other candidates. Similarly, each state's score gives its location in relation to each of the other states.

Figure 5, section A, indicates how many delegates have particular attitudinal scores along this summary index. About twenty delegates,

FIGURE 5. *Arena of Competition within the Republican Party*

A. Actual attitudinal scores of delegates

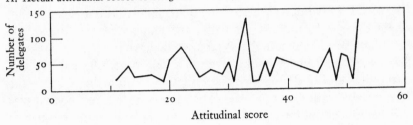

B. Attitudinal scores grouped by fives

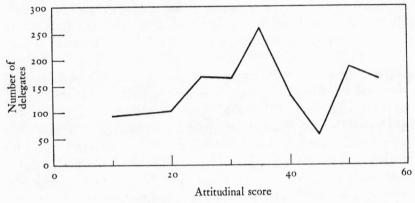

C. Attitudinal scores grouped by tens

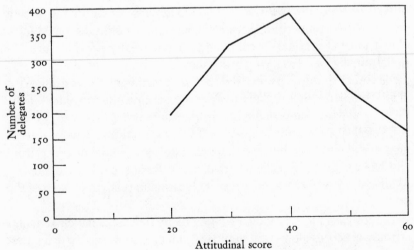

for example, have scores of 2 5, about seventy delegates have scores of 47, and so forth. However, it is difficult to discern any pattern with these ungrouped data. If, however, the scores are grouped by fives as in section B, a fairly clear trimodal pattern may be seen. (The lower scores represent "conservative" postures and the higher scores "liberal" stances on this summary index.) It is apparent from this figure that, although the greatest number of delegates are at a middle-of-the-road position, there is a distinct difference between the conservative and liberal elements of the Republican party. There is a clear gap on the liberal side, so that most liberals appear to be further down the scale. On the conservative side, the distribution of the delegates is more even. Obviously suggestive of a Hotteling-Downs spatial analysis, this view of the arena of competition within the party has some important tactical consequences. Before turning directly to these implications, however, the reader's attention is directed to section C of Figure 5 to remind him that such grouping is an arbitrary process. Here the scores are grouped by tens, and a unimodal distribution emerges. Our suggestion is, however, that something akin to section B resembles the cognitive maps of politicians, and that these politicians act on the basis of such a conception of the arena of competition—neither such a crude picture as in section C nor such a detailed picture as in section A.

The tactical implications of this arena of competition for the Republican party in 1968 may be envisioned by imagining the chances of differently located contenders. A liberal candidate could quickly gain support from "natural allies," but would have difficulty "getting across the gap" into the center of the party to recruit enough votes to win. A center candidate is in the most favored position, provided he can move quickly enough to avoid being blocked by strong contenders on either side. Since there are more votes on the conservative side, it is particularly important that he not have strong conservative opposition.[20] If there is no center candidate, or if the center is weak, a strong conservative candidate can form a fairly sizable coalition among his natural allies; then he may move on to winning size by negotiating with center groups from a position of strength. These possibilities for center and conservative candidates, incidentally, suggest why a very

20. Here is a theoretical answer to the rhetorical question, posed at the beginning of this chapter, concerning why Nixon wanted to move against Reagan in the South at a time when the Nixon coalition was relatively strong.

similar collection of state delegations ended up in a center coalition
around Nixon in 1968 and in a conservative coalition around Goldwater in 1964.

The relative strength of a conservative candidate may be illuminated by one of the real advantages of simulation: the opportunity it
offers us to conduct quasi experiments by altering certain conditions
and then observing the consequences. In Version 1, we permitted all
states to be available as recruits for the three coalitions. But to see
what might have occurred had all the favorite-son candidates held
out, we withdrew the favorite-son states from the roster of actors in
Version 2. What happens if the coalitions have to attain winning size
when there are fewer potential recruits? The outcomes of the twenty-
five runs under these circumstances are shown in Table 1. Without
the favorite-son states to draw upon, the Nixon coalition was blocked

TABLE 1. *Outcomes of Computer Simulations of Republican Nomination,
1968, Version 2*

Run number	Outcome	Nixon	Rockefeller	Reagan
1	Nomination blocked	398	331	406
2	Nomination blocked	639	126	370
3	Nixon wins			
4	Nomination blocked	549	142	444
5	Nomination blocked	461	156	518
6	Nomination blocked	549	156	430
7	Nomination blocked	461	156	518
8	Nomination blocked	555	126	454
9	Nomination blocked	398	331	406
10	Nixon wins			
11	Nomination blocked	549	156	430
12	Nomination blocked	639	126	370
13	Nomination blocked	486	243	406
14	Nomination blocked	436	269	430
15	Nixon wins			
16	Nomination blocked	398	331	406
17	Nixon wins			
18	Nixon wins			
19	Nomination blocked	573	156	406
20	Nomination blocked	573	156	406
21	Nomination blocked	436	307	392
22	Nomination blocked	601	142	392
23	Nomination blocked	600	165	370
24	Nomination blocked	600	165	370
25	Nomination blocked	412	331	392

on twenty of twenty-five runs.[21] To indulge once more in the risky venture of predicting from this model, we would say that moving from Version 1 to Version 2 decreases Nixon's chances of winning from 64 percent to 20 percent. Moreover, inspection of the votes on the blocking runs shows that the Reagan coalition emerged strong enough to stop the front runner. The reasons for this are the relative strength of the conservative candidate noted above, and the location of the favorite-son states. Many of these states were relatively liberal; withdrawing them from the roster of available actors created a contest between the centrist Nixon coalition and the conservative Reagan coalition. The Nixon coalition emerged as the larger on fifteen of the twenty blocking runs, but none of the candidates—Nixon, Reagan, or Rockefeller—was able to attain winning size.

Conclusions

How do these simulated outcomes correspond to real-world events? The import of our analysis has been that the Nixon nomination was likely, but by no means a sure thing; that Nixon's danger lay not in Rockefeller's candidacy, but rather in Reagan's; and that if Governor Reagan had been able to start adding southern groups to his coalition, his threat to Nixon would have become very real indeed.

If one cuts below the bland statements of confidence issuing from the front runner's headquarters, there is evidence that coalition leaders saw the situation in precisely this way. Theodore H. White reports that Reagan strategist F. Clifton White felt he was very close to prying a hundred southern votes away from Richard Nixon. Of the Louisiana state chairman, the Reagan leader said: "He's on the wire, I know he's on the wire, there were tears in his eyes when he said goodbye, he agrees with everything we say—but he can't get off his commitment to Nixon." And of the Florida state chairman, F. Clifton White despaired: "He drives me out of my cotton-picking mind. He won't go with us unless a majority in his delegation goes for us; we're three votes short of the majority and I've just got to drag him across that line."[22] An account of Nixon's relations with southern groups has revealed that the Reagan threat was taken so seriously that Strom

21. This provides reasons for the interest of the Nixon coalition in obtaining votes in Maryland and New Jersey.

22. White, *Making of the President 1968*, p. 280.

Thurmond and Harry Dent were summoned to a special meeting with Richard Nixon and John Mitchell at 10 P.M. the first evening of the convention. There Thurmond was authorized to tell southern delegates "that Nixon would oppose busing for school integration, that he favored gradualism as a means to desegregation, and that he would name a Vice Presidential candidate acceptable to the South." A former Thurmond aid told how this message was conveyed: "Harry [Dent] would sell Strom [Thurmond] as the statesman who had put his long career on the line for Southern Republicanism, and then Strom would sell Nixon as a winner whom the South could trust."[23] And when Nelson Rockefeller called Richard Nixon to congratulate him, he said, in part: "Your strategy was perfect, you handled it perfectly. . . . Ronnie didn't do as well as I thought, I was counting on him for a little more muscle."[24]

Another way of comparing model outcomes to real-world results is to look at "predictions" as to which coalitions given states would join. Since one ought to predict correctly 50 percent of the time on the basis of chance, our model must do better to be judged successful. Table 2 presents two such comparisons. The predictions in the top section are based on attitudinal distance alone. Here each state is automatically assigned to the most proximate coalition, which increases the correct judgments to a little more than five out of eight. Next the actual pluralities are compared with the model "prediction" from the Version 1 runs. This increases our success to nearly four chances out of five. The proportion of success is not only enough greater than what might be expected by chance; it is also enough better than the attitudinal-distance "predictions" to assure us that we increase our accuracy by adding the size consideration and dynamic features of our model.

Finally, how does this model compare with other coalition theories found in the literature? Some four distinctive points about the coalition theory have informed this analysis. (This is not to claim that they are unique to our approach.) First of all, it is dynamic. Most other coalition theories have been essentially static, attempting prediction solely in terms of final outcomes rather than of the processes by which

23. James Boyd, "Harry Dent, the President's Political Coordinator," *New York Times Magazine* (Feb. 1, 1970), p. 13.
24. White, *Making of the President 1968*, p. 290.

TABLE 2. *Comparison of Predictions of Two Models with Actual Votes of 47 States, Republican National Convention, 1968*[a]

Candidate and model	Number of states that went as predicted	Number of states that did not go as predicted	Actual number of states won by candidate
Attitudinal-distance model[b]			
Nixon	24.5	3	38
Rockefeller	6	4	7
Reagan	0	9.5	2
Total	30.5	16.5	47
Percentage	*64.8*	*35.2*	*100*
Version 1 model[c]			
Nixon	32	4	38
Rockefeller	4	1	7
Reagan	1	5	2
Total	37	10	47
Percentage	*78.7*	*21.3*	*100*

a. Each state is assigned to the candidate receiving the plurality of votes cast by its delegation.

b. Of the 3 states that did not go for Nixon as predicted, 1 went to Rockefeller, 2 to Reagan. The 4 states that did not go for Rockefeller as predicted went to Nixon. The 9.5 states that did not go for Reagan as predicted went to Nixon. Fractions in number of states indicate a tie in prediction for Alabama in model.

c. Of the 4 states that did not go for Nixon as predicted, 3 went to Rockefeller, 1 to Reagan. The state that did not go for Rockefeller as predicted went to Nixon. The 5 states that did not go for Reagan as predicted went to Nixon.

coalitions are achieved.[25] Second, our theory gives emphasis to the goals of the actors, the attitudes that may motivate them to join a coalition, as well as to the size of the proto-coalitions. This corresponds more accurately than alternative models, we think, to the facts of political life. What motivation does an extreme conservative have to join a very liberal proto-coalition and convert it into a winning coalition when he does not approve of what that coalition intends to do? This may be a trivial point in economic coalitions, in which monetary resources can be equally divided, but not in politics. Third, this theory has been operationalized with a relatively large number of actors. To

25. The obvious reason for this static emphasis has been a reliance on game-theoretic, and in some cases graph-theoretic, concepts. Leiserson's review of game theory notes this as one of coalition theory's most severe shortcomings. See his "Game Theory and the Study of Coalition Behavior" in S. Groenings, E. W. Kelly, and M. Leiserson (eds.), *The Study of Coalition Behavior* (Holt, Rinehart and Winston, 1970).

be sure, much can be learned about the processes of coalition-forma-
tion with three-man experiments, but there are enough political processes embracing large numbers of actors to make it worthwhile to
push some theories in this direction. Fourth, and perhaps most important of all, in this theory it makes a difference *who* joins the coalition. The actors are not thought of as interchangeable. And this concern with the composition of the coalition as well as its size has a
rather significant consequence. It enables us to discuss (although we
have not done so here) what the coalition is likely to do after it is
formed. Most of our coalition theories are, in fact, theories of coalition formation. And while coalition formation is undoubtedly important, it is, in most cases, episodic. If coalition theory is to take its
proper place in the range of political theory, it must become possible
to discuss what the formed coalitions do with the power they have
achieved.[26]

26. Hayward Alker, in whose seminar on mathematical political analysis this analysis
was begun, has called for the development of individually tailored, nonrational, multilevel,
process-specific theories. We hope that this is such a one.

Chapter Six

☆

Delegate Turnover at National Party Conventions, 1944–68

LOCH K. JOHNSON *and* HARLAN HAHN

As THE GROUP whose official responsibility is to select presidential nominees, delegates to the national party conventions perform a critical role in American politics. Despite the importance of their task, however, relatively little attention has been devoted to the study of convention delegates. "In view of the obvious significance of the nominating process," David Truman observed in 1952, "it is astonishing that we know almost nothing of a systematic character about how nominations are made, and about the role of groups in connection with them."[1] Although some progress has been made in the analysis of national conventions in recent years,[2] the scope of the research has been limited by the lack of basic facts concerning delegate participation.

The purpose of this chapter is to present the results of a study of delegate tenure and turnover at the Republican and Democratic national party conventions from 1944 through 1968. While this investigation represents only one approach to the study of participants at the national nominating conventions, the data provide some new insights into basic questions about American political parties and the process of making presidential nominations.

Note. The authors would like to thank Leena Sepp Johnson and Bruce Sheppard for their assistance in the preparation of this chapter.

1. David B. Truman, *The Governmental Process* (Knopf, 1952), p. 288.
2. See the bibliographic appendix to this chapter.

Why Study Delegate Turnover?

Personnel turnover is important to the study of change and development in virtually any political institution, including national conventions.[3] Among the most significant properties of any group or organization is the stability—or instability—of its personnel. The growth in the average length of service of members of the House of Representatives has drastically altered Congress, for example, and is sometimes thought to help account for the effectiveness of that institution compared with most state legislatures and national parliaments whose personnel changes more rapidly. Similarly, administrative agencies whose staffs are made up of lifetime careerists behave differently from those run by neophytes. In voluntary organizations, experienced members have organizational commitments different from those of the inexperienced. Even communities or geographical regions characterized by rapid population growth or out-migration often exhibit characteristics different from those of stable and settled areas.

In the same way, one would expect national party conventions to be influenced by the past experience of their personnel. Either the return of numerous experienced delegates or the sudden appearance of many new and unfamiliar activists might have a critical effect on the processes and results. Battle-scarred veterans of previous national party meetings would be likely to behave differently from those who have not acquired earlier convention experience.

Second, turnover is closely related to the critical issue of survival for any organization. In the United States, the two major parties have demonstrated a remarkable capacity to sustain themselves for an extended period of time. A partial explanation for their impressive longevity may lie in the ability of the parties to replenish their ranks. Although turnover may be dysfunctional in many institutions that attempt to maintain continuity and expertise, since parties can prosper only by winning elections they are constantly compelled to broaden their appeal and attract new sources of support.

Furthermore, if political parties are to perform their functions of selecting nominees and soliciting the support of voters, they must attract the manpower they need. In fact, the recruitment of a large number of party activists to fill important positions and to perform other

---

3. For literature with specific comments on delegate turnover at national party conventions, see the section "On Delegate Turnover" in the appendix to this chapter.

essential duties, both during campaigns and on less dramatic occasions, may be more critical than the nomination of candidates or even the attainment of legislative and other policy objectives. There is a need "for party leadership to consider the party workers as a clientele as much in need of wooing as the party's voters."[4] Recruitment may become increasingly pivotal as patronage and other rewards and punishments traditionally dispensed by political machines begin to disappear. As Sorauf notes, "The party, in order to maintain its organizational health, has to replenish constantly the store of incentives it needs to purchase additional labor to produce its party functions."[5] Perhaps one of the most appealing of those incentives is admission to the highest decision-making assemblies of the party. Thus the promotion of party workers to the status of convention delegates could be an important inducement to increased party activity.[6]

The role of parties in fostering activism, however, raises a serious issue. While political parties may be continuously expanding organizations that depend on a persistent influx of new enthusiasts for both their survival and their success, an extremely high rate of turnover might present a threat to the existence of the organization. Consequently, the recruitment of a large proportion of new party activists may be either an important sign of organizational strength and vitality or a signal of imminent decay.[7] The study of turnover may offer a means of exploring the adaptability, strength, and potential for survival of party organizations.

Third, the study of convention attendance patterns allows a longitudinal and comparative analysis of the parties at both national and state levels. Research on delegate participation provides a means of assessing the dynamic nature of political parties and of reducing the inevitable limitations of research conducted at a single point in time.[8]

4. Frank J. Sorauf, *Political Parties in the American System* (Little, Brown, 1964), p. 11.

5. Ibid., p. 89.

6. Convention delegates may of course be drafted by presidential aspirants as well as by party organizations. See Joseph A. Schlesinger's discussion of candidates as party "nuclei" in James G. March (ed.), *Handbook of Organizations* (Rand McNally, 1965), pp. 764–801.

7. Compare Samuel J. Eldersveld, *Political Parties: A Behavioral Analysis* (Rand McNally, 1964), p. 11.

8. For an impressive longitudinal study of the nominating conventions that uses the state delegations as units of analysis, see Frank J. Munger and James Blackhurst, "Factionalism in the National Conventions, 1940–1964: An Analysis of Ideological Consistency in State Delegation Voting," *Journal of Politics*, Vol. 27 (May 1965), pp. 375–94.

Examining variations in delegate turnover rates at a series of national conventions may make it possible to identify evidence of major disruptions or persistent regularities that reflect crucial features of the nominating process.

This research also provides a method of examining important and continuing attributes of state political parties. Unlike other common sources of political data, such as surveys or voting statistics, turnover rates offer composite measures of the organizational characteristics of state parties that are for the most part unrelated to other environmental conditions. The retention or replacement of delegates to the national conventions is one of the few unobtrusive measures of institutional attributes that are comparable for all state parties.

Finally, this approach permits a comparative study of differences between the two major political parties. In a survey of rank-and-file party members and delegates to the 1956 conventions, for example, McClosky, Hoffmann, and O'Hara disclosed that Republicans were more likely than Democrats to disapprove of the political positions of their convention representatives.[9] Since this research revealed noticeable discrepancies between the policy preferences of voters and leaders within each party in a single election year, similar differences might also be found in the voting behavior of experienced and inexperienced Republican and Democratic delegates in a series of national conventions.

This study first examines the total turnover of delegates at Republican and Democratic nominating conventions from 1944 to 1968;[10] second, the nature of state and regional delegate participation, as well as major factors that might affect variations in turnover, such as the method of selecting delegates; and finally, the impact of turnover on delegation voting behavior.

9. Herbert McClosky, Paul J. Hoffmann, and Rosemary O'Hara, "Issue Conflict and Consensus Among Party Leaders and Followers," *American Political Science Review*, Vol. 54 (June 1960), pp. 406–27.

10. This study is devoted solely to an examination of delegate turnover at the national party conventions. As a result, it does not encompass an analysis of delegate characteristics. Several recent commissions, however, have studied the issue of representation in the nominating process. See the report of the Commission on the Democratic Selection of Presidential Nominees, chaired by Senator Harold Hughes of Iowa, *The Democratic Choice* (Washington: Commission on the Democratic Selection of Presidential Nominees, 1968); and the report of the Commission on Party Structure and Delegate Selection, chaired by Senator George S. McGovern of South Dakota, *Mandate for Reform* (Washington: Democratic National Committee, 1970).

Delegate Turnover at National Party Conventions

Data for this study were compiled from the official rosters of delegates to the Democratic and Republican national conventions during the period from 1940 to 1968. The rosters, which included more than 50,000 delegates and alternates, were examined to determine the previous convention experience of delegates at each national party meeting.[11]

The results of this analysis disclosed a high total turnover of delegates at Republican and Democratic nominating conventions between 1944 and 1968. Sixty-three percent of Democratic and 65 percent of Republican delegates during this period had not previously attended a national party meeting. The attendance records of returning delegates in both parties were also comparable. Among the Democrats, only 21.7 percent of the delegates had participated in one earlier convention during those years, 8.7 percent had attended two, and 6.6 percent had attended three or more. Similarly, 21.3 percent of the Republican delegates had attended one prior convention, 7.9 percent had attended two, and 5.8 percent had attended three or more. The largest percentage of delegates at both party conventions were thus without previous experience in the nomination of presidential candidates. National convention delegates are frequently depicted as lost and bewildered; since few of them are experienced participants in the nominating process, the data provide little reason to doubt the accuracy of the description.

Furthermore, the parties have been able to secure a steady and continuing influx of new party activists at every nominating convention.

11. The rosters of convention delegates and alternates are printed in the official proceedings of the two parties for each convention. Similarities in names were resolved beyond a reasonable doubt in nearly all cases by reference to city addresses, which are listed in the rosters. Since one of the major objectives of this research was to explore the effect of previous convention experience on *delegate* behavior in specific years, attendance at earlier conventions (either as a delegate or as an alternate) rather than at any convention during the twenty-eight-year period was used as the definition of "experience." For example, when the effect of experience on delegate behavior at the 1960 conventions was analyzed, only the 1940–56 attendance records were examined for the names of delegates and alternates who also attended the 1960 party meeting as delegates. In the same way, for the 1968 analysis the 1940–64 attendance records were examined for names that also appeared in the 1968 record. Previous attendance as an alternate was included in the definition, since the participant acquired prior convention experience even as an alternate. Limitations on resources precluded the extension of the research to conventions before 1940; thus, to permit the analysis of as many conventions as possible, 1944 was used as the initial year for the examination of delegate turnover.

The figures below record the percentage of inexperienced delegates at
each of the Republican and Democratic national conventions by year: [12]

	1944	*1948*	*1952*	*1956*	*1960*	*1964*	*1968*	*Mean*
Republican conventions	70.0	63.9	63.6	64.9	61.4	66.4	65.3	65.1
Democratic conventions	69.0	64.1	67.2	67.3	58.4	53.5	62.7	63.7

Delegate participation in all Republican and Democratic conventions
showed comparable patterns. The proportion of new delegates at each
convention did not differ by more than 9 percentage points in the Republican party or by more than 16 percentage points in the Democratic party. The difference between the mean turnover rates for the
two parties was only 1.4 percentage points.[13] David, Goldman, and

12. Since the data for this study were based on Democratic and Republican conventions from 1940 through 1968, delegates to the 1944 conventions had the opportunity to
attend a maximum of two conventions, while delegates to the 1968 conventions might conceivably have participated in as many as eight. Although the necessity of selecting an arbitrary date as a start for any time series study might have affected trends in convention
attendance by year, the effect of this factor seemed to be minimal in this investigation. As
the data reveal, the largest proportion of delegates at each of the conventions during this
period, including the later as well as the earlier years, had not been selected to attend a
prior convention. Moreover, the percentage of returning delegates did not increase pro-
gressively with each succeeding convention. In the Democratic conventions, the proportion of experienced delegates increased by only 6.3 percentage points between 1944 and
1968, and this trend was reversed in the conventions of 1952, 1956, and 1968. Similarly, in
the Republican meetings, the percentage of repeating delegates increased by merely 4.7
percentage points between 1944 and 1968, and a progressive increase was not reflected in
the delegate composition of the conventions of 1956 and 1964.

13. Comparisons were also made between the mean percentage of inexperienced delegates at the conventions and a statistical estimate of the mean error that might have been
produced by restrictions on the time span of the study. Two methods were used to increase
the accuracy of such estimates. The first obtained a probability distribution function to fit
the observed distribution of previous convention attendance for delegates at each convention. The binomial index of dispersion test indicated the need for a contagious model, and
Pólya's urn model fit the observed distributions. For a discussion of Pólya's urn model,
also known as the Pólya-Eggenberger distribution, see Norman L. Johnson, *Discrete
Distributions* (Houghton Mifflin, 1969), pp. 229–32; William Feller, *An Introduction to
Probability Theory and Its Applications*, Vol. 1 (Wiley, 1968), pp. 120–21. For each convention year, data were used to secure estimates of the parameters of Pólya's model. The
model then was used to estimate the distribution of prior convention attendance for a time
span of seven earlier conventions. Because of limitations on degrees of freedom, however,
this technique did not permit the computation of an estimate for the 1944 conventions. The
difference between the observed mean turnover rate and the estimate derived by this
method was 7.8 percentage points for the Republican and 7.6 percentage points for the
Democratic convention. The second method employed six constants that were postulated
as possible corrections in the observed percentage of inexperienced delegates who might

Bain noted that the nearly equivalent recruitment levels "attest to the institutional stability of the party system and to the considerable similarity of the delegate selection practices of the two parties."[14]

Although the recruitment patterns in both parties were relatively uniform, slight variations in delegate participation rates occasionally reflected political events. In 1964, for example, the influx of Goldwater enthusiasts was reflected in a 5-point increase in Republican convention turnover. The greatest increase in the proportion of new delegates attending a convention within a party, however, emerged in the Democratic meeting of 1968, when that party was widely criticized for failing to represent contemporary ideas or new faces in its delegate composition.[15] Some evidence also suggests that the mean

---

have attended from one to six previous conventions for which data were not collected. For each pair of conventions, the difference in the observed percentage of inexperienced delegates was expressed as a combination of one or more of these six constants. Least-squares techniques were then used to obtain estimates of the values of the constants. The difference between the observed mean turnover rate and the estimate derived by the second method was 2.2 percentage points for the Republicans and 10.1 percentage points for the Democrats. The differences obtained by the two methods thus did not seem to affect the interpretation of delegate participation in the national conventions presented in this chapter.

14. Paul T. David, Ralph M. Goldman, and Richard C. Bain, *The Politics of National Party Conventions* (Brookings Institution, 1960), p. 21.

15. It is interesting to compare the 1944–68 time series data presented here with the figures on 1972 delegate turnover reported by the press. According to several sources, approximately 70 percent of the Republican delegates and 80 percent of the Democratic delegates in 1972 were attending their first national party convention. Although these figures are somewhat inflated since they are based on a comparison with 1968 delegates only rather than the 1940–68 *cumulative* experience recorded in this chapter, they represent roughly a 5 percent increase over the average for recent Republican conventions and a 16 percent increase for the Democratic party. This dramatic rise in the percentage of new party activists attending the 1972 Democratic meeting presumably represents, at least in part, the results of attempts to broaden participation in the selection of Democratic convention delegates. These efforts were initiated by the 1968 convention's adoption of the credentials committee majority report requiring state parties to give "all Democratic voters . . . a full, meaningful and timely opportunity to participate" in the selection of delegates. This "mandate for reform" was carried out by the Democratic Commission on Party Structure and Delegate Selection. (See *Mandate for Reform*.)

For press reports on 1972 Democratic delegate turnover, see the following: *Newsweek* (Aug. 28, 1972), reporting 79.0 percent newcomers; *Time* (July 10, 1972), 85.0 percent newcomers; *Washington Post* (July 8, 1972), 80.0 percent newcomers; *New York Times* (Aug. 20, 1972), 89.0 percent newcomers. The Democratic National Committee reported a figure of 80.0 percent to the authors in October 1972. The press percentages for Republican newcomers were as follows: *Newsweek* (Aug. 28, 1972), 70.5 percent; *New York Times* (Aug. 20, 1972), "more than 67.0 percent." The Republican National Committee reported a figure of 67.7 percent in October 1972.

percentage of experienced delegates was lower in years when parties enjoyed high prospects of electoral success—or when they actually won an election—than at conventions in which the party's expectations were less sanguine.[16]

These data do not offer strong evidence of party rigidity. In general, the most striking features of the delegate participation patterns were their similarities rather than their differences. The ebb and flow of delegates has tended to be high but to vary within a narrow range. Variations in delegate turnover did not seem to indicate either the presence of party ossification or an imminent danger of institutional decay. In fact, convention participation seemed to reflect the porous nature of American parties. The national conventions have allowed the relatively free and open movement of delegates between the state parties and the nominating process. The large proportion of inexperienced delegates at each of the national conventions, therefore, appeared to signify organizational strength and vitality rather than atrophy or disintegration.

Delegate Turnover by State and Region

Although delegate participation rates in both party conventions displayed relatively similar patterns, significant differences were found in the turnover of personnel among separate state delegations. Figures 1 and 2 indicate the average delegate turnover rates by state in Republican and Democratic national conventions from 1944 through 1968.

In the Democratic party, the mean delegate turnover rates ranged from 82.1 percent in South Dakota to 43.3 percent in Delaware. The

16. The mean turnover rate for conventions nominating a winning candidate was 62.7 percent, that of conventions selecting a losing candidate 65.6 percent. If the 1960 and 1968 elections, in which the prospects for electoral victory seemed unclear, are excluded, conventions held when party prospects were high (by the Democrats in 1944 and 1964, and by the Republicans in 1948, 1952, and 1956) recorded a mean turnover rate of 63.0 percent; for those held in years in which party fortunes appeared to ebb (by the Democrats in 1948, 1952, and 1956, and by the Republicans in 1944 and 1964), the rate was 67.0 percent. Slight variations were also found when the conventions were classified by other features of the strategic situation in each election year. An examination of the distinction between parties in power and parties attempting to capture control of the presidency yielded the following mean turnover rates: conventions of the in-party with an incumbent president securing renomination (62.9 percent) and not seeking renomination (63.8 percent), and conventions of the party out of power (65.0 percent).

comparable figures for the Republican conventions extended from a high of 86.5 percent in Montana to a low of 45.3 percent in New York. The majority of state party delegations consisted mostly of participants who were attending their first national conventions; only two states in the Republican party and three in the Democratic party selected delegations in which an average of half or more of the members had attended any prior national party meetings.[17] Few states placed a high premium on earlier convention experience in selecting delegates; on the contrary, state parties generally seemed to pursue the goal of involving a large number of new activists in each contest. Republican conventions included an especially large number of states in which the average proportion of inexperienced delegates was very high. Although the Democratic party had mean turnover rates that exceeded 80 percent in only two states, ten delegations in the Republican conventions surpassed that figure.[18] State parties have differed in the extent to which they seek either to promote new activists to positions as convention delegates or to protect entrenched party leaders from a deluge of unfamiliar and inexperienced workers.

Perhaps even more important than the variations among states are the strong regional configurations presented in Figures 1 and 2.[19] Regional analysis is useful in the study of many aspects of American politics, including national party conventions.[20] The choice of presi-

17. The Republican delegations with low mean turnover rates were New York (45.3 percent) and West Virginia (45.8 percent); their counterparts in the Democratic conventions were Delaware (43.3 percent), Rhode Island (46.2 percent), and Illinois (49.7 percent).

18. The Democratic delegations were South Dakota (82.1 percent) and Washington (80.9 percent); the Republican delegations included North Dakota (86.5 percent), Montana (86.2 percent), Wyoming (85.7 percent), South Dakota (83.9 percent), Iowa (83.9 percent), Washington (83.7 percent), Missouri (83.7 percent), Oklahoma (82.3 percent), Alaska (80.9 percent), and Idaho (80.5 percent).

19. Following the regional breakdown used by David, Goldman, and Bain, *Politics of Conventions* (except for Alaska and Hawaii, which they placed in a "non-state" category), we have grouped the states in this project as follows:

Northeast—Maine, New Hampshire, Vermont, Massachusetts, Rhode Island, Connecticut, New York, New Jersey, Delaware, Maryland, Pennsylvania, West Virginia. *South*—Virginia, North Carolina, South Carolina, Georgia, Florida, Kentucky, Tennessee, Alabama, Mississippi, Arkansas, Louisiana, Oklahoma, Texas. *Midwest*—Ohio, Michigan, Indiana, Illinois, Wisconsin, Iowa, Minnesota, Missouri, North Dakota, South Dakota, Nebraska, Kansas. *West*—Montana, Idaho, Wyoming, Colorado, Utah, Nevada, New Mexico, Arizona, Washington, Oregon, California, Alaska, Hawaii.

20. Raymond E. Wolfinger and Fred I. Greenstein, in "Comparing Political Regions: The Case of California," *American Political Science Review*, Vol. 63 (March 1969), p. 74,

FIGURE 1. *Average Percentage of Delegate Turnover by State and Region at Democratic National Conventions, 1944–68*

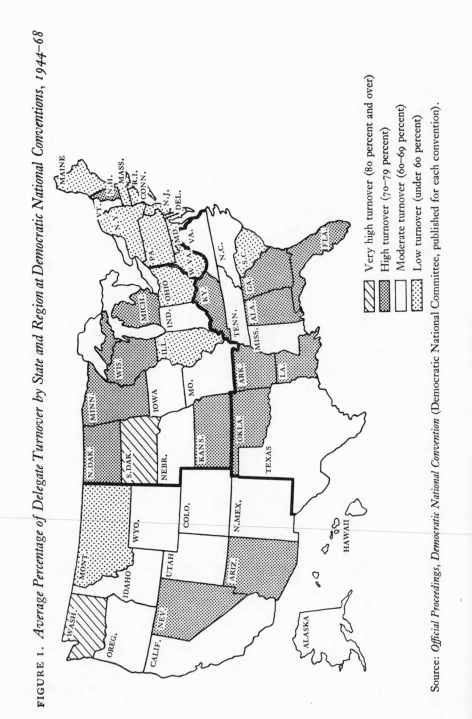

Very high turnover (80 percent and over)

High turnover (70–79 percent)

Moderate turnover (60–69 percent)

Low turnover (under 60 percent)

Source: *Official Proceedings, Democratic National Convention* (Democratic National Committee, published for each convention).

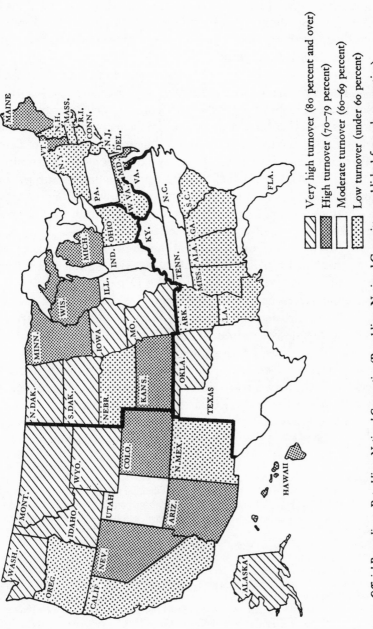

FIGURE 2. *Average Percentage of Delegate Turnover by State and Region at Republican National Conventions, 1944–68*

Very high turnover (80 percent and over)

High turnover (70–79 percent)

Moderate turnover (60–69 percent)

Low turnover (under 60 percent)

Source: *Official Proceedings, Republican National Convention* (Republican National Committee, published for each convention)

dential and vice-presidential nominees has usually reflected an effort to achieve regional balance, and sectional traditions or interests have often left a distinctive imprint on convention platforms and proceedings. Moreover, regional boundaries seemed to delineate major differences in delegate experience.

In the Democratic party, the salient regional pattern was the high level of convention experience compiled by state delegations from the Northeast; the mean proportion of returning delegates from this region was nearly 9 percentage points higher than the comparable figure for any other section of the nation. While moderate levels of delegate experience characterized a majority of the states in the West, turnover rates in the Midwest failed to reflect a predominant pattern. In the South, however, seven of thirteen states exhibited a high average of delegation turnover, perhaps illustrating what V. O. Key has termed the "multifaceted, discontinuous, kaleidoscopic, fluid, transient" nature of Democratic party organizations in that area of the country.[21]

In the Northeast and in the Midwest, Republican turnover rates were comparable to those found in the Democratic party: seasoned convention veterans were most prevalent in the Northeast, while delegation participation patterns in the Midwest again were variegated. In the West, however, Republican delegations tended to exhibit high or very high turnover rates rather than the moderate levels characteristic of western Democratic delegations, while southern states were generally split between low and moderate turnover. In large measure, this division probably reflected the trends that have emerged in the Republican party in the South, especially the decline in the proportion of experienced southern delegates from 44.6 percent in 1952 to 27.3 percent in 1956.[22]

---

point out that "one of the more fertile sources of data for systematic comparative political studies is in the regional differences that abound within political systems." On regionalism at the national party meetings, see David, Goldman, and Bain, *Politics of Conventions*, esp. Chap. 14.

21. V. O. Key, Jr., *Southern Politics in State and Nation* (Knopf, 1949), p. 302.

22. This pattern may have been stimulated by a group of prominent Republican leaders, including Lucius D. Clay, Thomas E. Dewey, Herbert Brownell, Leonard Hall, and Henry Cabot Lodge, Jr., who decided to concentrate on "the recruitment of 'Eisenhower-type' delegates to the Republican national convention of 1956, particularly from southern states where Republican party organizations had previously been controlled by the Taft faction of the party, and also with the recruitment of 'Eisenhower-type' Republicans to run in 1956 in the congressional districts that the party had lost by close margins in 1954." See David, Goldman, and Bain, *Politics of Conventions*, p. 53.

In addition to the strength of the regional patterns, other factors may help explain variations in delegate recruitment rates among the states. Competitive two-party systems, for instance, were associated with high levels of experienced delegates in the Democratic party, while state delegations to the Republican conventions from one-party southern states tended to have a large percentage of returning convention representatives, especially in the early years examined here.[23] The data appear to provide some support for the proposition that parties with relatively centralized structures may exhibit lower rates of delegation turnover than highly decentralized ones. Of particular importance was the comparatively low mean turnover of delegates in Illinois, a state known for its integrated party system. At Democratic conventions, for example, an average of 54.3 percent of the Illinois delegates had represented the state at one or more earlier national conventions. By contrast, an average of 32.2 percent of the delegates from California, a state prominent for its decentralized party institutions, had attended at least one prior Democratic convention.[24]

Another important characteristic of state party structures is the method of choosing convention delegates. In fact, perhaps the principal innovation in the selection of presidential candidates during this century, the party primary, was specifically adopted to prevent party "bosses" from dominating state conventions and to promote the par-

---

23. The classification of party competition employed in this analysis was developed by Austin Ranney, "Parties in State Politics," in Herbert Jacob and Kenneth N. Vines (eds.), *Politics in the American States* (Little, Brown, 1965), pp. 61–100. At Democratic conventions, the lowest mean turnover was recorded in competitive states (61.1 percent), followed by modified one-party Democratic states (66.2 percent), predominantly one-party Democratic states (67.8 percent), and modified one-party Republican states (70.6 percent). On the other hand, in the Republican party, competitive two-party states displayed a slightly higher mean turnover rate (68.3 percent) than modified one-party Democratic states (67.2 percent), and modified one-party Republican states exhibited the greatest turnover rate (77.1 percent). The lowest mean turnover rate at Republican conventions was revealed by one-party Democratic states in the South (57.7 percent). In many respects, therefore, the association between delegate participation and party competition seemed to be strongly affected by the regional differences that have permeated both major party conventions.

24. An examination of numerous other social, economic, and political attributes, such as population growth, the percentage of foreign-born residents, per capita income, voter turnout, and similar measures failed to disclose any clear or significant associations between those variables and mean delegate turnover by state. See Loch K. Johnson, "Delegate Selection to the National Party Conventions, 1944–1968" (Ph.D. dissertation, University of California, Riverside, 1969), pp. 148–85.

ticipation of new or inexperienced citizens in the nominating process.[25] It was anticipated that the involvement of party rank-and-file in the election of delegates to the national conventions would eliminate, or at least reduce, the predominant influence of party regulars in the choice of presidential candidates.

The evidence, however, does not confirm this expectation. The following table reports the mean turnover of delegates selected by direct appointment, state or district conventions, and presidential preference primaries at Republican and Democratic national conventions from 1944 to 1968:[26]

| | | Percentage of turnover ||
Method of selection	Number	Republicans	Democrats
Appointment	2	66.1	72.9
Convention	34	71.2	64.6
Primary	14	61.1	63.7

The most striking feature is the high average level of convention participation by delegates elected in presidential primaries. Although the pattern was somewhat stronger among the Republicans, states with primaries picked fewer new delegates on the average than states that chose their representatives either at conventions or by direct appointment in both parties. Moreover, at each of the Republican and Democratic national conventions from 1944 through 1968, presidential primaries yielded lower turnover rates than the convention system of recruiting delegates.

To the extent that the perpetuation of experienced delegates limits the entrance of new workers into the nominating process, the goal of progressive reformers who embraced the direct primary as a means of encouraging increased participation in the selection of candidates ap-

25. See Louise Overacker, *The Presidential Primary* (Macmillan, 1926); and James W. Davis, *Presidential Primaries: Road to the White House* (Crowell, 1967).

26. Although the procedure for selecting national convention delegates is a confusing and inadequately studied subject, the definition of selection methods used in this study is based on the material presented in Nelson W. Polsby and Aaron B. Wildavsky, *Presidential Elections: Strategies of American Electoral Politics* (2d ed., Scribner's, 1968), pp. 112–14. In the few states that select delegates by more than one procedure, the method by which a majority of the delegates were selected determined the predominant selection procedure used in the table above. Since few states have relied on the direct appointment procedure to select delegates, no firm generalizations can be made concerning its relation to delegate turnover. The principal comparison is therefore between the convention and primary method of selecting delegates to national party meetings.

pears to have fallen short of the mark. As Key concluded, "Under the direct primary the party organization remained and adapted its methods to the new machinery of nominations. Whatever the form of nominating procedure, its operation has required the collaboration of men working in concert toward common ends, and they are usually professional politicians, who perform a task that has to be accomplished to operate government."[27]

The findings of this study indicate that high convention turnover rates are more likely to result from delegate selection in state conventions than from recruitment through presidential primaries. In any event, the search for a final explanation of state and regional variations in turnover would seem to require a more extensive investigation than the study of methods of delegate selection. This quest might profitably be focused on an examination of the structural characteristics of political parties in each of the fifty states.

Delegate Turnover and Voting Behavior

While delegate turnover appears to reflect important organizational characteristics of state parties, the impact of participation on voting behavior at the conventions may provide an even more critical insight into the American nominating process. To examine this question, simple product-moment coefficients of correlation were computed between the percentage of the vote by state for different candidates on all divisive convention roll calls and the proportion of delegates with varying degrees of prior convention experience. This analysis of voting for Democratic presidential nominees is presented in Table 1.

In several Democratic conventions, delegation support for various candidates was related to levels of convention experience. In 1948, for example, the vote for President Truman was inversely related to the proportion of new delegates, but it was directly associated with the percentage that had attended one or more prior conventions. At the 1952 Democratic convention, however, support for Senator Estes Kefauver was directly related to the percentage of delegates who had attended only one convention, and inversely related to the proportion with longer attendance records. The votes for both Averell Harriman

27. V. O. Key, Jr., *Politics, Parties, and Pressure Groups* (5th ed., Crowell, 1964), p. 394.

TABLE 1. *Coefficients of Correlation between State Delegation Turnover and Support for Presidential Candidates at Democratic National Conventions, Selected Years, 1948–68*

Year and ballot	Delegates attending		
	1 convention	*2–3 conventions*	*4 or more conventions*
1948			
First ballot (before and after shift)			
Harry S. Truman	−.31[a]	.31[a]	—
Richard B. Russell	.13	−.13	—
1952			
First ballot			
Estes Kefauver	.24[a]	−.21	−.21
Richard B. Russell	.01	.01	−.05
W. Averell Harriman	−.14	.06	.30[a]
Adlai E. Stevenson	−.25[a]	.17	.37[b]
Second ballot			
Estes Kefauver	.25[a]	−.22	−.23
Richard B. Russell	.05	−.03	−.08
W. Averell Harriman	−.13	.05	.29[a]
Adlai E. Stevenson	−.24[a]	.17	.33[b]
Third ballot			
Estes Kefauver	.25[a]	−.23	−.21
Richard B. Russell	.01	.01	−.06
Adlai E. Stevenson	−.18	.08	.40[b]
1960			
First ballot			
Adlai E. Stevenson	.04	.01	−.10
Stuart Symington	−.05	.09	−.05
Lyndon B. Johnson	−.07	.13	−.09
John F. Kennedy	−.18	.03	.36[b]
1968			
First ballot			
Eugene McCarthy	.28[a]	−.26[a]	−.15
Goerge S. McGovern	−.19	.23	.01
Hubert H. Humphrey	.05	−.02	−.08

Sources: Voting data 1948–52—Richard C. Bain and Judith H. Parris, *Convention Decisions and Voting Records* (2d ed., Brookings Institution, 1973), App. C; 1960—*Official Proceedings*, p. 168; 1968—*New York Times*, Aug. 29, 1968.

a. Significant at the 0.05 level.
b. Significant at the 0.01 level.

and Adlai Stevenson indicated a contrasting association: as the proportion of new delegates within a state delegation increased, support for Harriman and Stevenson declined; an increase in the percentage of experienced delegates was associated with a growing vote in favor of both. In large measure, those relations seemed to denote some of the major sources of strength for each presidential aspirant. According to one account of this convention, Kefauver "had no backing from the power blocs or party leaders, and his only chance for the nomination was to go directly to the voters."[28] By contrast, many party stalwarts tended to favor the candidacies of either Harriman or Stevenson.

In the two subsequent conventions, however, the vote for several major Democratic candidates did not appear to be closely associated with delegate turnover. Perhaps the most striking results from this period were produced by the analysis of the vote for John F. Kennedy in 1960. Support for Kennedy was inversely associated with the percentage of new delegates, but it was directly related to the proportion of delegates with extensive convention experience.[29] In 1968, a direct relationship was found between the percentage of inexperienced delegates and the vote for Senator Eugene McCarthy, which seemed to be consistent with general appraisals of his major sources of support. But the proportion of new delegates in that year was inversely related to the backing for Senator George McGovern; this may have reflected the support he attracted among former Kennedy partisans.

In general, the examination of voting in Republican conventions yielded similar results. As Table 2 indicates, delegation turnover was strongly related to the vote for several Republican contenders, while a less discernible association was found between this measure and the balloting on other candidates. The 1948 GOP convention, for example, produced a close association between the percentage of inexperienced delegates and the vote for Harold E. Stassen, perhaps substantiating the observation that "few professional politicians took [Stassen's] candidacy very seriously."[30] Conversely, there was a direct relationship between increasing delegate experience and support

28. Herbert Eaton, *Presidential Timber* (Macmillan, 1964), p. 455.

29. Although Kennedy naturally received strong support from the Northeast, 54 percent of his vote in the 1960 convention was cast by state delegations from the West and Midwest.

30. Eaton, *Presidential Timber*, p. 411.

TABLE 2. *Coefficients of Correlation between State Delegation Turnover and Support for Presidential Candidates at Republican National Conventions, Selected Years, 1948–68*

Year and ballot	Delegates attending		
	1 convention	*2–3 conventions*	*4 or more conventions*
1948			
First ballot			
Harold E. Stassen	.34[a]	−.34[a]	—
Thomas E. Dewey	−.09	.09	—
Robert A. Taft	−.19	.19	—
Second ballot			
Harold E. Stassen	.32[b]	−.32[b]	—
Thomas E. Dewey	−.06	.06	—
Robert A. Taft	−.20	.20	—
1952			
First ballot (before shift)			
Dwight D. Eisenhower	−.05	.01	.11
Robert A. Taft	−.11	.10	.08
First ballot (after shift)			
Dwight D. Eisenhower	−.08	.05	.09
Robert A. Taft	−.07	.03	.10
1964			
First ballot (before shift)			
Nelson A. Rockefeller	−.19	.15	.14
William Scranton	−.07	.03	.09
Barry M. Goldwater	−.07	.04	.09
First ballot (after shift)			
Nelson A. Rockefeller	−.04	.11	−.13
William Scranton	.27[b]	−.31[b]	−.01
Barry M. Goldwater	−.23	.13	.27[b]
1968			
First ballot			
Nelson A. Rockefeller	−.29[b]	.13	.44[c]
Ronald Reagan	.03	−.06	.04
Richard M. Nixon	.06	−.08	.02

Sources: Voting data 1948–52—Bain and Parris, *Convention Decisions and Voting Records*, App. C; 1964—*Official Proceedings*, pp. 366–67, 373–74; 1968—*New York Times*, Aug. 8, 1968.

a. Significant at the 0.01 level.
b. Significant at the 0.05 level.
c. Significant at the 0.001 level.

for Robert A. Taft and, to a lesser extent, for Thomas E. Dewey. Although the battle between Taft and Dwight D. Eisenhower in 1952 did not seem to be greatly affected by delegation turnover,[31] this factor appeared to have an important impact on voting for several other Republican candidates.

In 1964, not only was delegate experience related to the vote for Nelson Rockefeller, but the correlations also indicated some noticeable shifts after the first ballot of the convention. When it became clear that Barry Goldwater had won the nomination, the inverse relationship between delegation turnover and support for Rockefeller was virtually erased, and the association between extensive convention experience and voting for Goldwater was strengthened appreciably. The evidence suggested that the lengthy convention experience of some delegates who had preferred Rockefeller led to a willingness to endorse Goldwater as the presidential nominee for the sake of party unity. Although turnover was unrelated to the vote for Richard Nixon or Ronald Reagan in 1968, increasing delegation experience again seemed to be directly associated with support for Rockefeller in this convention.

While the limited evidence provided by convention votes precludes the framing of definitive conclusions, the data suggest that increasing convention experience was directly related to support for many seasoned campaigners in both parties, including Truman, Harriman, Stevenson, Kennedy, Taft, and Rockefeller. Conversely, a relatively high proportion of inexperienced delegates seemed to be associated with the vote for several political newcomers such as Stassen in 1948, Kefauver in 1952, and McCarthy in 1968.

The candidate preferences expressed by delegates in nominating conventions have not only reflected specific choices in different election years, but also denoted persistent factional cleavages at national party meetings. In their 1965 study, Munger and Blackhurst found that the votes of state delegations at both Republican and Democratic conventions from 1940 to 1964 tended to form a definite pattern that may reflect an ideological spectrum.[32] Figure 3 employs positions on

31. Accounts of this convention indicate that both candidates had extensive support from seasoned party regulars. See, for example, Richard C. Bain and Judith H. Parris, *Convention Decisions and Voting Records* (2d ed., Brookings Institution, 1973), p. 279; and David, Goldman, and Bain, *Politics of Conventions*, p. 81.

32. Munger and Blackhurst, "Factionalism in the National Conventions."

FIGURE 3. *Positions on Munger-Blackhurst Scale of Convention Voting and Average State Delegation Turnover at Republican and Democratic National Conventions, 1944–68*

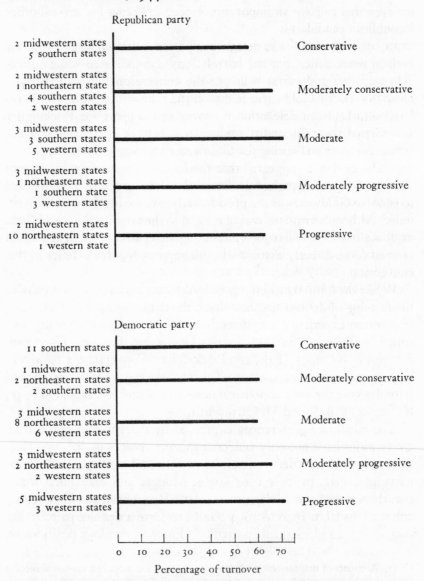

Source: Frank Munger and James Blackhurst, "Factionalism in the National Conventions, 1944–1964: An Analysis of Ideological Consistency in State Delegation Voting," *Journal of Politics*, Vol. 27 (May 1965), pp. 375–94.

the Munger-Blackhurst scale to examine the association between mean state delegation turnover rates and the ideology of state delegations at both national party conventions.

State delegations classified according to the Munger-Blackhurst scale disclosed sharply contrasting levels of convention experience, especially between the parties.[33] In the Democratic party, the largest proportion of inexperienced delegates were recruited by states representing either conservative or progressive positions on the Munger-Blackhurst scale of convention voting. At the Republican conventions, by contrast, the highest levels of delegation turnover were manifested by states with moderate or "middle-of-the-road" voting orientations. Thus the more experienced delegations in the two parties tended to occupy different positions on the Munger-Blackhurst scale; the experienced Republican delegations assumed polar positions, while the experienced Democratic delegations concentrated at the center.[34]

These results seem to bolster the proposition that Republican party regulars have tended to favor less moderate political positions than seasoned veterans at Democratic conventions. Patterns of participation in state party delegations are thus not only associated with convention voting behavior, but reveal salient variations between the two major political parties in America.[35]

33. As Munger and Blackhurst (ibid.) observed, ideological positions in convention voting coincided partially with regional boundaries. This phenomenon was most notable in the extreme conservative wings of both parties, which represented primarily states from the South. Removing this conservative category from the analysis, however, does not appreciably alter the findings. In the Democratic party, "middle-of-the-road" states revealed low mean turnover; in the Republican party, the converse was true. (Munger and Blackhurst classify the Democratic delegations into six groups; for the comparative purposes of this chapter, their two moderate categories are combined into one, providing five groupings for each party from "conservative" through "progressive.")

34. This evidence may contain some interesting implications about the "middle-of-the-road" position pursued by most successful party candidates. In the Democratic party, presidential aspirants who hope to gain the backing of experienced delegations may be encouraged to adopt a stance near the center of the political spectrum. In a similar effort to acquire the support of seasoned party regulars, Republican presidential hopefuls may find themselves in the awkward position of attempting to straddle the polar wings of the party. Although the methods of appealing to the convention veterans in the two parties may be different, the net effect has probably been to promote the moderate and frequently bland character of American presidential politics.

35. See also McClosky, Hoffmann, and O'Hara, "Conflict and Consensus"; and John W. Soule and James W. Clarke, "Issue Conflict and Consensus: A Comparative Study of Democratic and Republican Delegates to the 1968 National Conventions," *Journal of Politics*, Vol. 33 (February 1971), pp. 72–91.

Summary and Discussion

This paper has examined tenure and turnover at both Republican and Democratic nominating conventions from 1944 through 1968. Delegate participation in the conventions disclosed highly similar and consistent patterns. In both political parties, and at most of the national conventions during this period, approximately two-thirds of the convention membership consisted of new delegates, while slightly more than one-third of the delegates had acquired convention experience in earlier election years. The nominating process has been characterized by the constant replenishment of delegate positions through the continuous admission of new activists to the national conventions of both political parties.

Variations in the percentage of experienced or inexperienced convention delegates were associated with delegate selection procedures, state party attributes, and regional patterns. In general, presidential primaries in both parties tended to select more experienced delegations than did either state-convention or direct-appointment procedures. Preliminary evidence indicated that turnover was associated with party competition and centralization. Moreover, convention attendance patterns tended to coincide with regional boundaries. In both parties, the Northeast produced delegations with the greatest amount of previous convention experience. While the Midwest and the West registered intermediate or diverse rates of participation, relatively high turnover characterized southern Democratic delegations, and somewhat lower attendance records were found in Republican delegations from the South. The southern Republican patterns show an increase in delegation turnover since the mid-fifties, when the party began to intensify its efforts to recruit new personnel in that region.

An examination of convention voting patterns also disclosed that delegate experience was related to the vote for several major candidates—especially challengers—at both Republican and Democratic national conventions. In addition, however, the investigation of persistent ideological orientations indicated major differences between the political parties. While states reflecting moderate tendencies in Democratic conventions exhibited relatively high levels of delegate experience, the delegations with the most extensive experience at

Republican conventions were found in states that assumed either conservative or progressive positions.

The high rate of delegate turnover creates advantages and disadvantages for the political parties in the selection of presidential nominees. National party conventions have been described as chaotic carnivals attended by an aimless and perplexed throng of delegates. The evidence of delegate inexperience presented here does little to belie the impression. Unlike many other major positions in American politics, in which a large number of officials are long-standing incumbents, convention seats are filled primarily by newcomers, and as a result the average delegate possesses few skills in the nominating process. Kessel has noted that "it is not unusual to find many of the groups involved in nomination politics behaving in a very tentative and hesitant fashion. This is because they are seeking their footing on unfamiliar terrain."[36] Lack of familiarity may make convention representatives either the pawns of party leaders or incorrigible mavericks.

On the other hand, high levels of turnover at the national conventions may enhance the legitimacy of leadership selection in America. One of the basic postulates of democratic theory is the extensive participation of citizens in crucial political decisions. In the nominating conventions, there appears to be little effort to restrict the access—at least of politically dominant groups in the population—to the highest decision-making assemblies of the parties. The selection of convention representatives seems to place more emphasis on the effort to promote opportunities for participation by party workers than to maximize political experience. Hence, the prospect of a continuous stream of new party activists representing all segments of the American public in both the Republican and Democratic national conventions may offer a delicate but crucial vehicle for preserving the strength and vitality of the party system and of the presidential nominations it produces.

36. John H. Kessel, *The Goldwater Coalition* (Bobbs-Merrill, 1968), pp. 27–28.

APPENDIX

This bibliographic note is intended to serve as a guide to further reading and research on the politics of presidential nominations. While this listing is by no means exhaustive, it includes the major academic research on American presidential nominations published in the past four decades. The journalistic literature on presidential nominations is simply too vast to cover here.

General Works

Bone, Hugh A. *American Politics and the Party System.* 4th ed. New York: McGraw-Hill, 1971.

Brogan, D. W. *Politics in America.* New York: Harper, 1954.

Carleton, William. "The Revolution in the Presidential Nominating Convention," *Political Science Quarterly,* Vol. 72 (June 1957), pp. 224–40.

David, Paul T., Ralph M. Goldman, and Richard C. Bain. *The Politics of National Party Conventions.* Washington: Brookings Institution, 1960.

Eaton, Herbert. *Presidential Timber.* Glencoe, Ill.: Free Press of Glencoe, 1964.

Herring, E. Pendleton. *The Politics of Democracy.* New York: Rinehart, 1950.

Kessel, John H. "The Nominating Game," in Demetrios Caraley (ed.), *Party Politics and National Elections.* Boston: Little, Brown, 1966.

Key, V. O., Jr. *Politics, Parties, and Pressure Groups.* 5th ed. New York: Crowell, 1964.

Martin, Ralph. *Ballots & Bandwagons.* Chicago: Rand McNally, 1964.

Moos, Malcolm C. "New Light on the Nominating Process," in Stephen K. Bailey and others (eds.), *Frontiers in Government and Politics.* Washington: Brookings Institution, 1955.

―――, and Stephen Hess. *Hats in the Ring.* New York: Random House, 1960.

Ogden, Daniel M., Jr., and Arthur L. Peterson. *Electing the President.* San Francisco: Chandler, 1968.

Polsby, Nelson W., and Aaron B. Wildavsky. *Presidential Elections.* 3d ed. New York: Scribner's, 1972.

Pomper, Gerald M. *Nominating the President: The Politics of Convention Choice.* Evanston: Northwestern University Press, 1963.

Sorauf, Frank J. *Political Parties in the American System.* Boston: Little, Brown, 1964.

Theoretical Perspectives

Costantini, Edmond. "Intraparty Attitude Conflict: Democratic Party Leadership in California," *Western Political Quarterly,* Vol. 16 (December 1963), pp. 956–72.

―――, and Kenneth H. Craik. "Competing Elites within a Political Party:

A Study of Republican Leadership," *Western Political Quarterly*, Vol. 22 (December 1969), pp. 879–903.

Gamson, William Anthony. "Coalition Formation at Presidential Nominating Conventions," *American Journal of Sociology*, Vol. 68 (1962), pp. 157–71.

McClosky, Herbert, Paul J. Hoffmann, and Rosemary O'Hara. "Issue Conflict and Consensus Among Party Leaders and Followers," *American Political Science Review*, Vol. 54 (June 1960), pp. 406–27.

Munger, Frank, and James Blackhurst. "Factionalism in the National Conventions," 1940–1964: An Analysis of Ideological Consistency in State Delegation Voting," *Journal of Politics*, Vol. 27 (May 1965), pp. 375–94.

Polsby, Nelson B. "Decision-Making at the National Conventions," *Western Political Quarterly*, Vol. 13 (September 1960), pp. 609–19.

———, and Aaron B. Wildavsky. "Uncertainty and Decision-Making at the National Conventions," in Nelson W. Polsby, Robert A. Dentler, and Paul A. Smith (eds.), *Politics and Social Life*. Boston: Houghton Mifflin, 1963.

Pomper, Gerald M. "Factionalism in the 1968 National Conventions: An Extension of Research Findings," *Journal of Politics*, Vol. 33 (August 1971), pp. 826–30.

Soule, John W., and James W. Clarke. "Amateurs and Professionals: A Study of Delegates to the 1968 Democratic National Convention," *American Political Science Review*, Vol. 64 (September 1970), pp. 888–98.

———. "Issue Conflict and Consensus: A Comparative Study of Democratic and Republican Delegates to the 1968 National Conventions," *Journal of Politics*, Vol. 33 (February 1971), pp. 72–91.

Background and Recruitment of Convention Delegates

Niemi, Richard G., and M. Kent Jennings. "Intraparty Communications and the Selection of Delegates to a National Convention," *Western Political Quarterly*, Vol. 22 (December 1968), pp. 29–46.

McKeough, Kevin L., and John F. Bibby. *The Costs of Political Participation: A Study of National Convention Delegates*. Study Number Fourteen. Princeton, N.J.: Citizens' Research Foundation, 1968.

Meadows, Paul, and Charles L. Braucher. "Social Composition of the 1948 National Conventions," *Sociology and Social Research*, Vol. 36 (September–October 1951), pp. 31–35.

Preconvention Campaigns

Converse, Philip E., Aage R. Clausen, and Warren E. Miller, "Electoral Myth and Reality: The 1964 Election," *American Political Science Review*, Vol. 59 (June 1965), pp. 220–46.

———, Warren E. Miller, Jerrold G. Rusk, and Arthur C. Wolfe. "Continuity and Change in American Politics: Parties and Issues in the 1968 Election," *American Political Science Review*, Vol. 63 (December 1969), pp. 1083–1105.

Davis, James W. *Presidential Primaries: Road to the White House.* New York: Crowell, 1967.

Harris, Louis. "Why the Odds Are Against a Governor's Becoming President," *Public Opinion Quarterly*, Vol. 23 (Fall 1959), pp. 361–70.

Larner, Jeremy. *Nobody Knows: Reflections on the McCarthy Campaign of 1968.* New York: Macmillan, 1970.

Orbell, John M., Robyn M. Dawes, and Nancy J. Collins. "Grass Roots Enthusiasm and the Primary Vote," *Western Political Quarterly.* Vol. 25 (June 1972), pp. 249–59.

Ranney, Austin. "Turnout and Representation in Presidential Primary Elections," *American Political Science Review*, Vol. 66 (March 1972), pp. 21–37.

Stavis, Ben. *We Were the Campaign.* Boston: Beacon, 1969.

Case Studies in Nomination Politics

Appleby, Paul A. "Roosevelt's Third-Term Decision," *American Political Science Review*, Vol. 46 (September 1952), pp. 754–65.

Bagby, Wesley. "The 'Smoke-Filled Room' and the Nomination of Warren G. Harding," *Mississippi Valley Historical Review*, Vol. 41 (March 1955), pp. 657–74.

Bunzel, John H., and Eugene C. Lee. *The California Delegation of 1960.* Inter-University Case Study No. 67. University: University of Alabama Press, 1962.

Chester, Lewis, Godfrey Hodgson, and Bruce Page. *An American Melodrama: The Presidential Campaign of 1968.* New York: Viking, 1969.

Cooke, Edward F. "Drafting the 1952 Platforms," *Western Political Quarterly*, Vol. 9 (September 1956), pp. 699–712.

Cosman, Bernard. *The Case of the Goldwater Delegates: Deep South Republican Leadership.* University, Alabama: Bureau of Public Administration, 1966.

Cummings, Milton C., Jr. (ed.). *The National Election of 1964.* Washington: Brookings Institution, 1966.

David, Paul T. "Purposes, Procedures, and Outcomes on the Cooperative Research Project on Convention Delegates," *American Political Science Review*, Vol. 47 (December 1953), pp. 1116–29.

———, Malcolm C. Moos, and Ralph M. Goldman. *Presidential Nominating Politics in 1952.* 5 vols. Baltimore: Johns Hopkins Press, 1954.

Hahn, Harlan. "The Republican Party Convention of 1912 and the Role of Herbert S. Hadley in National Politics," *Missouri Historical Review*, Vol. 59 (July 1965), pp. 407–23.

Johnson, Walter. *How We Drafted Adlai Stevenson.* New York: Knopf, 1955.

Kessel, John H. *The Goldwater Coalition.* New York: Bobbs-Merrill, 1968.

Morison, S. E. "The First National Nominating Convention," *American Historical Review,* Vol. 27 (July 1912), pp. 744–63.

Pomper, Gerald M. "New Jersey Convention Delegates of 1964," *Southwestern Social Science Quarterly,* Vol. 48 (June 1967), pp. 24–34.

Squires, J. Duane. "A Delegate's View of the Republican Convention of 1952," *New England Social Studies Bulletin,* Vol. 10 (March 1953), pp. 4–10.

Sullivan, Mark. "The Nomination of Warren Gamaliel Harding," in *Our Times, The Twenties,* Vol. 6. New York: Scribner's, 1935.

Tillett, Paul (ed.). *Inside Politics: The National Conventions, 1960.* Dobbs Ferry, N.Y.: Oceana, 1962.

Walters, Everett. "The Ohio Delegation at the National Republican Convention of 1888," *Ohio State Archaeological and Historical Quarterly,* Vol. 56 (July 1947).

White, Theodore H. *The Making of the President 1960.* New York: Atheneum, 1961.

———. *The Making of the President 1964.* New York: Atheneum, 1965.

———. *The Making of the President 1968.* New York: Atheneum, 1969.

Wildavsky, Aaron B. "The Goldwater Phenomenon: Purists, Politicians, and the Two-Party System," *Review of Politics,* Vol. 27 (July 1965), pp. 386–413.

Financing Presidential Nominations

Alexander, Herbert E. *Financing the 1960 Election.* Princeton, N.J.: Citizens' Research Foundation, 1962.

———. *Financing the 1964 Election.* Princeton, N.J.: Citizens' Research Foundation, 1962.

———. "Financing the Parties and Campaigns," in Paul T. David (ed.), *The Presidential Election and Transition 1960–1961.* Washington: Brookings Institution, 1961.

Bibby, John F., and Herbert E. Alexander. *The Politics of National Convention Finances and Arrangements.* Princeton, N.J.: Citizens' Research Foundation, 1968.

Heard, Alexander. *The Costs of Democracy.* Chapel Hill: University of North Carolina Press, 1960.

Perspectives on Reform

David, Paul T. "Reforming the Presidential Nominating Process," *Law and Contemporary Problems,* Vol. 27 (Spring 1962), pp. 159–77.

Dauer, Manning J., and others. "Toward a Model State Presidential Primary Law," *American Political Science Review*, Vol. 50 (March 1956), pp. 138–53.

Lederle, John W. "National Conventions: Canada Shows the Way," *Southwestern Social Science Quarterly*, Vol. 25 (September 1944), pp. 130–38.

Leventhal, Harold. "The Democratic Party's Approach to Its Convention Rules," *American Political Science Review*, Vol. 50 (June 1956), pp. 553–68.

Mandate for Reform. Washington: Democratic National Committee, 1970.

Parris, Judith H. *The Convention Problem: Issues in Reform of Presidential Nominating Procedures*. Washington: Brookings Institution, 1972.

Proxmire, William, "Presidential Primaries: Pro," and David S. Broder, "Presidential Primaries: Con," in John Owens and P. J. Staudenraus (eds.), *The American Party System: A Book of Readings*. New York: Macmillan, 1955.

Rose, Richard. "Between Miami Beach and Blackpool," *Political Quarterly*, Vol. 43 (October–December 1972), pp. 414–24.

Rosenthal, Albert J. *Federal Regulation of Campaign Finance: Some Constitutional Questions*. Princeton, N.J.: Citizens' Research Foundation, 1972.

The Democratic Choice. Washington: Democratic National Committee, 1968.

Wildavsky, Aaron B. "On the Superiority of National Conventions," *Review of Politics*, Vol. 24 (July 1962), pp. 307–19.

Zeidenstein, Harvey. "Presidential Primaries—Reflections of 'The People's Choice'?" *Journal of Politics*, Vol. 32 (November 1970), pp. 856–74.

On Delegate Turnover

David, Paul T., Ralph M. Goldman, and Richard C. Bain. *The Politics of National Party Conventions*. Washington: Brookings Institution, 1960.

Fisher, Marguerite J., and Betty Whitehead. "Women and National Party Organization," *American Political Science Review*, Vol. 38 (October 1944), pp. 895–903.

Guide to Black Politics '72: The Democratic and Republican National Conventions (Parts 1 and 2). Washington: Joint Center for Political Studies, Summer 1972.

Hahn, Harlan. "Turnover in Iowa State Party Conventions: An Exploratory Study," *Midwest Journal of Political Science*, Vol. 11 (February 1967), pp. 98–105.

Kessel, John H. *The Goldwater Coalition*. New York: Bobbs-Merrill, 1968.

Marvick, Dwaine, and Samuel J. Eldersveld. "National Convention Leadership: 1952 and 1956," *Western Political Quarterly*, Vol. 14 (March 1961), pp. 176–94.

Polsby, Nelson W., and Aaron B. Wildavsky. *Presidential Elections*. 3d ed. New York: Scribner's, 1972.

Basic Data Sources

Bain, Richard C., and Judith H. Parris. *Convention Decisions and Voting Records*. 2d ed. Washington: Brookings Institution, 1973.

Nomination and Election of the President and Vice President of the United States, Including the Manner of Selecting Delegates to National Political Conventions. Washington: U.S. Government Printing Office, published each election year.

Official Proceedings, Democratic National Convention. Washington: Democratic National Committee, published for each convention.

Official Proceedings, Republican National Convention. Washington: Republican National Committee, published for each convention.

Porter, Kirk, and Donald B. Johnson. *National Party Platforms 1840–1956*. Urbana: University of Illinois Press, 1956.

The Presidential Nominating Conventions 1968. Washington: Congressional Quarterly Service, 1968.

☆

Chapter Seven

☆

The Biases of the Electoral College: Who Is Really Advantaged?

JOHN H. YUNKER *and* LAWRENCE D. LONGLEY

THE POLITICS of electoral college reform has been permeated in recent years by contradictory assessments of the biases of the electoral college.[1] There seems to be widespread agreement among both scholars and politicians that the effective voting power for president of the 350,000 residents of Omaha, Nebraska, is not the same as that of the 350,000 residents of Oakland, California. But there is no agreement on whether the inhabitants of small or of large states have the advantage.[2]

These biases arise because the contemporary electoral college is more than just "an archaic and undemocratic counting device."[3] It is an institution whose "consequences come about because of the way

Note. The research on which this chapter is based was considerably assisted by a National Science Foundation–COSIP Grant to Lawrence University.

1. This question is, of course, only one of many issues surrounding electoral reform and proposals for the abolition of the electoral college. Such controversies as whether the electoral college serves as an essential prop for federalism, provides vital support for the American two-party system, or localizes and neutralizes election fraud—as well as the broader question of whether the electoral college should be retained—are not examined here. These questions are considered, however, in another study: Lawrence D. Longley and Alan G. Braun, *The Politics of Electoral College Reform* (Yale University Press, 1972), esp. Chaps. 3 and 4.

2. For a comprehensive review of conventional wisdom on the biases of the electoral college, see Longley and Yunker, "Who Is Really Advantaged by the Electoral College— and Who Just Thinks He Is?" (paper presented at the 67th annual meeting of the American Political Science Association, Sept. 7–11, 1971). See also Longley and Braun, *Politics of Electoral College Reform*, Chap. 4.

3. John D. Feerick, "The Electoral College—Why It Ought to Be Abolished," *Fordham Law Review*, Vol. 37 (October 1968), p. 43.

the College operates to aggregate votes."[4] Among the distinctive structural features of the electoral college that give rise to biases are:[5]

1. The "constant two" constitutional allocation of two electoral votes to every state, regardless of size (corresponding to its Senate representation), in addition to electoral votes equal to its number of congressmen. In the case of states with quite low populations, this can lead to startling results. During the elections of the 1960s, for example, Alaska, with one-half the population of Delaware, enjoyed an equal number of electoral votes—the constitutional minimum of three.

2. The "unit rule" extraconstitutional provision (sometimes termed the "winner-take-all" feature) that the candidate who receives a plurality of votes in a state wins all that state's electoral votes. The result of this feature is that a candidate can win all the electoral votes of states carried with even the slimmest of margins, while losing millions of popular votes in other states carried by the opposition. In 1924, for example, Democratic nominee John W. Davis received 136 electoral votes from states in which he had obtained 2 million popular votes, and no electoral votes from other states in which he had received 6 million popular votes.[6]

3. The assignment of electoral votes (other than the "constant two") to states on the basis of population rather than voter turnout. In 1968, Connecticut and South Carolina had eight electoral votes each, based on their similar populations, yet the number of voters in Connecticut exceeded that in South Carolina by more than 590,000.[7] On a regional level, the effect of this feature would appear to work to the advantage of the South. In the 1960 election, the South had 17.8

4. Syndicated column by Nelson W. Polsby, distributed by the *Los Angeles Times* News Service, Nov. 20, 1969.

5. See Neal R. Peirce, *The People's President: The Electoral College in American History and the Direct-Vote Alternative* (Simon and Schuster, 1968), p. 137; Allan P. Sindler, "Presidential Election Methods and Urban-Ethnic Interests," *Law and Contemporary Problems*, Vol. 27 (Spring 1962), p. 216; Joseph F. Kallenbach, "Our Electoral College Gerrymander," *Midwest Journal of Political Science*, Vol. 4 (May 1960), p. 166; Robert G. Dixon, Jr., *Democratic Representation: Reapportionment in Law and Politics* (Oxford University Press, 1968), pp. 565–66; and John D. Feerick, "The Electoral College—Its Defects and Dangers," *New York State Bar Journal*, Vol. 40 (August 1968), pp. 319–20. These features of the electoral college are discussed in detail in Longley and Braun, *Politics of Electoral College Reform*, Chap. 1.

6. Feerick, "Electoral College—Its Defects and Dangers."

7. William T. Gossett, "Direct Popular Election of the President," *American Bar Association Journal*, Vol. 56 (March 1970), p. 227.

percent of the national popular vote, but controlled 27.2 percent of the nation's electoral votes. It seems to be a curious feature of the electoral college that low levels of voter participation are rewarded.

4. The assignment of electoral votes on the basis of census population figures, which reflect population shifts only at ten-year intervals. As a result, states that grew fast during the 1960s, such as Arizona, California, Colorado, Florida, and Texas, did not find their new population reflected in their electoral vote until the 1970 census. Since that census established the electoral votes for each state for the presidential elections of 1972, 1976, and 1980, population changes after 1970 will not be reflected in the electoral college until 1984.

These features ensure that the electoral college will always provide an imperfect reflection of the popular vote for president. To say that the electoral college introduces random distortions into the election of the president is, however, only a half-truth, for it also contains a variety of systematic biases conferring advantages on some voters and imposing disadvantages on others.

Various approaches find that different groups and interests are advantaged or disadvantaged under the present mechanism for electing the president. Among the voters often seen as advantaged are minority groups (especially black voters), urban and ethnic voters, and inhabitants of "swing" states, metropolitan areas, and the South. For the most part, arguments dealing with these demographic groups have been based on the premise that either large states or small states have an advantage. Consequently, the interpretations have been subject to much the same controversy surrounding the big-state, small-state debate. It is the purpose of this chapter to reconcile the contradictory assessments concerning the biases of the electoral college and to determine systematically "who is really advantaged."

The Voting Power Approach

For more than a century and a half, both reformers and opponents of reform have attempted to demonstrate the effects of the electoral college through the use of rhetorical argument supported by simple arithmetic. In the past decade, however, more sophisticated analyses have appeared.[8] Recent advances in game theory and the mathemati-

8. Research on the contributions of Riker, Shapley, and Mann (see below) to the literature on voting power under the electoral college was originally conducted by Alan Braun for Longley and Braun, *Politics of Electoral College Reform*, Chap. 4.

cal analysis of voting power have made possible inquiry into the consequences of the present electoral college on two levels. On the one hand, a determination of *the relative power of the states* in the present electoral college has been made by Irwin Mann and Lloyd S. Shapley.[9] On the other hand, John F. Banzhaf III has calculated *the relative power of individual citizen-voters within each state* in the electoral college and in various alternative systems.[10] The work of William Riker and Lloyd S. Shapley serves as a valuable transition.[11]

Mann and Shapley developed a fifty-one-person, weighted majority game to evaluate the electoral college. Defining the power index of a state as "the chance that a state has of being 'pivotal' on a ballot—i.e., of casting the deciding vote for or against a proposal [or a candidate],"[12] they used the resulting power indices to demonstrate that "power, in any reasonable sense of the word, is *not* automatically proportional to voting strengths."[13]

In their estimate, although a slight systematic bias in favor of the large states is created by the unit rule, it does not exceed a 10 percent variation in power per electoral vote among the states. They concluded that this slight big-state advantage is of less importance than the small-state advantage afforded by the "constant two" electoral votes:

> To take the most extreme case, New York has 15 times as many electoral votes as Nevada, and their power indices are in the ratio 16½ : 1, reflecting the big-state bias. But the number of Congressmen (the nominal measure of population) of the two states are in the ratio 43 : 1, and the actual populations (1950 census) are in the ratio 93 : 1. At best, the two biases cancel each other only for the half-dozen or so most populous states.[14]

9. Irwin Mann and L. S. Shapley, *Values of Large Games VI: Evaluating the Electoral College Exactly*, Memorandum RM-3158-PR (Santa Monica: RAND Corporation, 1962).

10. John F. Banzhaf III, "One Man, 3.312 Votes: A Mathematical Analysis of the Electoral College," *Villanova Law Review*, Vol. 13 (Winter 1968), pp. 303–46. The Banzhaf article was later reprinted in *Electoral College Reform*, Hearings before the House Judiciary Committee, 91 Cong. 1 sess. (1969), pp. 309–52; and *Electing the President*, Hearings before the Senate Judiciary Committee, 91 Cong. 1 sess. (1969), pp. 823–66.

11. William H. Riker and Lloyd S. Shapley, *Weighted Voting: A Mathematical Analysis for Instrumental Judgments*, Memorandum P-3318 (RAND Corporation, 1966).

12. Irwin Mann and L. S. Shapley, "The A Priori Voting Strength of the Electoral College," in Martin Shubik (ed.), *Game Theory and Related Approaches to Social Behavior* (Wiley, 1964), p. 153. This definition is based on the assumption that all combinations of states are equally likely. The computations used "monte carlo" techniques, while the computations in Mann and Shapley, "Values of Large Games," were made with the aid of a computer and were therefore more accurate.

13. Mann and Shapley, *Values of Large Games*, p. 3.

14. Mann and Shapley, "A Priori Voting Strength," pp. 154, 159.

The latter argument is plausible only if citizens, instead of states, are taken as players in the theoretical model, and if the power of a citizen to affect the outcome of his state's vote is assumed to be inversely proportional to the state's population. When the analysis using states as players (in which New York has a 16.5 : 1 advantage over Nevada) and the simple analysis using citizens as players (in which Nevada has a 93 : 1 advantage over New York) are combined, Nevada has a net advantage of 5.6 : 1.

Mann and Shapley's calculations were based on a free-agent model of the electoral college. As Riker and Shapley noted, however, in a later article, the electoral college is a delegate model; if an elector casts his vote as instructed by the voters he represents, he is a delegate representative, and his vote merely reflects the decision of a plurality of his constituents. When the analysis shifts from a free-agent model with states as players to a delegate model with citizens as players, "the citizens' power indices are multiplied by a factor proportional to the square-root of their district population."[15] The reason for the additional bias in favor of large states is that, when citizens are regarded as players, a citizen's voting power is inversely proportional not to his constituency's population but to the *square root* of his constituency's population.[16] Although Riker and Shapley did not attempt to calculate the electoral college power indices for the citizens in each state, Mann and Shapley speculated that the bias in favor of voters in the large states "might be as much as double the one seen by treating the states as players."[17]

Banzhaf has calculated the power indices of "citizen-voters" in each state for the present electoral college and has found greater disparities than had been anticipated by Mann and Shapley. The term

---

15. Riker and Shapley, *Weighted Voting*, pp. 24, 26.

16. Multiplying the power indices by the square root of the district population is, for the electoral college, equivalent to the statement that a citizen's ability to affect the outcome of the election in his district is *inversely* proportional to the square root of his district's population. For Riker and Shapley, the "power ratio," P_w, is equal to the "power index," ϕ_w, divided by the district's population, W: $P_w = \phi_w/W$.

We, however, are interested in the net biases of the electoral college, and thus are concerned only with the effect of the delegate model on the power ratio. The power index measures only the bias introduced by the fifty-one-state game (the free-agent model). Multiplying the square root of the district's population gives $P'_w = \phi_w\sqrt{W/W}$, or $P'_w = \phi_w/\sqrt{W}$. This latter expression—essentially Banzhaf's formulation—indicates that a citizen's ability to affect the result of a national election is inversely proportional to the square root of his district's population and proportional to the free-agent bias, ϕ_w.

17. Mann and Shapley, *Values of Large Games*, p. 9.

"citizen-voters" is used to indicate that Banzhaf's calculations were, of necessity, based on 1960 census figures, rather than on the number of actual voters; he noted, however, that the method is reasonable since electoral votes are also apportioned according to census figures. Neither Banzhaf's calculations nor the distribution of electoral votes takes into account such factors as the number of registered voters in a state, the number of voters who actually participate in an election, or population changes between censuses.

Banzhaf defined voting power as simply "the ability to affect decisions through the process of voting." Voting power, he postulated, "can be most easily measured by comparing the opportunities each voter has to affect the outcome. If all voters have an equal chance to affect the outcome in a given voting situation, we say that they have equal voting power. However, if some voters have a greater chance than others, we say that the voting powers are unequal."[18]

Banzhaf's analysis of the present electoral college involved three steps. First, a determination was made of the chance that each state has of casting the pivotal vote in the electoral college (Mann and Shapley's indices). Second, Banzhaf determined the number of voting combinations (out of all possible combinations of citizen-voters) in which a given citizen-voter can, by changing his vote, alter the way in which his state's electoral votes will be cast. Third, the results of the first step were combined with the results of the second, to determine "the chance that any voter has of affecting the election of the President through the medium of his state's electoral votes."[19] These calculations were normalized (with the power index of the state whose citizens have the least voting power set at one, and all other states having voting powers greater than one); the result was an index of the voting power of each citizen in relation to that of voters residing in other states.

Banzhaf's calculations differed from those of Mann and Shapley in that Banzhaf assumed that the voting power of an individual voter in an n-person constituency is inversely proportional to the *square root* of n, not merely inversely proportional to n, as had been assumed in Mann and Shapley's analysis.[20] If an individual's voting power were inversely proportional to his constituency's population, the big-state

18. Banzhaf, "One Man, 3.312 Votes," p. 307.
19. Ibid., p. 313.
20. Ibid., p. 316. For a detailed mathematical derivation of this conclusion, see pp. 314–17, nn. 32–34.

advantage would be outweighed by the small-state advantage from the "constant two"—as Mann and Shapley had earlier concluded about Nevada and New York.

Empirical Findings: Large versus Small States

Banzhaf's results, represented in Table 1, show specifically that the chance that a citizen-voter in New York will determine the outcome of a presidential election is 3.312 times that of a citizen-voter in the District of Columbia. The table gives the 1960 census population of each state, the electoral votes allotted each state in the 1964 and 1968 elections, and the resulting voting power indices of a citizen-voter in each of the states.[21] The table also includes two columns providing additional statistical interpretations of the relative voting power column. These columns (4 and 5) are useful in comparing the voting power of states for a given plan and, as will be shown later, in comparing the voting powers of each state under each of four electoral plans—the present electoral college, and the proportional, district, and direct-vote reform plans.[22] The fourth column lists the percentage deviations from average voting power per state for the citizen-voters of each of the states. The average voting power per state is calculated by dividing the sum of the relative voting power indices for the fifty states and the District of Columbia by the total number, fifty-one.

It seems more appropriate to Banzhaf's analysis, however, that a second measure, percentage deviation from average voting power per citizen-voter, be calculated in addition to the data on average voting power per state. Consequently, these data were newly derived and are contained in the fifth column of Table 1. The average voting power per citizen-voter is calculated by multiplying the number of citizen-voters in a state (which, for calculative purposes, Banzhaf as-

21. The voting power indices, as well as the following statistical interpretations of the data, apply to the "automatic plan" of electoral college reform, as well as to the present system, since that reform would not affect the structural characteristics of the electoral college, but would merely abolish individual electors. Electoral votes would be assigned as at present, and the unit rule would be written into the Constitution.

22. Table 1 is basically Banzhaf's Table 1 with the addition of the last column, "percentage deviation from average voting power per citizen-voter," and with the omission of an essentially irrelevant column, "percent excess voting power"—the percentage by which voting power for each state's voters exceeds that of the most deprived voters. See Banzhaf, "One Man, 3.312 Votes," p. 329.

TABLE I. *Voting Power in the Present Electoral College, Arranged by Size of Population of State*

State[a]	(1) Electoral votes, 1964, 1968	(2) Population, 1960 census	(3) Relative voting power[b]	(4) Percentage deviation from average per state[c]	(5) Percentage deviation from average per citizen-voter[d]
Alaska	3	226,167	1.838	9.2	−17.4
Nevada	3	285,278	1.636	−2.8	−31.9
Wyoming	3	330,066	1.521	−9.6	−41.9
Vermont	3	389,881	1.400	−16.8	−54.1
Delaware	3	446,292	1.308	−22.3	−65.0
New Hampshire	4	606,921	1.499	−10.9	−44.0
North Dakota	4	632,446	1.468	−12.8	−47.0
Hawaii	4	632,772	1.468	−12.8	−47.0
Idaho	4	667,191	1.429	−15.1	−51.0
Montana	4	674,767	1.421	−15.5	−51.9
South Dakota	4	680,514	1.415	−15.9	−52.5
Dist. of Columbia	3	763,956	1.000	−40.6	−115.8
Rhode Island	4	859,488	1.259	−25.2	−71.4
Utah	4	890,627	1.237	−26.5	−74.5
New Mexico	4	951,023	1.197	−28.9	−80.3
Maine	4	969,265	1.186	−29.5	−82.0
Arizona	5	1,302,161	1.281	−23.9	−68.5
Nebraska	5	1,411,330	1.231	−26.9	−75.3
Colorado	6	1,753,947	1.327	−21.1	−62.6
Oregon	6	1,768,687	1.321	−21.5	−63.4
Arkansas	6	1,786,272	1.315	−21.9	−64.1
West Virginia	7	1,860,421	1.506	−10.5	−43.3
Mississippi	7	2,178,141	1.392	−17.3	−55.0
Kansas	7	2,178,611	1.392	−17.3	−55.0
Oklahoma	8	2,328,284	1.541	−8.4	−40.0
South Carolina	8	2,382,594	1.524	−9.5	−41.6
Connecticut	8	2,535,234	1.477	−12.2	−46.1
Iowa	9	2,757,537	1.596	−5.2	−35.2
Washington	9	2,853,214	1.569	−6.8	−37.5
Kentucky	9	3,038,156	1.521	−9.6	−41.9
Maryland	10	3,100,689	1.675	−0.4	−28.8
Louisiana	10	3,257,022	1.635	−2.9	−32.0
Alabama	10	3,266,740	1.632	−3.0	−32.3
Minnesota	10	3,413,864	1.597	−5.1	−35.1
Tennessee	11	3,567,089	1.721	2.3	−25.4

TABLE I (*continued*)

State[a]	(*1*) Electoral votes, *1964, 1968*	(*2*) Population, *1960 census*	(*3*) Relative voting power[b]	(*4*) Percentage deviation from average per state[c]	(*5*) Percentage deviation from average per citizen-voter[d]
Georgia	12	3,943,116	1.789	6.3	−20.6
Wisconsin	12	3,951,777	1.788	6.2	−20.7
Virginia	12	3,966,949	1.784	6.0	−21.0
Missouri	12	4,319,813	1.710	1.6	−26.2
North Carolina	13	4,556,155	1.807	7.4	−19.4
Indiana	13	4,662,498	1.786	6.1	−20.8
Florida	14	4,951,560	1.870	11.1	−15.4
Massachusetts	14	5,148,578	1.834	9.0	−17.7
New Jersey	17	6,066,782	2.063	22.6	−4.6
Michigan	21	7,823,194	2.262	34.4	4.6
Texas	25	9,579,677	2.452	45.7	12.0
Ohio	26	9,706,397	2.539	50.9	15.0
Illinois	26	10,081,158	2.491	48.0	13.4
Pennsylvania	29	11,319,366	2.638	56.8	18.2
California	40	15,717,204	3.162	87.9	31.8
New York	43	16,782,304	3.312	96.8	34.8

Source: Adapted from John F. Banzhaf III, "One Man, 3.312 Votes: A Mathematical Analysis of the Electoral College," *Villanova Law Review*, Vol. 13 (Winter 1968), p. 329. Column 5 is newly calculated.

a. Includes the District of Columbia.

b. Ratio of voting power of citizens of state compared with voters of the most deprived state.

c. Percentage by which voting power deviated from the average per state of the figures in col. 3. Minus signs indicate less than average voting power.

d. Percentage by which voting power deviated from the average per citizen-voter of the figures in col. 3. Minus signs indicate less than average voting power.

sumes to be the state's population) times the relative voting power of the citizen-voters in that state. The sum of these fifty-one products (including that for the District of Columbia) is then divided by the total number of citizen-voters in the nation (that is, its population) to obtain the national average per citizen-voter. We feel that this second measure more adequately evaluates voting power, since Banzhaf had used citizen-voters, not states, as players in his basic model.[23]

The graphic presentation of the data in Figure 1 is helpful in illus-

23. Banzhaf recognized that this average was as valid as the per-state average; however, for a variety of reasons, he chose not to use it. See ibid., p. 313.

FIGURE 1. *Percentage Deviations from Average Voting Power per Citizen-Voter of States under the Electoral College, the Proportional Plan, the District Plan, and the Direct Vote Plan*

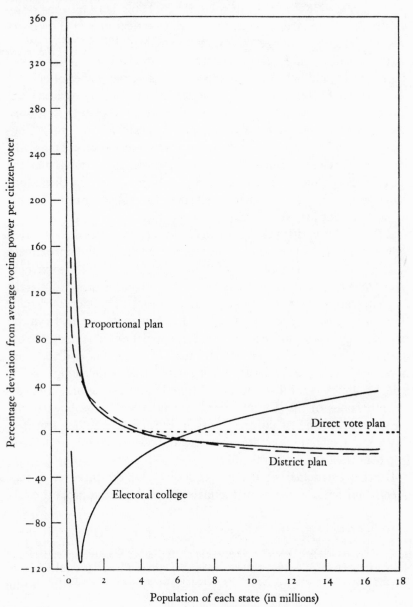

trating the disparities of the present electoral college system. In this figure, the populations of the various states are measured along the horizontal axis, and the percentage deviations from average voting power per citizen-voter (from column 5 in Table 1) of citizens residing in each state are represented on the vertical axis.[24] The curve labeled "electoral college" shows a steady decrease in voting power of the smallest states up to a state population of one million. For states with more than one million people, the voting power of citizens increases almost linearly. The advantage for the large states, however, when multiplied by the high number of citizen-voters in these states, results in a very high *average* voting power for all citizen-voters. Consequently, citizen-voters in only seven states exceed the average voting power, while citizen-voters in forty-three other states and the District of Columbia are relatively disadvantaged. The deviations range from — 115.8 percent for residents of the District of Columbia to 34.8 percent for New Yorkers.

The relative voting power of citizens in specific states departs from an exact linear relationship because electoral votes only approximate state populations. The citizens of the very small states at the extreme left of the graph have a relative voting power that is disproportionately large in comparison with the population of each. The increased relative voting power of the residents of the small states stems from the two electoral votes that are not based on population. The relative voting power of the citizens of the District of Columbia is disproportionately low, since the District has a population large enough to entitle it to four electoral votes, but is limited to three electoral votes by the provisions of the Twenty-third Amendment.[25] The linearly increasing advantage of citizen-voters in the more populous states— those with populations greater than one million—is a result of the unit rule feature of the electoral college.

Banzhaf calculated similar power indices for the three most frequently proposed reforms of the electoral college, the proportional,

---

24. The comparable graphs for the per-state average are available upon request from the authors. See Longley and Braun, *Politics of Electoral College Reform*, Chap. 4, for a similar set of four graphs in which the populations of the various states are measured along the horizontal axis, but in which the relative voting power indices (from column 3 in Tables 1, 2, 3, and 4) of citizens residing in each state are represented on the vertical axis.

25. The Twenty-third Amendment grants the District of Columbia the "number of electors of President and Vice President equal to the whole number of Senators and Representatives in Congress to which the District would be entitled if it were a State, but in no event more than the least populous State."

district, and direct-vote plans. These alternatives result in biases different from those arising under the electoral college, since each of the plans aggregates popular votes in a unique manner. The proportional plan would abolish the unit rule by dividing a state's electoral vote in proportion to the popular vote in that state to the nearest one-thousandth of an electoral vote. The distribution of electoral votes would be maintained as at present but the office of elector would be abolished. In most of its versions, the district plan would keep the institution of the electoral college but would abolish the unit rule except for the constant two votes corresponding to the two senators in each state. The other votes would be decided district by district—a sort of miniature winner-take-all system. The districts need not be, although they probably would be, congressional districts. Finally, the direct-vote plan would abolish the electoral college, including unit voting and the constant two. Under this plan, the president would be elected by a nationwide popular vote, with neither states, electors, nor any other mechanism serving an intermediary role.

Banzhaf's analysis of the proportional plan demonstrates a bias significantly different from that of the electoral college. Since the proportional system departs from the electoral college system in that the electoral vote of a state is divided proportionally to reflect the actual differences in sentiment within the state, each citizen-voter would be a member of a multimillion-person electoral college. As such, each citizen's vote would affect a minute fraction of the state's electoral votes. This fraction would be equal to the number of the state's electoral votes divided by the number of voters who cast ballots in the state. The most important consequence of the proportional plan would be to abolish the unit rule, and thus to eliminate the near-linear trend of the relative voting power's increasing directly with the size of the population. The relative voting power of citizens in small states, however, would still be inflated because of the two added electoral votes corresponding to their Senate representation. There would be no unit rule to counteract this trend; the result would therefore be a bias markedly favoring inhabitants of the small states. The result of the proportional plan, then, would be to transform the present electoral college system, with its countervailing biases, into a system with a single, systematic bias.[26]

Table 2 shows the extent of this small-state bias. In addition,

26. Banzhaf, "One Man, 3.312 Votes," p. 319.

TABLE 2. *Voting Power under the Proportional Plan, Arranged by Size of Population of State*

	(1)	(2)	(3)	(4)	(5)
State[a]	Electoral votes, 1964, 1968	Population, 1960 census	Relative voting power[b]	Percentage deviation from average per state[c]	Percentage deviation from average per citizen-voter[d]
Alaska	3	226,167	5.212	218.7	342.1
Nevada	3	285,278	4.132	152.7	250.5
Wyoming	3	330,066	3.571	118.4	202.9
Vermont	3	389,881	3.023	84.9	156.4
Delaware	3	446,292	2.641	61.5	124.0
New Hampshire	4	606,921	2.590	58.3	119.7
North Dakota	4	632,446	2.485	52.0	110.8
Hawaii	4	632,772	2.484	51.9	110.7
Idaho	4	667,191	2.356	44.0	99.8
Montana	4	674,767	2.329	42.4	97.5
South Dakota	4	680,514	2.310	41.2	95.9
Dist. of Columbia	3	763,956	1.543	−5.6	30.9
Rhode Island	4	859,488	1.829	11.8	55.1
Utah	4	890,627	1.765	7.9	49.7
New Mexico	4	951,023	1.653	1.1	40.2
Maine	4	969,265	1.622	−0.8	37.6
Arizona	5	1,302,161	1.509	−7.7	28.0
Nebraska	5	1,411,330	1.392	−14.9	18.1
Colorado	6	1,753,947	1.344	−17.8	14.0
Oregon	6	1,768,687	1.333	−18.5	13.1
Arkansas	6	1,786,272	1.320	−19.3	12.0
West Virginia	7	1,860,421	1.478	−9.6	25.4
Mississippi	7	2,178,141	1.263	−22.8	7.1
Kansas	7	2,178,611	1.263	−22.8	7.1
Oklahoma	8	2,328,284	1.350	−17.4	14.5
South Carolina	8	2,382,594	1.319	−19.3	11.9
Connecticut	8	2,535,234	1.240	−24.2	5.2
Iowa	9	2,757,537	1.282	−21.6	8.7
Washington	9	2,853,214	1.239	−24.2	5.1
Kentucky	9	3,038,156	1.164	−28.8	−1.3
Maryland	10	3,100,689	1.267	−22.5	7.5
Louisiana	10	3,257,022	1.206	−26.2	2.3
Alabama	10	3,266,740	1.203	−26.5	2.0
Minnesota	10	3,413,864	1.151	−29.6	−2.4
Tennessee	11	3,567,089	1.212	−25.9	2.8

TABLE 2 (*continued*)

	(*1*)	(*2*)	(*3*)	(*4*)	(*5*)
				Percentage	*Percentage deviation*
	Electoral		*Relative*	*deviation*	*from average*
	votes,	*Population,*	*voting*	*from average*	*per*
*State*ᵃ	*1964, 1968*	*1960 census*	*power*ᵇ	*per state*ᶜ	*citizen-voter*ᵈ
Georgia	12	3,943,116	1.196	−26.9	1.4
Wisconsin	12	3,951,777	1,193	−27.0	1.2
Virginia	12	3,966,949	1.189	−27.3	0.8
Missouri	12	4,319,813	1.092	−33.3	−7.4
North Carolina	13	4,556,155	1.121	−31.4	−4.9
Indiana	13	4,662,498	1.096	−33.0	−7.0
Florida	14	4,951,560	1.111	−32.1	−5.8
Massachusetts	14	5,148,578	1.068	−34.7	−9.4
New Jersey	17	6,066,782	1.101	−32.7	−6.6
Michigan	21	7,823,194	1.055	−35.5	−10.5
Texas	25	9,579,677	1.025	−37.3	−13.1
Ohio	26	9,706,397	1.053	−35.6	−10.7
Illinois	26	10,081,158	1.013	−38.0	−14.1
Pennsylvania	29	11,319,366	1.007	−38.4	−14.6
California	40	15,717,204	1.000	−38.9	−15.2
New York	43	16,782,304	1.007	−38.4	−14.6

Source: Adapted from Banzhaf, "One Man, 3.312 Votes," p. 330. Column 5 is newly calculated.

a. Includes the District of Columbia.

b. Ratio of voting power of citizens of state compared with voters of the most deprived state.

c. Percentage by which voting power deviated from the average per state of the figures in col. 3. Minus signs indicate less than average voting power.

d. Percentage by which voting power deviated from the average per citizen-voter of the figures in col. 3. Minus signs indicate less than average voting power.

Figure 1 illustrates the range of percentage deviations from average voting power per citizen-voter under the proportional plan. Because the voters in large states are most disadvantaged, the average voting power (1.179) is low in comparison with that under the electoral college (2.158). Voters in fifteen large states that include 65 percent of the national population have below-average voting power, while voters in thirty-five states and the District of Columbia—35 percent of the population—have above-average voting power.[27] Deviations

27. *Electoral College Reform*, Hearings, p. 373.

range from −15.2 percent for Californians to 342.1 percent for Alaskans.

Banzhaf also analyzed the district system and calculated the relative voting power of citizens under its provisions. In this calculation, there were three steps. First, he determined the chance a citizen-voter has of decisively affecting the way his two at-large state votes will be cast. This chance is inversely proportional to the square root of the state population. Second, he calculated the chance each citizen-voter has of casting the deciding ballot within his district. This chance is proportional to the inverse of the square root of the district population. Third, these two calculations were combined to determine the citizen-voter's relative voting power under a district system. Once again the conclusion was that there would be a significant bias in favor of the residents of the small states.[28] Banzhaf noted, however, that his district plan calculations were based on the assumption that districts would be equal in size, and suggested that the effect of variations in district size would be to increase the disparities.

Table 3 depicts the voting power disparities of the district system. The net effect of reducing the unit rule to the level of congressional districts and retaining the constant two electoral votes per state is to greatly increase the relative voting power of citizens of the smallest states and to significantly reduce that of citizens of the larger states. Again, as in the proportional system, relative voting power would generally vary inversely with the size of the population. The disparity between the citizens of the smallest and the largest states would not be as great, however, as under the proportional plan.

Figure 1 also illustrates the percentage deviations from average voting power per citizen-voter under the district plan. As in the proportional plan, the average of 1.220 for the district plan is lower than that for the electoral college. Citizens in thirteen large states, including more than 61 percent of the nation's population, are below average in voting power. Thirty-nine percent of the total population in thirty-seven states and the District of Columbia have above-average voting power.[29] Deviations vary from −18.1 percent for New Yorkers to 151.8 percent for Alaskans.

Finally, Banzhaf's analysis demonstrated that abolishing the intermediate electoral votes, as in the direct-vote plan, would equalize vot-

28. Banzhaf, "One Man, 3.312 Votes," p. 320.
29. *Electoral College Reform*, Hearings, p. 373.

TABLE 3. *Voting Power under the District Plan, Arranged by Size of Population of State*

State[a]	(1) Electoral votes, 1964, 1968	(2) Population, 1960 census	(3) Relative voting power[b]	(4) Percentage deviation from average per state[c]	(5) Percentage deviation from average per citizen-voter[d]
Alaska	3	226,167	3.075	99.1	151.8
Nevada	3	285,278	2.738	77.3	124.2
Wyoming	3	330,066	2.546	64.8	108.5
Vermont	3	389,881	2.342	51.6	91.8
Delaware	3	446,292	2.189	41.7	79.3
New Hampshire	4	606,921	2.137	38.3	75.0
North Dakota	4	632,446	2.093	35.5	71.4
Hawaii	4	632,772	2.092	35.5	71.3
Idaho	4	667,191	2.038	31.9	66.9
Montana	4	674,767	2.026	31.2	65.9
South Dakota	4	680,514	2.018	30.6	65.3
Dist. of Columbia	3	763,956	1.673	8.3	37.0
Rhode Island	4	859,488	1.795	16.2	47.0
Utah	4	890,627	1.764	14.2	44.5
New Mexico	4	951,023	1.707	10.5	39.8
Maine	4	969,265	1.691	9.4	38.5
Arizona	5	1,302,161	1.594	3.2	30.6
Nebraska	5	1,411,330	1.532	−0.9	25.5
Colorado	6	1,753,947	1.472	−4.7	20.6
Oregon	6	1,768,687	1.466	−5.1	20.1
Arkansas	6	1,786,272	1.459	−5.5	19.5
West Virginia	7	1,860,421	1.514	−2.0	24.0
Mississippi	7	2,178,141	1.399	−9.4	14.6
Kansas	7	2,178,611	1.399	−9.4	14.6
Oklahoma	8	2,328,284	1.422	−8.0	16.5
South Carolina	8	2,382,594	1.405	−9.0	15.1
Connecticut	8	2,535,234	1.362	−11.8	11.5
Iowa	9	2,757,537	1.364	−11.7	11.7
Washington	9	2,853,214	1.341	−13.2	9.8
Kentucky	9	3,038,156	1.299	−15.9	6.4
Maryland	10	3,100,689	1.337	−13.5	9.5
Louisiana	10	3,257,022	1.304	−15.6	6.8
Alabama	10	3,266,740	1.302	−15.7	6.6
Minnesota	10	3,413,864	1.274	−17.5	4.3
Tennessee	11	3,567,089	1.291	−16.5	5.7

TABLE 3 *(continued)*

State[a]	(1) Electoral votes, 1964, 1968	(2) Population, 1960 census	(3) Relative voting power[b]	(4) Percentage deviation from average per state[c]	(5) Percentage deviation from average per citizen-voter[d]
Georgia	12	3,943,116	1.267	−18.0	3.8
Wisconsin	12	3,951,777	1.266	−18.0	3.7
Virginia	12	3,966,949	1.264	−18.2	3.5
Missouri	12	4,319,813	1.211	−21.6	−0.8
North Carolina	13	4,556,155	1.214	−21.4	−0.6
Indiana	13	4,662,498	1.200	−22.3	−1.7
Florida	14	4,951,560	1.197	−22.5	−2.0
Massachusetts	14	5,148,578	1.174	−24.0	−3.8
New Jersey	17	6,066,782	1.162	−24.7	−4.8
Michigan	21	7,823,194	1.108	−28.3	−9.3
Texas	25	9,579,677	1.070	−30.7	−12.4
Ohio	26	9,706,397	1.080	−30.1	−11.5
Illinois	26	10,081,158	1.059	−31.4	−13.3
Pennsylvania	29	11,319,366	1.043	−32.5	−14.6
California	40	15,717,204	1.004	−35.0	−17.8
New York	43	16,782,304	1.000	−35.3	−18.1

Source: Adapted from Banzhaf, "One Man, 3.312 Votes," p. 331. Column 5 is newly calculated.

a. Includes the District of Columbia.

b. Ratio of voting power of citizens of state compared with voters of the most deprived state.

c. Percentage by which voting power deviated from the average per state of the figures in col. 3. Minus signs indicate less than average voting power.

d. Percentage by which voting power deviated from the average per citizen-voter of the figures in col. 3. Minus signs indicate less than average voting power.

ing power throughout the country. The disparities in relative voting power that are embedded in the present electoral college system, and would be inherent in the proportional or district plans, are the natural result of weighted voting systems. His conclusion is obvious: "Of all systems, both present and proposed, the direct election is the only plan which guarantees to each citizen the chance to participate equally in the election of the President."[30]

Besides illustrating the inequities inherent within the electoral college system and two of the three alternative reform plans, Figure 1

30. Banzhaf, "One Man, 3.312 Votes," p. 322.

also provides an opportunity for direct comparison of the plans. This is made possible by the fact that each curve in the composite figure is based on the percentage deviations from average voting power per citizen-voter. The comparison could not have been made using the basic relative voting power data on the vertical axis. To illustrate, a relative voting power of 1.0 under the electoral college is not equal to a 1.0 under the other three plans, since the absolute probabilities of a citizen-voter's affecting the outcome of an election are computed differently for each of the four systems. Thus, this absolute probability that a citizen-voter in a state with a relative voting power of 1.0 under the electoral college system will be pivotal in the election is not equal to that of a citizen-voter in a state with a 1.0 power index under any of the other three plans. Consequently, in order to compare the four electoral systems in a single figure, we have used the percentage deviations from average voting power per citizen-voter data on the vertical axis. The deviations provide a measure of the extent of advantage or disadvantage a state incurs under the electoral college and the other three systems.

Along with Tables 1–3, Figure 1 shows that the fourteen smallest states, ranging in population from 226,167 (Alaska) to 951,023 (New Mexico), plus the state of West Virginia (population, 1,860,421) are most advantaged by the proportional plan.[31] These fourteen states would enjoy the greatest positive percentage deviation from the average per citizen-voter under the proportional plan. Similarly, the twenty-two states ranging in population from 969,265 (Maine) to 3,966,949 (Virginia), plus the District of Columbia (population, 763,956) are most advantaged by the district plan; six states, ranging in population from 4,319,813 (Missouri) to 6,066,782 (New Jersey), are most advantaged by the direct vote plan; and the seven largest states, ranging in population from 7,823,194 (Michigan) to 16,782,304 (New York) are most advantaged by the existing electoral college system.

This voting power analysis has filled a major gap in the literature concerning the effect of state residency on citizens' voting power under the electoral college and the three reform plans. Before the effects of the electoral college system and of the various alternatives had been quantitatively measured, some reformers had argued that the present

31. West Virginia is anomalous in the general trend among states, since it just qualified, on the basis of its population during the 1960s, for seven electoral votes.

system gives a great advantage to the citizens of the large states; according to the Banzhaf analysis, this argument appears to be generally correct—at least for the seven largest states.[32] Others had argued that the present system gives a disproportionate advantage to the citizens of small states; this argument appears to be partially correct. Although the argument that the citizens of the small and medium-sized states—such as Alabama, Colorado, Florida, Iowa, Minnesota, Nebraska, Oregon, Utah, and Wisconsin—are disadvantaged under the present system, has rarely, if ever, been advanced, this analysis would seem to indicate that this is the case.

Voting Power of Demographic Groups

Those who have supported the view that urban ethnic groups are advantaged by the electoral college have generally started by assuming that it favors large states, and that urban ethnic groups and other minorities are concentrated in America's large cities, which are in turn concentrated in the large states. Under Banzhaf's assumptions, citizens in large states do indeed have greater relative voting power than citizens in smaller states, but the Banzhaf data as presented do not confirm the assumption that urban ethnic groups are located primarily in the large states with high voting power.

To test this hypothesis, we have used the Banzhaf power indices to compare the average voting power of various groups under the electoral college with the average voting power of the total population. The groups chosen were placed in three categories: residency, ethnic and occupational, and regional. Residency groups include residents of urban areas, standard metropolitan statistical areas (SMSAs), central cities, suburbs, and rural areas (including rural nonfarm and rural farm areas).[33] The average voting power of urban residents for the

32. The citizens of the seven largest states have an advantage over the citizens of the remaining forty-three states and the District of Columbia. As Figure 1, in conjunction with Table 1, shows, a citizen of one of these seven states has greater than average voting power. In other states, the effects of the unit rule are outweighed by the effects of the "constant two" votes.

33. Data on urban and rural populations are from U.S. Bureau of the Census, *Congressional District Data Book (Districts of the 88th Congress)—A Statistical Supplement* (1963). The measures of central cities, SMSAs, and suburban populations are taken from Bureau of the Census, *U.S. Census of Population: 1960*, Vol. 1: *Characteristics of the Population*, Pt. A, "Number of Inhabitants" (1961). Since SMSAs are made up of central cities, other urban areas, and rural areas, we have defined suburbs as urban areas other than central cities within SMSAs.

present electoral college, for example, was calculated by multiplying each state's relative voting power index (Table 1, column 3) by the number of its urban residents. The sum of these products for all fifty states and the District of Columbia, divided by the total number of urban residents in the nation, equals the average voting power per urban resident. Finally, the percentage deviation of this average from the average per citizen-voter was obtained.

The percentage deviation gives an indication of how this particular group in the electorate fares in comparison with other groups, as well as with the electorate as a whole. Since the analysis attempts to assess the strength of the argument that certain groups in the electorate exert inordinate voting power under the electoral college system, national averages for various groups have been calculated. Even the more sophisticated argument that these groups hold the balance of power in only a few large, closely competitive states is challenged by the data. Albert Rosenthal, for example, reasons:

> Seven of the eight largest cities in the country are located in the seven largest states—New York, California, Pennsylvania, Illinois, Ohio, Texas, and Michigan. These states have a total of 210 electoral votes— only 60 less than the 270 needed to elect a President—and with the possible exception of Texas, they are closely balanced between the two parties (in the last five Presidential elections [prior to 1967], each backed one party three times and the other twice). All seven have a greater proportionate urban population than the country as a whole, and the percentage of Negroes in their metropolitan areas, already high, is rising.[34]

Rosenthal's claim concerning the advantages enjoyed by urban and black voters under the electoral college must be qualified in a number of ways. First, it has been suggested that the central cities of urban areas are not the key to populous states with large blocs of electoral votes. As William J. D. Boyd has pointed out, "No center city contains the necessary 50 percent of the people to dominate the state. . . . It now appears that no city will ever attain that dominance. The United States is an urban nation, but it is not a big-city nation. The suburbs own the future."[35] The advantage asserted for urban areas is likely to benefit suburban, rather than central city, interests. It may

34. Albert J. Rosenthal, "Rooting for the Electoral College," *New Leader*, Vol. 51 (Oct. 21, 1968), p. 16.

35. Quoted in League of Women Voters of the United States, *Who Should Elect the President?* (Washington, D.C.: LWV, 1969), p. 55.

very well be the case, however, that both suburbs and central cities are advantaged by the existing electoral system.

Second, it has been pointed out that the majority of blacks may not live in big cities, or in big states. Millions of them live in the medium to small states of the South and other regions. As a result, Neal Peirce has argued, "If there were a direct vote system, blacks in Mississippi could combine their votes with those of blacks in Chicago, or Alabama blacks could see their votes counted equally with those of Negroes along the Eastern seaboard. *Instead of being a big-city bloc, Negroes would become a national bloc.*"[36]

Under the present electoral college, we find, suburban residents are the most advantaged, at 9.1 percent above the national average per citizen-voter. The other groups follow, residents of central cities at 8.0 percent, SMSA residents at 7.2 percent, and urban residents at 4.2 percent. Rural residents are the most disadvantaged, at −9.6 percent. Within the rural groups, the two subgroups—rural nonfarm and rural farm—are disadvantaged at −8.0 percent and −14.6 percent, respectively.

The ethnic and occupational groups examined were blacks, foreign stock, and blue-collar workers.[37] People of foreign stock have a voting power average 10.2 percent above the national average, blue-collar workers 2.5 percent above the average, and blacks, surprisingly, 5.1 percent below average.

Finally, percentage deviations for some regional groups of states were calculated.[38] The electoral college, we find, is most favorable to residents of states in the Far West—26.5 percent above the national average. The East is also above the national average, at 14.2 percent,

---

36. *Electoral College Reform*, Hearings, p. 522. Emphasis added.

37. Data on foreign-stock population (foreign natives plus children of one or two foreign-born parents) and black populations are from Bureau of the Census, *Congressional District Data Book*. Data on blue-collar workers are 1968 figures from U.S. Department of Labor, *Manpower Report of the President* (1970), p. 276.

38. The regional data are from the 1960 census. The Mountain states are defined as Arizona, Colorado, Idaho, Montana, Nevada, New Mexico, Utah, and Wyoming. The South is defined as Alabama, Arkansas, Florida, Georgia, Kentucky, Louisiana, Mississippi, North Carolina, Oklahoma, South Carolina, Tennessee, Texas, and Virginia. The Midwest is defined as Illinois, Indiana, Iowa, Kansas, Michigan, Minnesota, Missouri, Nebraska, North Dakota, Ohio, South Dakota, and Wisconsin. The East is defined as Connecticut, Delaware, Maine, Maryland, Massachusetts, New Hampshire, New Jersey, New York, Pennsylvania, Rhode Island, Vermont, and West Virginia. The Far West is defined as Alaska, California, Hawaii, Oregon, and Washington.

while the Midwest, South, and Mountain states are all below the national average, at −4.2 percent, −15.4 percent, and −38.4 percent, respectively.

These data seem to confirm the urban-ethnic hypothesis, at least in an aggregate sense. Urbanized areas, like central cities, have better than the national average voting power, while rural voters are relatively disadvantaged. People of first- or second-generation ethnic background—that is, of foreign stock—were also found to be advantaged, as conventional wisdom suggests. Blue-collar workers, too, are slightly advantaged.

The findings for two groups, however, somewhat contradict the hypothesis. Black citizens have less than average voting power because of their high concentrations in small and medium-sized states such as Alabama, Georgia, Louisiana, and Mississippi, as well as the District of Columbia and the central cities of large states. Furthermore, suburban residents are slightly more advantaged than residents of SMSAs or central cities. Conventional wisdom usually overlooks these important consequences of the electoral college system.

As previous analysis suggests,[39] the South appears to be disadvantaged by the electoral college and would stand to gain from the direct-vote proposal. It should be noted, however, that the bias has nothing to do with the small turnout in southern states or with the supposed bloc voting of southerners for the Democratic party; it merely measures the disadvantage stemming from the effect of the unit rule and the constant two. To the extent that the voter turnout as a percentage of the total population of a state is smaller in southern states than in states throughout the rest of the nation, the voting power of those citizens actually voting in the South is enhanced. The power of any such state as a whole, however, is not enhanced, since its electoral vote count remains the same. On the contrary, the voting power of citizens in a southern state that votes en masse for one party's candidate is significantly reduced, since its citizens are less likely to cast a pivotal vote in the election of that state's electors. With the decline of the Solid South phenomenon in the past decade and the effective enfranchisement of many black voters, the net effect of the electoral college on the South is probably adequately expressed by the effect of the unit rule and the constant two.

39. See, for example, Nelson W. Polsby and Aaron B. Wildavsky, *Presidential Elections: Strategies of American Electoral Politics* (3d ed., Scribner's, 1971).

We have also examined the effect of the three most frequently proposed reform plans on the a priori voting power of these groups. The direct-vote plan, of course, introduces no deviations from average voting power; all citizen-voters would have the same voting power.

The proportional and district plans, however, produce marked deviations. For the residency groups previously discussed, the biases are in the opposite direction from those introduced by the electoral college. The proportional plan gives rural citizens a voting power 5.2 percent above average, rural farm residents 6.2 percent, and rural nonfarm residents 4.8 percent. On the other hand, all the metropolitan groups would be disadvantaged by the proportional plan: urban areas (−2.3 percent), central cities (−4.2 percent), SMSAs (−4.7 percent), and suburbs (−6.0 percent).

The biases of the district plan for these groups are very similar. Rural citizens are 4.3 percent above the district plan's average voting power, rural farm residents 6.2 percent and rural nonfarm residents 3.7 percent. Metropolitan groups have biases no more than 0.5 percent different from those for the proportional plan: urban areas (−2.1 percent), central cities (−3.8 percent), SMSAs (−4.2 percent), and suburbs (−5.6 percent).

Blue-collar workers, people of foreign stock, and blacks are slightly disadvantaged by both the proportional and the district plans. For the proportional plan, blacks are 2.2 percent below the national average voting power, people of foreign stock 2.6 percent below, and blue-collar workers 3.3 percent below. With only small differences, the district plan places all three groups at a disadvantage: blacks (−0.1 percent), blue-collar workers (−2.6 percent), and people of foreign stock (−3.7 percent).

The regional group averages are also similar for the proportional and district plans—in many ways the opposite of the biases created by the present electoral college. For the proportional plan, the Mountain states (6.0 percent) were found to be the only region above average voting power. The others are slightly disadvantaged: the South (−1.0 percent), the Far West (−2.5 percent), the East (−2.9 percent), and the Midwest (−3.8 percent). For the district plan, the biases range from 45.8 percent for the Mountain states and 2.6 percent for the South to −2.0 percent for the Midwest, −4.3 percent for the East, and −6.4 percent for the Far West.

Since conventional wisdom has little to say about the particular biases imposed on these groups by the proportional and district plans, the new data may serve as a starting point for the formulation of new conclusions. We find rural voters to be advantaged, while citizens in metropolitan areas are, in general, slightly disadvantaged. These conclusions are the opposite of our findings about the electoral college. The ethnic and occupational groups we examined were all slightly disadvantaged by both the proportional and district plans. Finally, the regional data reveal only slight biases in both plans, except that the Mountain states are greatly advantaged by the district plan.

Critique of the Voting Power Approach

While the voting power approach, as revised and extended above, results in the best available mathematical estimates of the biases of the electoral college and of its alternatives, it is possible to be misled by the results.

Banzhaf did not list the absolute probabilities that a citizen-voter has of affecting the outcome of an election; instead, he normalized the absolute probabilities at 1.0 to illustrate the relative differences among citizens of the various states. It appears to us that Banzhaf's dependence on relative measures of voting power, to the neglect of absolute measures, distorts the meaning of his results in such a way as to exaggerate differences in power found in large electorates. Perhaps in the analysis of smaller groups, such as committees, legislatures, and courts, the pivotal power concept is more appropriate. But in absolute terms, the chance a citizen in a state has of changing the outcome of the election is very small in comparison with, for example, the chance that a Supreme Court justice has of changing the outcome of a case. Hence, the *relative* power differences, although they are evident in the present electoral college and proposed systems other than the direct-vote plan, may be severely outweighed by the extremely low *absolute* chances that a citizen will affect the outcome. In other words, although any citizen has little individual voting power in the pivotal sense, there are small, but real, differences in relative voting power.

Even more important, the voting power approach rests on the sometimes unrealistic assumptions of game theory. If the only significant vote is the vote that breaks a tie, the definition of voting power used by Mann, Shapley, Riker, and Banzhaf is a meaningful one, and their calculations provide us with a true indication of the voting power disparities that are inherent in the rules governing the present electoral college and the proposed alternatives. But as Mann and Shapley concede:

> It is obvious that all these interpretations rest on *ceteris paribus* assumptions; in particular we are forced to insist that the players (i.e., the states) all be independent agents, free from prior commitments and uninfluenced by considerations outside the stated objectives of the game. These unrealistic assumptions would at once invalidate any attempt to apply the power indices in an actual Presidential campaign. The only conceivably valid direct application of these numbers would be a study of the electoral vote system itself, as a timeless, Constitutional entity.[40]

In similar fashion, Banzhaf did not intend to imply by his use of the concept of "pivotal power" that a voter is necessarily conscious of his pivotal role in an election. There is no way for the voter to know *before* the election if, and in combination with what other voters, he can be pivotal. A voter is likely, therefore, not to act as an "independent agent," voting in full awareness of his pivotal possibilities, if there are any.

An equally important criticism of the pivotal power concept is directed against the assumption: "If a coalition has a majority, then extra votes do not change the outcome. For any vote, only a minimal winning coalition is necessary."[41] The objection is that "power inheres only in precisely marginal votes; a vote in which one side outnumbers the other by more than one is power-free by definition."[42] More specifically, there may well be reason to assign some power value to voters who, although not pivotal, contributed to the winner's coalition. The basis of the idea of the "minimal winning coalition" lies in the assumption that a rational candidate wishes to obtain a following only as large as is necessary to win—no larger, and certainly no smaller.

Models of this sort assume "that players had perfect information, that is, that they knew precisely who belonged to which coalition. With this knowledge they could, of course, aim at creating exactly

---

40. Mann and Shapley, "A Priori Voting Strength," p. 154.
41. L. S. Shapley and Martin Shubik, "A Method for Evaluating the Distribution of Power in a Committee System," reprinted in John C. Wahlke and Heinz Eulau (eds.), *Legislative Behavior: A Reader in Theory and Research* (Free Press, 1959), p. 358.
42. Robert J. Sickels, "The Power Index and the Electoral College: A Challenge to Banzhaf's Analysis," *Villanova Law Review*, Vol. 14 (Fall 1968), p. 95.

minimum winning coalitions." The political world does not, however, offer perfect information or total certainty:

> Since the members of a winning coalition may be uncertain about whether or not it is winning, they may in their uncertainty create a coalition larger than the actually minimum winning size. When this occurs, the members cannot be said to have behaved irrationally for their behavior can be interpreted as a purely rational attempt to ensure that they win rather than lose. . . . In short, the rejection of an optimal payoff in favor of a subjectively certain payoff may be regarded as a rational act of maximization in an uncertain world.[43]

Finally, Banzhaf's analysis can be criticized on the grounds that it does not deal with the question of how, if at all, the electoral college affects the relative degree to which voters are able to exert influence over a candidate's issue positions. Banzhaf's analysis, in its concern with voting power, is devoid of any political theory of election dynamics and of the effect of issues. In a fashion analogous to the way in which Luce and Rogow treated congressional power distributions, we can discuss voting power in the electorate. Rewards are seen as obtained by voters for voting for a certain candidate, and voting power is defined in terms of a quantitative assessment of these rewards. Since the rewards are not necessarily real but are conceived by the voters, such rewards must be individual, not collective; yet it is nearly impossible to exclude voters outside the winning coalition from receiving rewards.[44] The supporters of George Wallace in the 1968 presidential election, for example, though not members of the winning coalition, probably felt rewarded in the sense that the two major party candidates addressed themselves, on various occasions, to the "law-and-order" issue.

Voting power analysis has produced a theoretical measure of a citizen's chances of affecting the outcome of a presidential election. Although its indices reflect "inequalities in voting power which are built into the systems,"[45] they do not take into account other factors, such as one-party dominance in a state and voter turnout, that may affect a citizen's voting power in any given election. The indices are

43. William H. Riker, *The Theory of Political Coalitions* (Yale University Press, 1962), pp. 47, 48.

44. Duncan Luce and Arnold A. Rogow, "A Game Theoretic Analysis of Congressional Power Distributions for a Stable Two-Party System," reprinted in Wahlke and Eulau, *Legislative Behavior*, pp. 362–71.

45. Banzhaf, "One Man, 3.312 Votes," p. 308.

intended to provide a long-range average of citizen voting power, under the assumption that the other factors vary from election to election while the kind of inequalities measured by this analysis remain fairly constant.[46] But some of these additional causes of inequalities in voting power are, in fact, relatively stable and predictable. How can one go about taking them into account, thereby improving the estimates of voting power?

Improving the Estimates

According to Banzhaf's formula, a person's voting power is equal to probability A, the chance that person has of casting the decisive popular vote within his state, *times* probability B, the chance that his state has of casting the decisive vote in the electoral college.

For greater realism and accuracy, Banzhaf's calculations of probability A should be modified to take into account the effects of voter turnout, the relative propensity of voters to shift their votes from one candidate to another, and the closeness of elections in various states.[47] It is obvious from Banzhaf's analysis that the smaller the voter turnout as a percentage of total population in a state, the greater the chance each citizen who actually votes in that state has of affecting the outcome of his state's election. Low voter turnout increases probability A, however, only for those who actually vote. On the one hand, it appears that voters in the states of the South with relatively low voter turnout are not as disadvantaged as we had calculated above; on the other, southerners who do not vote, many blacks among them, are at a further disadvantage.

Probability A is also affected by the relative propensity of voters to change their votes from one candidate to another; specifically, it is increased for voters who are "swing voters," defined as "those who cannot be taken for granted."[48] Alexander M. Bickel has identified liberal urban groups as "swing voters" in arguing that "the system is in effect malapportioned in favor of cohesive interest, ethnic or racial

46. The indices calculated in Banzhaf's analysis and used here are based on the 1960 census figures. Census figures for 1970 have resulted in a reallocation of electoral votes among the states, with consequent changes in power indices for states and various demographic groups. An examination of these changes has been made by John H. Yunker and Lawrence D. Longley, "The Changing Biases of the Electoral College" (forthcoming).

47. The authors are indebted to Donald R. Matthews for this suggestion.

48. Letter to the editor from James Tobin, *New Republic* (Oct. 11, 1969), p. 32.

groups within those big states, which often go very nearly en bloc for a candidate, and can swing the state's entire electoral vote."[49]

Yet the moorings of these "liberal" groups to one party seem more secure than those of most other voting groups. The true "swing" groups would seem more likely to be groups that are undergoing a political transition, such as backlash and suburban groups, rather than the traditionally Democratic blocs of urban, blue-collar, and black voters.[50] Merely being a part of the winning coalition does not necessarily mean that a group will be credited with being the decisive element—especially if its support has been taken for granted. At best, "the problem with a swing-vote theory . . . is that a number of voting groups can be identified as crucial,"[51] and the groups most likely to be so credited are those *not* traditionally part of the partisan coalition. As Senator Birch Bayh has observed, "The influence of minorities, as a result of the unit rule, is exaggerated by Professor Bickel simply because these groups are not composed of 'swing' voters who can entice the major party candidates to bargain for their votes. It is a fact of political life, known alike to Democratic and Republican politicians, that these minorities traditionally vote Democratic."[52]

The swing voter hypothesis is, to a considerable degree, caught up in the big state hypothesis: that the truly important states are those that are closely competitive and have large blocs of electoral votes. As Allan Sindler argued in 1962, "States safe for either party merit relatively less attention from both parties; attention must be concentrated on those states in which the election outcome is uncertain and, within that category, on those states in which large blocs of electoral votes are at stake."[53]

To test this argument empirically, we have computed correlation coefficients (Pearsonian r's) for the relation between a state's population size and the degree of its competitiveness in each of the postwar presidential elections from 1948 to 1968. The degree of competitiveness within a state was defined as the popular vote margin between the

49. "Wait a Minute!" *New Republic* (May 10, 1969), pp. 11–13.

50. See Neal R. Peirce, "The Case Against the Electoral College," *New Republic* (Feb. 11, 1967), p. 12; Peirce, *People's President*, pp. 282–83; and Wallace S. Sayre and Judith H. Parris, *Voting for President: The Electoral College and the American Political System* (Brookings Institution, 1970), pp. 47–48.

51. Sayre and Parris, *Voting for President*, p. 46.

52. "Electing a President—The Case for Direct Popular Election," *Harvard Journal on Legislation*, Vol. 6 (1969), p. 132.

53. Sindler, "Election Methods," p. 218.

top two contenders in each state as a percentage of the total popular vote cast in the state. A significant negative correlation would have confirmed the swing hypothesis. In fact, the correlations for all but one election were negative: −0.09 for 1948, −0.33 for 1952, −0.18 for 1956, −0.25 for 1960, 0.02 for 1964, and −0.33 for 1968. Only two correlations, however, were significant at the 0.05 level—those for 1952 and 1968; none was significant at the 0.01 level. The relation between state population size and degree of competitiveness appears not to be systematic but to vary from election to election, and when it is perceptible, it is rather small. No liberal urban advantage, or any other advantage imputed to the electoral college, that is based on the swing voter hypothesis, is confirmed by the data.

Perhaps the liberal urban advantages can be supported in other ways. Charles W. Bischoff, for example, has used a curious method of calculating the partisan biases occurring in various elections. As described by Neal Peirce, Bischoff's method basically:

> postulated a range of uniform shifts in the percentages of popular votes received by major party candidates in each election. The impact of these assumed shifts on the electoral vote results was then calculated for each election. . . . The method further assumes that the percentage reduction occurred uniformly in each state, with a corresponding increase in the popular vote for the opposing major-party candidate. . . . Minor-party votes in each election were assumed to remain unchanged. . . . By repeating this experiment with different percentages, Bischoff discovered the minimum percentage of the major-party vote needed by each party to win an electoral college majority in the elections between 1920 and 1964.[54]

Of course, the most obvious criticism of this approach concerns its assumption that

> an increase in the popular support for a major presidential candidate would be distributed among the states in the same proportions as his actual strength was distributed. Some assumption about vote distribution is necessary for these projections, and this one is probably the most reasonable neutral assumption. However, a presidential candidate who actually lost an election by a wide margin would probably have needed a very different _sort_ of appeal to win an electoral victory.[55]

Nevertheless, this type of analysis may have some value in assessing the biases experienced by various strategic groups such as blacks

54. Peirce, _People's President_, pp. 142–43.
55. Carleton W. Sterling, "The Political Implications of Alternative Systems of Electing the President of the United States" (Ph.D. dissertation, University of Chicago, 1970), p. 130.

and ethnic minorities. From the results of polls on the voting of group members for president, with breakdowns by states, and assuming uniform shifts in the candidates' appeal to the group, it would be possible to derive measures of the degree to which such groups could have been pivotal in critical elections. Such an analysis would be very costly in time and money. The approach is somewhat presumptuous, moreover, in postulating a shift in popular sentiment within one group without a change in the voting behavior of other members of the voting public.

One means of forming a more realistic estimate of probability B, the chance that a given state has of casting a pivotal vote in the electoral college, might be to investigate whether the electoral votes of large states were indeed more pivotal in postwar presidential elections than their electoral vote totals alone would allow.

John Banzhaf, by request of the House Judiciary Committee, presented at its 1969 hearings a list of states that *alone* could have affected the outcome of an election in the period from 1860 to 1968. In the postwar period, only New York with 45 electoral votes in 1960 and California with 40 electoral votes in 1968 could alone have changed the outcome of an election. Both New York and California were also "competitive" states; Kennedy carried New York in 1960 with 52.5 percent of the popular vote and Nixon carried California in 1968 with 47.8 percent of the popular vote, 51.7 percent of the major two-party vote. In only one other election in this century could a single state have changed an election outcome: in 1916, eleven states were each in a pivotal position.[56] There are few cases in which a single state could have been pivotal; when such a case occurs, it is usually a large state.

Probability B should also be modified, if necessary, to accommodate the argument that

> if there are salient differences between large- and small-state voters, and if the former are more "valuable" in forming winning coalitions, then there are forces in operation to retard the nationalization of politics. Parties and candidates will bid more heavily for large-state votes while discounting the support of those in less populous states. Small-state voters are likely to find themselves in a kind of permanent opposition to winning coalitions.[57]

56. *Electoral College Reform*, Hearings, p. 360.
57. Max S. Power, "A Theoretical Analysis of the Electoral College System and Proposed Reforms" (Ph.D. dissertation, Yale University, 1971), pp. 203–04. This view is not necessarily the one accepted by Power.

The voting power of a state is higher if that state is relatively more likely to be a member of the winning coalition without regard to the partisan or ideological affiliation of the winning candidate. We have attempted to test empirically the circumstantial evidence supporting the contention that large states are more likely than small states to cast their electoral votes for the winning candidate. The number of states in the winning and losing coalitions for all the postwar presidential elections (1948–68) have been calculated and arranged according to state population size by quartiles:

	Quartile 1	Quartile 2	Quartile 3	Quartile 4
Member of winning coalition	56	48	46	58
Member of a losing coalition	16	26	29	17

Quartile 1 contains the number of states in each coalition among the largest one-fourth of the states. Quartiles 2, 3, and 4 contain increasingly smaller states. A simple chi-square test was applied to the data to test the null hypothesis that state population size is not appreciably related to its being a member of the winning or losing coalition;[58] at the 0.05 level of significance, this hypothesis could not be rejected. Consequently, a state's chances of being in the winning coalition does not seem to be affected by its size.

Conclusions

We have attempted to quantify and describe the biases of the electoral college and of the various reform plans. Large states, metropolitan area residents (including residents of central cities, SMSAs, and especially suburbs), population of foreign stock, blue-collar workers, and the regions of the Far West and the East were found to be advantaged by the electoral college.

Voters in low voter turnout states, "swing voters," voters in highly competitive states, and voters in states that are consistently in the winning coalition are more advantaged than Banzhaf's analysis reveals; the magnitude of this additional advantage is, however, uncer-

---

58. For 3 degrees of freedom, the chi-square value is 7.4. The null hypothesis is rejected if and only if the chi-square value exceeds 7.8 for 3 degrees of freedom at the 0.05 level of significance. Since the chi-square value is 7.4, the null hypothesis is not rejected.

tain. Unfortunately, it is also difficult to identify the demographic groups that benefit in the aggregate from any one of these modifications.

We have approached the study of these biases in a positivistic rather than a normative manner. Those who would defend the electoral college, however, solely on the grounds that it protects certain favored interests—whether large states, small states, or specific demographic groups—are guilty of the grossest sort of political cynicism. As Neal Peirce has stated:

> To say that the Electoral College should be retained to defend liberalism or big cities leads one down two odious roads: first, a political opportunism in which one would rather have a minority President he agrees with than a popularly chosen one he disagrees with; and secondly, a possibly fatal misreading of the political tea leaves, in which one assumes that the political balances and realities of the past decades will hold true for the 1970's and time to come.[59]

An assessment of the value of the electoral college (and other reform plans) as a total institution is left for other writings and writers. We have found the electoral college an institution that operates with noteworthy inequity—it favors some interests and hurts others. While the biases of the electoral college are not cumulative and unidirectional, they are significant and introduce a complex element of citizen inequality into the American political system.

59. *Electoral College Reform*, (Supplemental) Hearings before the Senate Judiciary Committee, 91 Cong. 2 sess. (1970), p. 230. See also *Electoral College Reform*, Hearings, p. 522.

☆

Chapter Eight

☆

Logic and Legitimacy: On Understanding the Electoral College Controversy

MAX S. POWER

THE CONTROVERSY about methods of presidential election, endemic in American political experience, has again entered an active phase.[1] In the past few years, moreover, two clear-cut opposing positions have come to dominate the debate. On the one hand, support for the present electoral college system as it operates remains formidable. On the other, advocacy of direct popular election of the president has gathered unprecedented strength and has largely superseded support

Note. This paper is based on research done for my doctoral dissertation, "A Theoretical Analysis of the Electoral College System and Proposed Reforms," submitted to Yale University, 1971. I am grateful to Robert A. Dahl and Douglas W. Rae for their many helpful suggestions and criticisms in that enterprise. Earlier drafts of this paper provoked helpful comments from several people. I wish particularly to thank Stanley L. Bach of the University of Massachusetts and Mark H. Sproule-Jones of the University of Victoria.

1. Since 1966, extensive hearings have been held on electoral college reform on both sides of Capitol Hill; the House has passed a constitutional amendment for direct election of the president; the American Bar Association has endorsed direct election, following a substantial study; two scholarly books devoted entirely to the question of electoral reform have appeared, together with a third, less scholarly tome by a famous author, and numerous shorter pieces. Reference is made in the following notes to all of these. For good accounts of the history of the debate over the electoral college, see two recent works, Neal R. Peirce, *The People's President: The Electoral College in American History and the Direct-Vote Alternative* (Simon and Schuster, 1968); Lawrence D. Longley and Alan G. Braun, *The Politics of Electoral College Reform* (Yale University Press, 1972); and an earlier work by Lucius Wilmerding, Jr., *The Electoral College* (Rutgers University Press, 1958).

for other reform proposals.[2] The case for direct election and the case against the electoral college system have thus come to coincide.[3]

In view of the attention devoted to the subject in Congress, the press, and academic circles, and the polarization around two opposing positions, one would expect the issues in dispute to be clearly joined. Yet protagonists of the opposing views often seem to be "talking past" one another. The reason is that the arguments for each position differ in nature.

It is suggested here that rigorous analysis of the case for direct election, together with its limits, will make these differences explicit. The basic argument for this sweeping reform—and against the electoral college system—is deductive and logical. The presidential election process, direct election advocates contend, must be made as "democratic" as possible.

Because the democratic process is epitomized by the election of the president, I will construct a formal analytical model that shows how primary democratic values are maximized in the election process. The analyst is at once struck by the agreement between the specific objections to the electoral college system, or claims for direct election, and the logical requirements of the formal model.

The limitations of the argument for direct election are of two kinds. The first is logical, to be found within the structure of the argument itself. Essentially, direct election provides no workable means for selecting a president from among more than two candidates. This problem is detailed here in part because it has been largely ignored in the controversy, but principally because consideration of the logical limits of the argument helps pinpoint the central issues in the conflict over electoral reform.

The second kind of limitation is contextual. By its very nature, the deductive argument for direct election is abstracted from reality,

2. A recent Gallup Poll found that 81 percent of its national sample favored direct popular election; *New York Times* (Nov. 24, 1968), p. 38. The House of Representatives passed a constitutional amendment providing for direct popular election by a vote of 339 to 70 on September 18, 1969, after rejecting alternative proposals by substantial margins. President Nixon, upon assuming office, endorsed the proportional plan, but then switched his support to direct popular election. For a summary of recent developments, see "Electing the President: Efforts to Revise System," *Congressional Quarterly Weekly Report*, Vol. 29 (April 23, 1971), pp. 944–47.

3. See Power, "Theoretical Analysis of the Electoral College System," Chap. 4, for a discussion of the relations among various reform proposals.

while proponents of the electoral college system are concerned primarily with contextual issues, with empirical rather than logical considerations. Though not always explicitly, their responses to advocates of direct election turn primarily upon the failure of the latter to take contextual questions into account.

The two positions are not, however, based on wholly different epistemological grounds. Each side is concerned, in the end, with maintaining and enhancing the legitimacy of that complex, powerful, and often mysterious office, the presidency of the United States.

The Case for Direct Popular Election

Once the idea of an executive independent of the legislature had won out at the Philadelphia Convention in 1787, it was generally accepted by the delegates that the legitimacy or authority of the presidency must in some way derive from the people.[4] The acceptance was not, however, unanimous; nor was there clear agreement on the means to secure such broadly based authority.

No majority could be found to support direct popular election of the president, the approach vigorously advanced by James Wilson of Pennsylvania[5] and others. Among the reasons for Wilson's failure was the considerable sentiment that the people lacked the information and the orientation toward national institutions and leaders necessary to a meaningful electoral choice.[6] This attitude led to acceptance of the indirect electoral college system. As Alexander Hamilton put it afterward in *The Federalist*, "A small number of persons, selected by their fellow-citizens from the general mass, will be most likely to possess the information and discernment requisite to such complicated investigations."[7]

James Madison, who supported direct election at the convention,

4. Charles C. Thach, Jr., *The Creation of the Presidency, 1775–1789: A Study in Constitutional History* (Johns Hopkins Press, 1969), Chaps. 4 and 5. See also Wilmerding, *Electoral College*, pp. 19–21.

5. Saul K. Padover, *To Secure These Blessings: The Great Debates of the Constitutional Convention of 1787, Arranged According to Topics* (Washington Square Press/Ridge Press, 1962), p. 346.

6. For a description of the limits of popular orientations toward the national government and its leaders in the early years of the republic, see James Sterling Young, *The Washington Community, 1800–1828* (Harcourt, Brace and World, 1966), Chap. 1.

7. *The Federalist* (Modern Library, n.d.), No. 69, pp. 441–42.

later espoused Hamilton's conception of the elector's function even as it was disappearing from political usage. The people, Madison wrote in 1823, were better able to judge electors, whom they could know, than presidential candidates, whom they could not.[8]

What had made Madison's view anachronistic, of course, was the practice of pledging electors to vote for party or (in the 1820s) factional candidates. The framers had simply not foreseen that parties would serve as means to organize the voters and inform them about preselected candidates.[9] A Senate committee buried the argument that the electors' intermediate judgment was necessary and emphasized the popular basis of presidential choice in an 1826 report:

> Electors, therefore, have not answered the design of their institution. They are not the independent body and superior characters which they were intended to be. They are not left to the exercise of their own judgment; on the contrary, they give their vote, or bind themselves to give it, according to the will of their constituents. They have degenerated into mere agents, in a case which requires no agency, and where the agent is useless, if he is faithful, and dangerous if he is not.[10]

In Jackson's electoral victory of 1828, Henry Jones Ford observed, "The subserviency of the electoral machinery to popular control was forever established."[11] So too was the notion that the presidency was to be the instrument for maximizing democratic values. As Ford put it, "In this country democratic progress found in the President its most convenient instrument. Public opinion suppressed the constitutional discretion of the electoral college, and made it a register of the result of the popular vote as taken by states. The President became the elect of the people, the organ of the will of the nation."[12]

---

8. Donald O. Dewey, "Madison's Views on Electoral Reform," *Western Political Quarterly*, Vol. 15 (March 1962), p. 141. For Madison's support of popular election during the convention, see Padover, *To Secure These Blessings*, p. 358.

9. Henry Jones Ford, *The Rise and Growth of American Politics* (Macmillan, 1898), pp. 150–61; Theodore J. Lowi, "Party, Policy, and Constitution in America," in William Nisbet Chambers and Walter Dean Burnham (eds.), *The American Party Systems* (Oxford University Press, 1967), p. 245.

10. S. Rep. 22, 19 Cong. 1 sess., cited in *The Electoral College: Operation and Effect of Proposed Amendments to the Constitution of the United States*, Staff Memorandum, Senate Judiciary Subcommittee on Constitutional Amendments, 87 Cong. 1 sess. (1961), p. 9 (hereinafter cited as *Senate Staff Memorandum*).

11. *Rise and Growth of American Politics*, p. 150. This development was the culmination of what Ford (Chap. 12) called "the nationalizing influence of party."

12. Ibid., pp. 213–14.

Perhaps the most eminent of this century's students of the presidency, Edward S. Corwin, expressed the relation between popular selection and presidential authority this way:

> In the National Government . . . the dogma of popular sovereignty had to adapt itself to the comparative rigidity of the national Constitution, and this it did by exalting and consolidating the power of the one national official who is—in a sense—elective by the people as a whole. The claim set up by Jackson to be the "People's Choice" has been reiterated, in effect, by his successors many times, and with decisive results for the presidential office.[13]

"Popular election," says Joseph E. Kallenbach, "is the foundation upon which the modern Presidency rests. Much of current constitutional theory and practice relative to the powers, functions, and relationships of the President to his party, to Congress, and to the outside world, springs from the proposition that he has a mandate from the people of the nation through popular election."[14]

The nature of the president's mandate—the method by which he is elected—is thus a matter of great importance; if the presidency is the instrument of popular sovereignty in the United States, the office ought to be filled according to specifically "democratic" principles. It is not surprising, therefore, that Kallenbach finds: "Recent attempts to reform the presidential electoral system have been directed primarily toward bringing the national popular vote results into closer focus upon the outcome of the election."[15]

The concern with popular sovereignty and majority choice is evident in recent indictments of the electoral college system. A commission of the American Bar Association listed these objections, among others:

> The electoral college method of electing a President of the United States is archaic, undemocratic, complex, ambiguous, indirect, and dangerous. Among other things, the present system allows a person to become President with fewer popular votes than his major opponent; grants all of a state's electoral votes to the winner of the most popular votes in the state;

13. *The President: Office and Powers* (2d ed., New York University Press, 1941), p. 30.

14. "Our Electoral College Gerrymander," *Midwest Journal of Political Science*, Vol. 4 (May 1960), pp. 162–63.

15. Joseph E. Kallenbach, *The American Chief Executive* (Harper and Row, 1966), p. 106.

[and] makes it possible for presidential electors to vote against the national candidate of their own party.[16]

Neal R. Peirce expresses the same concerns when he warns:

In any election the electoral college can misfire with tragic consequences. It can frustrate the will of the people, sending a man to the White House whom they have specifically rejected by a majority of their votes on election day. It can cause prolonged chaos and uncertitude by throwing an election into the House of Representatives. . . . [I]t could raise serious questions about the sincerity of our democratic ideals.[17]

The Populistic Model

Popular sovereignty and majority rule—these are the fundamental premises of the case against the electoral college system and for direct popular election, as well as the premises on which Robert A. Dahl has constructed his model of "populistic democracy."[18] In fact, the arguments of the Bar Association commission, Peirce, and other advocates of direct election may be summarized by paraphrasing Dahl's chain of definitions for majoritarian democracy. As this is done, the simplifying assumption is made that a presidential election is a choice between two candidates only. After the populistic model has been elaborated, this assumption will be removed.[19]

Definition 1. An institution is democratic if and only if the process of selecting its personnel is compatible with the condition of popular sovereignty and the condition of political equality.

Definition 2. The condition of popular sovereignty is satisfied if and only if it is the case that, whenever there is a contest for filling an office, the candidate selected is the candidate preferred by the members of the group or society.

16. "Electing the President: Recommendations of the American Bar Association's Commission on Electoral College Reform," *American Bar Association Journal*, Vol. 53 (March 1967), p. 220. See the similar language of James MacGregor Burns, "A New Course for the Electoral College," *New York Times Magazine* (Dec. 18, 1960), p. 10.

17. *People's President*, p. 25.

18. *A Preface to Democratic Theory* (University of Chicago Press, 1956), Chap. 2.

19. The two-alternative assumption greatly simplifies analysis at this point. At the same time it does not do too much violence to the reality of the arguments about the electoral college. These arguments generally accept the assumption implicitly except when they turn to those features of the present system or proposed reforms that touch specifically on the problems raised by "minor party" candidates.

Definition 3. The condition of political equality is satisfied if and only if the preference of each member is assigned an equal value in settling contests for office.

Proposition 1. The only rule compatible with decision making in a populistic democracy is the majority principle.

Definition 4, the rule. The principle of majority rule prescribes that in a choice between alternative candidates the candidate preferred by the greater number is elected.[20]

There is a set of formal requirements that a decision-making process must meet if it is to assure majority rule. These are Kenneth O. May's set of necessary and sufficient conditions for simple majority choice between two alternatives. As these conditions embody Dahl's (and the aforementioned critics') "populistic" premises, collectively they are called the populistic model.

May's conditions are elaborated in useful symbolic terms. The "group decision function" that meets May's four conditions is derived solely from the preferences of individuals within the relevant electorate, or group. Symbolically, the group decision function, D, $= f(D_1, D_2, \ldots, D_n)$, where D_i, for individual i, can be a preference for alternative x over alternative y (xP_iy), for y over x (yP_ix), or indifference between x and y (xI_iy). By using the "dummy" variables 1, -1, and 0 respectively, individual preferences can be summed to give a group choice.[21] The group decision, D, $= \sum(D_i)$.

The conditions that make up my model are:[22]

Condition 1, Decisiveness. The group decision function is defined and single-valued for every given set of N individuals. That is, the method used in arriving at the group decision must be *always decisive*.

Condition 2, Anonymity. The group decision function is a symmetric function of its arguments. The orderings of D_i—the assignments of subscripts (names)—makes no difference in the outcome.

That is, the system of counting preferences will yield the same result for a given set of preferences no matter how the actual counting proceeds. If, for instance, we have a group of three individuals, whose

20. Dahl, *Preface to Democratic Theory*, pp. 37–38.

21. Kenneth O. May, "A Set of Independent Necessary and Sufficient Conditions for Simple Majority Decision," *Econometrica*, Vol. 20 (October 1952), pp. 680–84. For simplicity's sake, I have avoided use of May's statement that the group decision function "maps the n-fold Cartesian product of $U \times U \times U \times \ldots \times U$ onto U, where $U = -1$, 0, 1."

22. Ibid., pp. 681–82.

preferences, D_1, D_2, and D_3, are 1, 0, and -1, respectively, the sum of D_i must equal 0 no matter what order the votes are taken in, or even if 1, 2, and 3 are relabeled. Hence the term "anonymity."

Condition 3, Neutrality. It does not matter if the names of the alternatives x and y, and thus the pluses and minuses of individuals' preferences, are interchanged; $f(-D_1, -D_2, \ldots, -D_n) = -f(D_1, D_2, \ldots, D_n)$. The method of counting votes is *neutral* between the alternatives.

Condition 4, Positive responsiveness. If the group decision function is indifferent or favorable to x, and one person changes his preference in a way favorable to x, the group decision will favor x. That is, if $D = f(D_1, D_2, \ldots, D_n) = 0$ or 1, and $D'_i = D_i$ for all $i \neq i_o$, and $D'_{i_o} > D_{i_o}$, then $D' = f(D_1, D_2, \ldots, D_n) = 1$.[23]

Condition 4 requires that an indifferent outcome would be broken if any one person voted differently, and the result would reflect that person's direction of change. By implication, the method of counting preferences is equally sensitive to each person's choice even if the outcome is not indifferent. If, for instance, alternative x is heavily favored, and one person changes his preference from y to x, the outcome will still be the group's election of x, but by a larger margin.

How are these abstract conditions related to specific presidential election procedures, present or proposed? The principal applications can be illustrated easily if each condition is examined in turn.

APPLICATION OF THE POPULISTIC MODEL IN THE CASE FOR POPULAR ELECTION

The first condition, decisiveness, is not very important if consideration is limited to elections between only two candidates. Such elections will be decisive whether they take place under the electoral college or under a system of direct popular election. In the next section, it will be seen that the condition becomes problematical when there are more than two candidates.

One point, however, must be stressed. Although a tie, an "indiffer-

---

23. Y. Murakami posits a similar condition for "strong monotonicity," which also demands that, if the group decision is indifferent or favorable to y, and individual i_o changes his preference in a way favorable to y, the group decision will favor y. If Condition 3, neutrality ("self-duality" in Murakami's terminology), holds, this additional requirement will necessarily be met if the original one stated for positive responsiveness is met. Murakami, *Logic and Social Choice* (Dover, 1968), pp. 35-36.

ent outcome," is formally "decisive" within the logic of the model, certain decisions, such as succession to the presidency, cannot admit such an outcome. Proposed electoral procedures thus sometimes incorporate a rule for tie-breaking; the alternative is to assume that the likelihood of ties is so remote, given a large electorate, that no formal provision for resolving them is necessary. Most tie-breaking devices, such as the chairman's deciding vote, have the drawback that they violate other conditions of the model, anonymity or neutrality.[24]

The condition of neutrality requires that the method of voting be neutral between the alternatives. One way of understanding this requirement is to say that it prohibits "fixed votes" or constants.

The group decision function, $D = f(D_1, D_2, \ldots, D_n)$, can be recast in terms of a "voting operator."[25] The "voting" for a group of five would be represented in this manner: $((D_1, D_2, D_3, D_4, D_5))$, and the outcome would depend on the individual D_i's, which might be 1, 0, or -1. If, however, constants are introduced, the neutrality of the voting procedure between the two alternatives is violated. Suppose the group of five voted under the following procedure: $((D_1, D_2, D_3, D_4, D_5, 1, 1, 1, 1, 1, 1))$. Alternative x, a preference for which is represented by 1, would win no matter what the group members' individual preferences were.[26]

Heredity, tradition, or any kind of outside intervention that "stacks" the voting procedure in favor of one candidate violates the condition of neutrality. The condition, in other words, is necessary and sufficient to ensure the "autonomy" of the decision-making process.[27] Interestingly, it was concern for the autonomy of the presidential selection process that led the framers of the Constitution eventually to reject election by the legislative branch.[28] As long as there

24. Ibid., pp. 39–42.

25. Ibid., pp. 19–20.

26. Thus any decision rule other than majority rule, such as a two-thirds rule, is inconsistent with neutrality. Ibid., pp. 33–34.

27. Ibid., pp. 31–33.

28. The reasons for rejecting election of the president by the legislature were very complex. The principal ones were a desire to make the president independent of the legislature while at the same time making him eligible for reelection, and a fear that foreign agents might influence the Congress, an ongoing body meeting in one place. See Clinton Rossiter, *1787: The Grand Convention* (Macmillan, 1966), pp. 198–99; John D. Feerick, "The Electoral College: Why It Was Created," *American Bar Association Journal*, Vol. 54 (March 1968), p. 254; Wilmerding, *Electoral College*, pp. 6–8.

are only two candidates, neither the present electoral college system nor direct popular election violates neutrality.

Condition 2, anonymity, is the strongest condition for equality that could be adopted here.[29] It requires that nothing about a voter affect the value of his vote in relation to those of others.

There are many ways in which greater or lesser degrees of inequality may be introduced into a voting procedure. Votes may be weighted according to attributes such as education or wealth;[30] the plural franchises that existed in Great Britain before 1948 to some extent reflected these values. The most common source of inequality among voters in our own day, however, and the one most relevant to a discussion of presidential election, is the use of indirect, or representative, electoral systems based on fixed geographical constituencies.

Any such indirect system of voting is incompatible with the condition of anonymity. Moreover, an indirect method of voting such as the electoral college is likely to incorporate features that violate a more general sense of voter equality. The symbolic "voting" can be used to illustrate both points.

To begin, in direct voting between two candidates, the preferences of a group of nine hypothetical citizens would be counted as follows: $((D_1, D_2, \ldots, D_9))$. However, in a representative or indirect system, the group might be divided into three "constituencies," each with a vote in the representative body, or electoral college. This may be displayed in this fashion:

$$((\ ((D_1, D_2, D_3)), ((D_4, D_5, D_6)), ((D_7, D_8, D_9))\ )).$$

The outside double parentheses in this formulation indicate that representatives (or electoral votes) are pledged.[31] There is a necessary relation between the outcome within each subgroup and the overall decision. To use a mathematical analogy, "the equation may be solved" from the inside out.

29. Murakami, *Logic and Social Choice*, p. 46.

30. See, for instance, John Stuart Mill, *Considerations on Representative Government*, edited by Currin V. Shields (Bobbs-Merrill, 1958), pp. 136–41.

31. This assumption is embedded both in popular belief and in the ballot forms in most states. In a large majority of the states, voters are given a direct ballot choice between presidential tickets—the names of candidates for elector do not even appear on the ballot. Where electoral slates are named, they are generally identified with presidential tickets. See Peirce, *People's President*, pp. 119–20, 342–49.

This example also incorporates equal apportionment, since each constituency has the same number of voters and of representatives. Equal apportionment is widely believed to ensure voter equality.[32] But it cannot assure anonymity.

Anonymity requires symmetry, which can be expressed symbolically:

$$f(D_1, \ldots, D_i, D_j, \ldots, D_n) = f(D_1, \ldots, D_j, D_i, \ldots, D_n),$$

for all i, j $(i, j = 1, 2, \ldots, n)$. Now if the preferences of the nine persons in the example are assumed to be distributed as follows:

$$((((1, 1, 1)), ((-1, 0, 1)), ((-1, -1, -1)))),$$

it is clear that symmetry is violated. The outcome of this voting would be 0, or indifference. But if the third and fourth persons were exchanged, the outcome would be 1, or the choice of x.[33] (Similarly, the exchange of the sixth and seventh persons would produce a decision of -1.) Thus, where a voter casts his vote may affect its value.

It is the asymmetry of indirect election that makes it possible for a minority to defeat a majority, even when majority rule prevails in each stage of voting. If the preferences are distributed as follows:

$$((((1, 1, -1)), ((1, 1, -1)), ((-1, -1, -1)))),$$

alternative x is selected in spite of the fact that five persons prefer y to x.

This is a fundamental point in the argument for direct popular election. It would "do away with the ever-present possibility of a person being elected President with fewer popular votes than his major opponent,"[34] a possibility built into the present electoral college system and into reform proposals that retain a geographically based method of indirect voting. Perhaps the best summary of the point was made by Representative William McCulloch of Ohio, who urged his colleagues to accept direct popular election in 1969:

32. The example corresponds to the standard of equality applied by American courts in recent years in congressional and legislative apportionment cases. See, for instance, *Wesberry* v. *Sanders*, 376 U.S. 1 (1964); *Reynolds* v. *Sims*, 377 U.S. 544 (1964). See also Robert G. Dixon, Jr., *Democratic Representation: Reapportionment in Law and Politics* (Oxford University Press, 1968), Chap. 11.

33. Murakami, *Logic and Social Choice*, pp. 41, 46.

34. "Electing the President: Recommendations," p. 220.

Everyone who subscribes to the neutral principles that Government should be representative, that every vote should count, that individual voting power should be equal, that winners should be declared winners and losers should be declared losers must also subscribe to the direct election proposal. No other proposal—and this is critically important—no other proposal contains those neutral principles.[35]

There is, however, a basis for the argument that an equally apportioned indirect electoral system assures equality of voter influence, although the equality is not unqualified. Anonymity, of course, requires unqualified equality. But if it can be shown *before* a particular preference distribution is given that every voter has an equal chance to cast a deciding vote, then a kind of equality exists. This is the standard for determining whether each voter has an equal chance of being "pivotal," a criterion devised by John F. Banzhaf III and other analysts of various vote-weighting and apportionment schemes.[36]

Even the less restrictive condition of equality cannot be met, however, without equal apportionment. If constituencies vary in size and in the number of electoral or representative votes assigned, each subgroup's collective decision has a different probability of influencing the final outcome. Such a system may be illustrated for a hypothetical group of eighteen voters:

$$((((D_1, D_2, D_3)), 2((D_4, D_5, \ldots, D_9)), 3((D_{10}, D_{11}, \ldots, D_{18})))).$$

The relative weight of units casting different-sized blocs of votes is not necessarily proportional to the blocs. Under the electoral college system, large states have a slightly disproportionate advantage.[37] Moreover, inequalities of influence occur in voting for electors in constituencies of varying sizes, and would occur even if electoral votes were allocated in exact proportion to population among the un-

35. *Congressional Record*, 91 Cong. 1 sess. (Sept. 10, 1969), p. H7750. (A misspelling in the text has been corrected.)

36. John F. Banzhaf III, "Multi-Member Districts—Do They Violate the 'One Man, One Vote' Principle?" *Yale Law Journal*, Vol. 75 (July 1966), pp. 1319–21; and the references to earlier analyses in Banzhaf, "One Man, 3.312 Votes: A Mathematical Analysis of the Electoral College," *Villanova Law Review*, Vol. 13 (Winter 1968), pp. 307–16. For a critique of Banzhaf's method, see Robert J. Sickels, "The Power Index and the Electoral College: A Challenge to Banzhaf's Analysis," *Villanova Law Review*, Vol. 14 (Fall 1968), pp. 92–96.

37. Irwin Mann and Lloyd S. Shapley, *Values of Large Games VI: Evaluating the Electoral College Exactly*, Memorandum RM-3158-PR (Santa Monica: RAND Corporation, 1962).

equal constituencies. This has been amply demonstrated elsewhere by John F. Banzhaf III, William H. Riker, and Lloyd S. Shapley.[38]

Of course, the electoral college system does not allocate electoral votes to states on an exactly proportional basis. Each state has two votes representing its Senate seats, and the remaining electoral votes are apportioned on the basis of seats in the House of Representatives, which are not quite proportional to population because state boundaries must be observed in their allocation. Altogether, there is no question that the present method of electing presidents produces inequalities in voter influence.

Using an a priori assumption that all distributions of preferences are equally likely, Banzhaf demonstrates that the net effect of variations in constituency size and unequal apportionment is to give disproportionate influence to voters in larger states.[39] This conclusion, derived quite abstractly by the use of a deductive model, coincides on the whole with that arrived at by observation and experience. Allan P. Sindler's conclusions are representative of the views of analysts who have taken the empirical approach.

> The presidential election strategy imposed on the major parties recognizes and acts on the inequality of voter influence. . . . The political rule of thumb that emerges may be simply put as follows: states safe for either party merit relatively less attention from both parties; attention must be concentrated on those states in which the election outcome is uncertain, and within that category, on those states in which large blocs of electoral votes are at stake. The latter group, that of key unsafe states, includes most of the populous, urbanized, ethnicized and industrialized states in the nation. Voters and interests in those states, therefore, are able to wield political influence disproportionate to their numbers especially if the groups involved maintain self-consciousness and high cohesion, e.g. certain ethnic and labor groups.[40]

To be sure, more systematic empirical studies have raised questions about the degree to which large-state voters, and especially ur-

38. Banzhaf, "Multi-Member Districts," pp. 1309–38; idem, "One Man, 3.312 Votes," p. 316 and passim; idem, "Weighted Voting Doesn't Work: A Mathematical Analysis," *Rutgers Law Review*, Vol. 19 (Winter 1965), pp. 317–43; William H. Riker and Lloyd S. Shapley, *Weighted Voting: A Mathematical Analysis for Instrumental Judgments*, Publication P3318 (RAND Corporation, 1966).

39. Banzhaf, "One Man, 3.312 Votes," esp. tables on pp. 329–31.

40. Sindler, "Presidential Election Methods and Urban-Ethnic Interests," *Law and Contemporary Problems*, Vol. 27 (Spring 1962), p. 218.

ban and ethnic voters, are advantaged. Kallenbach's calculations, based on the distribution of electoral votes, the closeness of party competition, and voter turnout, show that not only large-state voters but also voters in such middle-sized states as Indiana, Iowa, and Missouri have an advantage.[41] Carleton W. Sterling, using a different approach, concludes that there is no consistent advantage for large-state voters insofar as they are taken to favor especially liberal (or Democratic) candidates.[42]

Whether such inequalities in influence are desirable is a question that commands no such agreement among those who, from different perspectives, agree that they exist. Advocates of direct election, who tend to take a deductive approach, attack all such inequalities. Defenders of the electoral college, most of whom take a contextual or empirical approach, believe that disproportionate influence for large-state voters is justified. Again, their grounds are contextual or experiential. (Supporters of the district and proportional plans, whose views seem at present to be secondary to the main debate, favor a different pattern of inequalities that advantage small-state voters. Their approach, however, is also contextual.)

Albert J. Rosenthal argues that a system favoring voters in large, generally urbanized states is justified because (1) the gains made by urban areas in legislative and congressional apportionment are not complete and assured; (2) large states will continue to be underrepresented in the U.S. Senate; and (3) the president must be especially sympathetic to the needs of our cities, which are "in trouble," and to disaffected blacks, who are more and more concentrated in large cities.[43]

Supporters of direct election challenge voter inequalities in principle, regardless of what groups might be favored. Kallenbach has written:

A system of voting which gives more potential weight to the opinions and

41. Kallenbach, "Our Electoral College Gerrymander," pp. 169–76.

42. "The Failure of Bloc Voting in the Electoral College to Benefit Urban Liberal and Ethnic Groups" (paper delivered at the 66th annual meeting of the American Political Science Association, Sept. 8–12, 1970).

43. Albert J. Rosenthal, "The Constitution, Congress, and Presidential Elections," *Michigan Law Review*, Vol. 67 (November 1968), p. 11. See also Alexander M. Bickel, *The New Age of Political Reform* (Harper and Row, 1968), pp. 6–12; and Irving Kristol and Paul Weaver, "A Bad Idea Whose Time Has Come," *New York Times Magazine* (Nov. 23, 1969), pp. 150–57.

attitudes of a voter who happens to live in one of the "strategic twelve" states than to one who resides elsewhere in the nation is difficult to justify from the standpoint of political equity and justice. If it be conceded that the choice of the President should be, and is, in essence, a *national* act. . . . The accident of place of residence should have no relevance in the choice of the one officer who has the whole nation as his constituency and whose attitudes and actions affect so profoundly the conduct of national affairs in which all are equally concerned.[44]

Something of the intensity with which such views are held is reflected in Louis W. Koenig's statement, "The pretension of distinguishing good groups from bad and of assigning greater electoral weight to the former than to the latter cannot be justified in democratic theory, nor can it long be asserted satisfactorily in practice,"[45] and in William T. Gossett's judgment, "Clearly, any election system that lessens the power of any individual's vote in order to enlarge another's, on whatever grounds, rationale or pretext, is inequitable, unjust and indefensible."[46]

This debate cannot be pursued here. Note, however, that it underscores the reliance of the case for direct election on populistic principles. Those who take the populistic position reject the arguments for inequality on a priori grounds. They may or may not agree that the present electoral system favors urban, ethnic, and minority groups, but they unite in the judgment that such considerations are irrelevant.

Condition 4, positive responsiveness, also provides a useful tool for understanding major elements in the argument for direct election. Its meaning becomes clearer once one realizes that it is a sufficient condition for "faithful representation"; that is, individual preferences are always faithfully reflected in the voting procedure. There are no negations.[47]

Positive responsiveness in fact imposes two analytically separable conditions. If in a given voting one person were able to change his

44. "Our Electoral College Gerrymander," p. 176. Kallenbach argues (p. 165) that the early emergence of the electoral vote stage as determinative in presidential elections was a large step in converting the process from a *federal* to a *national* act. Direct election would presumably be a natural continuation of the trend.

45. *The Chief Executive* (rev. ed., Harcourt, Brace and World, 1968), p. 51.

46. "Electing the President: New Hope for an Old Ideal," *American Bar Association Journal*, Vol. 53 (December 1967), p. 1105.

47. Murakami, *Logic and Social Choice*, pp. 35–37.

preference, three things might happen. First, the group decision might reflect his change of mind directly. If the group's decision had been indifference, it would change to favor the candidate to whom the person had become more favorable; by implication, if the group's decision had not been indifferent, the balance of votes would nevertheless reflect the change. Second, the person's change might have no effect, the outcome of the group's decision remaining unaltered. Third, the voter's change, say, from a preference for y to a preference for x, might be reflected by a social decision more favorable to y than it had been. Positive responsiveness requires that the first situation prevail, and prohibits the other two. A less restrictive condition, labeled "simple monotonicity" by Murakami,[48] prohibits only the third outcome.

The present electoral college system does not formally meet even the second, or weaker, condition, since electors are not constitutionally bound to vote for the presidential ticket to which they are pledged. Many states have enacted laws binding electors, but the constitutionality of such laws is in doubt.[49] Convention has kept electors faithful in most cases,[50] but there have been isolated cases in which electors, by exercising discretion, have introduced "negatives" into the voting process.[51]

Most supporters of the present electoral college system believe that "the ever-present possibility that electors may substitute their own will for the will of the people," in President Lyndon Johnson's

48. Ibid., pp. 37–39.

49. For a comprehensive account of the legal and constitutional situation regarding the pledging of electors, see Rosenthal, "Constitution, Congress, and Presidential Elections," pp. 16–38. Rosenthal suggests that Congress might enforce electors' party pledges, thus forestalling the need to amend the Constitution. In 1969, however, Congress decided to accept the vote of Dr. Lloyd Bailey, a North Carolina Republican elector, for George Wallace. *Congressional Record*, 91 Cong. 1 sess. (Jan. 6, 1969), pp. H45-70, S11-60.

50. The *Senate Staff Memorandum* lists eight violations of party pledges by electors since 1789, out of approximately 14,000 electoral votes cast (p. 9). The 1968 case made a ninth. "Unpledged" electoral slates have been presented in some southern states in recent years. See Gerald Pomper, "The Southern 'Free Elector' Plan," *Southwestern Social Science Quarterly*, Vol. 45 (June 1964), pp. 16–25, for an account of these efforts to exploit the legal independence of electors.

51. More serious was the purported "plot" to get a number of electors, Republican and Democratic, to abandon their parties' candidates in the 1960 election, which stimulated extensive hearings by a Senate subcommittee in 1961. See *Nomination and Election of the President and Vice President*, Hearings before the Senate Judiciary Subcommittee on Constitutional Amendments, 87 Cong. 1 sess. (1961), esp. Pt. 3, pp. 562–656.

words, "should be foreclosed."[52] Supporters of direct election of course agree. But a constitutional amendment effecting only this reform falls so far short of their demands that they have little interest in supporting it.

Even if the faithfulness of electors were assured, the indirect electoral college system could not meet the condition of positive responsiveness. To repeat the simple example of indirect voting:

$$((\,((1,\,1,\,1)),\,((-1,\,0,\,1)),\,((-1,\,-1,\,-1))\,)),$$

of which the outcome would be 0, or indifference. A change by any of the members of the second "constituency" would break the indifference, but a change by one person in either of the others would not. The division of voters into fixed subgroups, by preventing symmetry, also prevents the realization of positive responsiveness.

By implication, of course, the result is that some votes for electors are "not counted" at the electoral vote stage. Senator Karl Mundt, a supporter of the district plan of reform, not of direct election, has argued, "This is an electoral college system by which the victor, the winner, can report at the electoral college level his success and at the same time take all of the votes of the loser—steal them, if you will—and add them to his own, and report these votes to the electoral college, in direct opposition to the way in which they were cast."[53]

To talk about "stealing" votes may be an exaggeration. In the example, the "faithless elector" has been banished and it is assumed that the "weaker" condition of monotonicity holds. No negative factors enter the voting. A voter's change from support of the winning ticket in his state to support of a losing ticket will neither help the former nor harm the latter. Any one person's change of preference is simply not likely to have an effect on the final outcome. This is quite enough to condemn the indirect system in the eyes of those who rest their case on popular sovereignty and majority rule.

The other side of the coin is that because the electoral college fails to meet the strong populistic condition of positive responsiveness, its pluralities are generally far more lopsided than popular-vote margins.

---

52. Message to Congress, Jan. 28, 1965, reprinted in *Congressional Quarterly Almanac, 1965*, Vol. 21 (Washington: Congressional Quarterly Service, 1966), p. 1408. An exception to the general consensus on this point may be found in Hall E. Timanus, "Should the Electoral College Be Abolished?" *Texas Bar Journal*, Vol. 30 (May 22, 1967), pp. 335–36, 370–74.

53. *Congressional Record*, 88 Cong. 2 sess. (Sept. 17, 1964), p. 21631.

Those who support the system argue that this has proved to be a considerable asset. Victors of such close elections as those in 1916, 1948, 1960, and 1968, it is argued, have had their legitimacy enhanced by substantial electoral vote tallies.[54]

THE LIMITS OF POPULISTIC LOGIC:
THREE-CORNERED ELECTIONS

In fourteen of the thirty-seven presidential elections since 1824 (the first year for which meaningful popular-vote figures are available), no candidate received an absolute majority of the popular votes cast.[55] In several others, candidates other than those of the "major" parties, while they did not deprive the leader of an absolute majority, gathered substantial shares of the popular vote. Although the populistic model has been useful in illuminating the case for direct popular election, it is nonetheless limited by the assumption that there are only two alternatives to choose between.

The premises of popular sovereignty and political equality, which are so precisely elaborated in the populistic model, become ambiguous when the number of alternatives is increased from two to three. There are two ways to extend populistic premises to elections among three or more candidates. Both have serious shortcomings in terms of these premises. One leads to logical entrapment, the other to the abandonment of majority rule.

The first extension appears straightforward enough. In the words of E. J. Nanson, who wrote many decades ago, "the fundamental condition which must be attended to in choosing a method of election is that the method adopted must not be capable of bringing about a result which is contrary to the wishes of the majority."[56] Suppose that the fourteen presidential elections mentioned above had been held under a system of direct popular election and that the popular vote totals had been the same in each case. Who "should have been" elected? The leading vote-getter? But he was always "rejected" by a majority.

54. Wallace S. Sayre and Judith H. Parris, *Voting for President: The Electoral College and the American Political System* (Brookings Institution, 1970), pp. 61–62; Kristol and Weaver, "A Bad Idea," p. 148.

55. The elections of 1824, 1844, 1848, 1856, 1860, 1880, 1884, 1888, 1892, 1912, 1916, 1948, 1960, 1968. See Peirce, *People's President*, App. A, pp. 302–08; and for 1968, James A. Michener, *Presidential Lottery* (Random House, 1969), App. D, pp. 230–33.

56. "Methods of Election," *Transactions and Proceedings of the Royal Society of Victoria*, Vol. 19 (May 10, 1883), p. 197.

In order to apply Nanson's condition satisfactorily, more would have to be known about individual voters' preference orderings than can be learned from a categorical ballot of the kind used in presidential elections.[57]

There are essentially two methods of voting that have been suggested to ascertain "true" majority preferences in elections among three or more candidates. Neither is satisfactory.

The first, comparison by pairs, was elaborated some two hundred years ago by the French mathematician, the Marquis de Condorcet:

> There is only one rigorous method of ascertaining the wish of a majority in an election. It consists in taking a vote on the respective merits of all the candidates compared two by two. . . . The method must select from more than two competitors the man supported as against any of the other competitors taken singly by more than half the voters who have expressed a preference between the two, if such a candidate there be.[58]

Comparison by pairs can be achieved either by successive votes between all pairs of candidates or by a single balloting in which each person indicates his order of preference among the candidates. The populistic model can be extended to accommodate comparison by pairs by the stipulation that, for any pair of alternatives, a group decision depends only on the voters' decisions concerning that pair,[59] and the requirement that the four original conditions of the model apply to each pair of alternatives.[60]

The trouble is that there may be no candidate supported by a majority against all other candidates. Paired voting will in some instances reveal a "voting paradox,"[61] also called the "Condorcet paradox," "Arrow paradox," or "cyclical majority." That is, while individual preference orderings may be assumed to be transitive, there may be an intransitive group decision,[62] in which case there is no unambigu-

---

57. Douglas W. Rae, *The Political Consequences of Electoral Laws* (Yale University Press, 1967), p. 17.

58. Quoted in G. van den Bergh, *Unity in Diversity: A Systematic Critical Analysis of All Electoral Systems* (London: B. T. Batsford, 1956), p. 54.

59. Murakami, *Logic and Social Choice*, pp. 83–84; Kenneth J. Arrow, *Social Choice and Individual Values* (2d ed., Wiley, 1963), pp. 27–28.

60. Murakami, *Logic and Social Choice*, pp. 54–58.

61. If sufficient rounds of voting are held. See ibid., p. 72, which cites "Black's Theorem": "The existence of a voting paradox is always revealed if there are as many rounds of voting as there are alternatives." The reference is apparently to Duncan Black, *The Theory of Committees and Elections* (Cambridge University Press, 1958), pp. 39–45.

62. Arrow, *Social Choice and Individual Values*, pp. 13–14 and Chap. 5; Dahl, *Preface to Democratic Theory*, p. 42, n. 9.

ous, or single-valued, outcome. The condition of decisiveness, while it holds in the voting for each pair, does not hold in the aggregate, so that the voting process will not necessarily produce a majority choice.

If it is assumed, as it was in discussing measures of voter equality above, that all combinations of preference are equally likely, then cyclical majorities in a certain proportion of cases must be expected.[63] There is no satisfactory way out of the dilemma. Kenneth J. Arrow demonstrates that only the imposition of a "dictator" will guarantee a decisive outcome.[64] This is of course antithetical to popular sovereignty and political equality.

If, on the other hand, all voters assume an inherent ordering among the alternatives, then all preferences are not equally likely, and voting paradoxes may be avoided. For example, presidential candidates might be placed on a "left-right" continuum by all voters. If so, voters' preferences would become "single-peaked"[65]—that is, there is some ordering of alternatives such that all voters' preference curves will be downward-sloping (or at least not upward-sloping) as one moves from first to second preferences and so on. For example, there are no voters in the following diagram who rank the alternatives in this way: a_1, a_4, a_2, a_3.

Alternatives

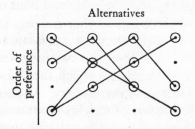

Order of preference

63. Oliver E. Williamson and Thomas J. Sargent, "Social Choice: A Probabilistic Approach," *Economic Journal*, Vol. 77 (December 1967), pp. 804–05, where the estimate is one in four for a large electorate. Others arrive at a more modest estimate, Guilbaud's number, 0.08774. See Mark B. Garman and Morton I. Kamien, "The Paradox of Voting: Probability Calculations," pp. 306–16, and Richard G. Niemi and Herbert F. Weisberg, "Mathematical Solution for the Probability of the Paradox of Voting," pp. 317–23, both in *Behavioral Science*, Vol. 13 (July 1968).

64. Arrow, *Social Choice and Individual Values*, pp. 51–59; Murakami, *Logic and Social Choice*, pp. 93–96.

65. Black, *Theory of Committees and Elections*, pp. 14–16. See the clear and suggestive discussion of this concept in Robert Paul Wolff, *In Defense of Anarchism* (Harper and Row, 1970), pp. 58–67. It is this assumption that underlies the spatial modeling of Anthony Downs in his *An Economic Theory of Democracy* (Harper and Row, 1957).

As a result, cyclical majorities would not occur. That is, the group's ordering of preferences would be transitive, just as each individual's ordering. Transitivity requires that with xP_iy and yP_iz, xP_iz must follow. If all individuals (i) order alternatives on the same dimension, the group decision will meet this requirement.

There is, however, a strong empirical case against the assumption that voters place presidential candidates on a single continuum. Studies made by the Survey Research Center at the University of Michigan indicate that voters place neither themselves nor the candidates on such a continuum.[66] Thus the dilemma posed by cyclical majorities remains.

The second method of voting proposed to ascertain "true" majority preferences circumvents voting paradoxes by making an overall comparison of individual voters' preference orderings.[67] The procedure is usually to assign each individual's first preference a certain weight, each second preference a lesser weight, and so on until the number of alternatives is exhausted; the points assigned each alternative are totaled, and the highest ranking candidate is elected. In place of the Condorcet criterion, one elaborated by the mathematician Jean Charles de Borda and by Duncan Black is used: that candidate is elected who stands highest overall, or on the average, in all voters' preference orderings.[68]

There are at least three serious shortcomings to this effort to extend majority rule to cover elections among more than two candidates. First, the premises of popular sovereignty and political equality provide no guidance to the relative weights that should be assigned to first, second, and succeeding preferences; weights may be assigned arbitrarily, but different sets of weights produce different outcomes. Disproportionate weights assigned first preferences, for instance, will produce results similar to those of simple plurality election.[69]

---

66. Donald E. Stokes, "Spatial Models of Party Competition," in Angus Campbell and others, *Elections and the Political Order* (Wiley, 1966), pp. 161–79. I think it is fair to say that the Survey Research Center's study of the three-way presidential race of 1968 supports Stokes's arguments. See Philip E. Converse and others, "Continuity and Change in American Politics: Parties and Issues in the 1968 Election," *American Political Science Review*, Vol. 63 (December 1969), pp. 1083–1105.

67. Murakami, *Logic and Social Choice*, p. 61.

68. Black, *Theory of Committees and Elections*, pp. 59 ff., where the Borda criterion and Borda's method of counting are elaborated. There is a discussion of other overall comparison methods in van den Bergh, *Unity in Diversity*, pp. 55–57.

69. Murakami, *Logic and Social Choice*, pp. 64–67.

If, however, Borda's method of assigning weights is accepted, the second drawback of overall comparison can be demonstrated. Borda suggested assigning a 0 to the lowest ranking alternative on each individual's preference schedule (assuming he orders all alternatives), a 1 to the next lowest, a 2 to the third lowest, and so on.[70] By this method, it is possible for a candidate who wins an absolute majority of first preference votes, as well as a majority against each other candidate, to lose. Using Duncan Black's method to calculate a Borda Count in which thirty-five voters select among three alternatives might lead to the following:[71]

| | Against | | | Borda |
	x	y	z	Count
x	—	(18, 17)	(18, 17)	36
For y	(17, 18)	—	(24, 11)	41
z	(17, 18)	(11, 24)	—	28

Here, candidate x has eighteen of thirty-five first-preference votes and defeats both y and z in paired voting, yet loses to candidate y under the Borda criterion, because y stands higher on the average in voters' preference schedules. This apparently conflicts with accepted notions of majority rule; it certainly violates the condition set down by Nanson.

The major shortcoming of the overall comparison method, however, is that it provides incentives for the rational voter to misrepresent his true preference ordering. In the example, those who prefer x to y and y to z may realize that expressing their sincere second preferences for y will harm x's chances for election. They may, therefore, give their second preferences to z in the hope of avoiding this outcome, or they may express no preferences beyond that for x.[72] The

70. Black, *Theory of Committees and Elections*, pp. 61, 157–58.

71. Ibid., p. 60. In a three-way contest, simply adding the number of votes each alternative receives against the other two produces the Borda Count for each. That is, in the example given, candidate x receives eighteen first-preference votes (thirty-six toward the Borda Count) and no second-preference votes. Third preferences are valued at 0, so x's total Borda Count is thirty-six. In the example:

> eighteen prefer x to y and, of these, twelve prefer y to z, six z to y;
> twelve prefer y to z and z to x;
> five prefer z to y and y to x.

The lack of second preferences defeats x.

72. "By expressing a further choice the elector may endanger his higher preference, thus possibly his first choice"; van den Bergh, *Unity in Diversity*, p. 55.

group decision, in Murakami's term, cannot be "stable" unless there are no strategic, or insincere, moves by which a voter or group of voters can improve the chances of the outcome they desire.[73]

Either approach to extending the populistic model to elections with more than two candidates by taking account of voters' preference orderings is bound to founder. Van den Bergh has summed up the dilemma:

> It is not difficult to realize that the two requirements which an electoral system should meet:
> 1. that the Condorcet criterion is satisfied—in other words, that the "wrong" candidate should never be struck out;
> 2. that a lower preference should not prejudice a higher one;
> are *incompatible*. This means that the *problem of selecting the right candidate out of three, which seems such a simple matter, is in reality insoluble*.[74]

The second path to promoting popular sovereignty and political equality in elections among more than two candidates avoids this logical morass. It is simple plurality choice, the approach chosen (with a qualification to be discussed below) by those who advocate direct popular election. Simple plurality election is compatible with the conditions of decisiveness, anonymity, and neutrality, but not with positive responsiveness, since a change of preference from x to y may advance z's cause rather than y's; a switch from Nixon to Wallace, for example, may favor Humphrey. But simple plurality election is at least monotonic: the change from x to y cannot help x or harm y.

Clearly, a simple plurality election need not come very close to meeting any standard of majority rule. A candidate who might well be defeated by another in paired voting can be elected; and that same candidate may not stand highest on the average in voters' preference orderings (for which we have, in any case, no evidence in a plurality election). In his later years, James Madison called attention to this weakness of simple plurality election. He feared that "it would permit the election of vastly inferior candidates. Thirty per cent of the voters—presumably the irresponsible third—might favor one candidate who would not even be considered by the rest of the voters," who might, in turn, divide their votes among other, superior candidates.[75]

There are, however, a number of points in favor of simple plurality

---

73. Murakami, *Logic and Social Choice*, pp. 74–81.
74. *Unity in Diversity*, p. 56. Italics in the original.
75. Dewey, "Madison's Views on Electoral Reform," p. 142.

election. First, it is "stable," giving no incentives for insincere voting.[76] Second, the procedure is simple and decisive. Third, it is familiar and legitimate to Americans. Fourth, it does adhere closely to
the conditions of the populistic model, maximizing popular sovereignty
and political equality even when "true" majority choice is apparently
impossible.

From a populist point of view, simple plurality election is obviously
superior to the present electoral college system, which meets neither
the condition of anonymity nor, in principle, the relatively weak condition of monotonicity. From this perspective the situation is perhaps
worse in three- or four-way contests. In all but one of the fourteen
elections in which no candidate has received an absolute majority of
popular votes, the present system has indeed produced an electoral
vote majority, but this is in no way necessarily tied to the popular-
vote plurality, as the 1888 election shows. Nor is a decisive outcome
necessary. If, as in 1824, no candidate receives an absolute majority
of electoral votes, the contingent procedure of voting by the House
comes into play; this procedure departs still more drastically from
anonymity and positive responsiveness, and it is not necessarily
decisive.[77]

The shortcomings of the present system clearly make simple plurality election preferable if it is assumed that the method of presidential election ought to be as democratic as possible. On the other hand,
under the present system the contingent procedure has not been called
into play since 1824, and the plurality or majority winner in popular
voting has won a majority of electoral votes since that time, except
for the aberrations of 1876 and 1888. From an empirical viewpoint,
there is little urgency for reform when simple plurality choice operates consistently in practice.

The qualification mentioned earlier with regard to the general acceptance of simple plurality choice in direct election of the president
is that most proposals incorporate a minimum vote requirement and
provide for a runoff election if no candidate receives the required
proportion of the popular vote.[78]

The requirement of an absolute majority may be construed as an

76. Murakami, *Logic and Social Choice*, p. 80; Thomas W. Casstevens, "A Theorem
about Voting," *American Political Science Review*, Vol. 52 (March 1968), pp. 205–07.

77. Power, "Theoretical Analysis of the Electoral College System," Chap. 5.

78. "Electing the President: Recommendations," p. 219. House Joint Resolution 681,
which passed the House on September 18, 1969, included a 40 percent minimum vote requirement. *Congressional Record*, 91 Cong. 1 sess. (Sept 18, 1969), pp. H8142–43.

effort to bring voters' preference orderings into play. From the fore-going discussion, it is clear that the runoff will not be a wholly satisfactory device for producing a "true" majority choice. The runoff procedure, which is familiar in many state primaries and in municipal elections, requires a second election between the two leading candidates if no candidate receives a majority (or other minimum vote share) in the first election. The weakness of this procedure is that it strikes out all lower ranking candidates. "It is quite possible," says van den Bergh, "that one of those dropping out is in reality the candidate most favored by the voters considered as a body."[79] Suppose that, in an election that requires a majority, candidates x and y each get 39 percent, while z gets only 22 percent. If all supporters of x and of y give their second preferences to z, the latter would defeat either x or y in a two-way contest. Yet under the runoff procedure, z is eliminated from competition.[80]

The direct popular election proposal advanced by the American Bar Association and other groups, and the proposal that passed the House of Representatives overwhelmingly in 1969, both provide 40 percent minimums. This appears to make little sense in populistic terms.

The 40 percent rule is justified on grounds other than those of the populistic model. This is nowhere better illustrated than in the colloquy that took place in the House of Representatives concerning the 40 percent rule. First, it is clear that the runoff procedure is not intended as a logical alternative to simple plurality choice. Chairman Emanuel Celler of the Judiciary Committee elaborated:

> MR. CELLER. I want to say . . . that the provision is not just 40 percent. That is only half the story. The provision is a plurality of the vote on condition that the plurality is at least 40 percent.
>
> In most States the Governors, Senators, Members of Congress, all high officials and low officials, are elected by simple plurality. It is the plurality that counts. . . .
>
> MR. MIKVA. Mr. Chairman, I wish to commend the chairman of the committee on his most recent remarks that 40 percent is the secondary

79. *Unity in Diversity*, p. 6.
80. Paul T. David has explored this problem thoroughly with regard to proposals for national nominating primaries. David uses the same theoretical insights from Arrow and Black that are employed here. See his "Reforming the Presidential Nominating Process," *Law and Contemporary Problems*, Vol. 27 (Spring 1962), pp. 161–65.

protection. The first protection is that the person must be a winner and receive a plurality.[81]

There are two rationales for the 40 percent rule and the runoff provision, both of which rely on premises other than those of popular sovereignty and political equality. The first is that such provisions will, it is believed, help maintain two-party competition. This was made clear by Chairman Celler when he responded to the argument of Representative Jacob H. Gilbert that "a majority of 50 percent would be the proper denomination to determine who should be the President of the United States, and not 40 percent, because then we are still dealing with a minority candidate or a minority President." Celler answered,

> We discarded the idea of 50 percent, because it would give rise to the proliferation of other parties. It would be to the advantage of other parties to endeavor to gather unto themselves as many votes as they could and then to try to make deals and try to cast their strength with one or the other of the candidates. . . . In order to forfend against that type of practice in the future the committee concluded that 40 percent would be proper.[82]

The second rationale is that a president needs a certain minimum level of support to carry out the functions of his office, that some pluralities would be too small to assure his legitimacy. Both rationales emerged in the following statements during the House debates. The first, by Representative Robert McClory, was made in support of a 35 percent minimum: "I believe that a 35-percent requirement would accomplish the twin task of preventing runoff elections and preserving the two-party system while at the same time providing a guarantee against the remote possibility of the election of a President who has only very minor national support."[83]

The ranking minority member of the Judiciary Committee, Representative William McCulloch, defended the 40 percent rule in these words: "The 40-percent figure is obviously a compromise. A higher

81. *Congressional Record*, 91 Cong. 1 sess. (Sept. 10, 1969), p. H7748. Opponents of the direct election plan attacked the 40 percent rule with special vigor throughout the House debates, usually on the majoritarian grounds that the populists had forsaken for simple plurality choice. The fact that almost all supporters of the direct election plan with a 40 percent rule expressed a fervent desire to avoid runoff elections suggests that they felt weakest on this point, on which their basic premises provide no clear guidance.
82. Ibid.
83. Ibid., p. H7754.

figure would encourage third parties and thus increase the possibility of a runoff which no one really desires. A lower figure would provide a very small mandate for the man elected President."[84]

There is a point of some interest implicit in this "legislative history." When those who accept the a priori logic of the case for direct popular presidential election find no applicable conclusion within that logic, they turn to empirical, or experiential, factors for help in reaching a usable solution to the electoral problem. In this case, empirical considerations of two-party competition and presidential legitimacy come into play. This suggests that the limits of the populistic approach to presidential election are not only theoretical; they derive also from the abstractness of the argument.

Put another way, the deductive argument for direct popular election loses some of its force when multicandidate elections are thoroughly analyzed. Simple plurality choice, while capable of strong justification in populistic terms, is not so compelling as the venerated principle of majority rule. Moreover, the logical scrutiny of the two principles makes clear just how far the former may depart from the latter.

Finally, the focus on the multicandidate election brings to the fore two contextual, or empirical, issues—the pattern of party competition and presidential legitimacy—upon which much of the current controversy turns. One can argue convincingly that the abstract logic of populism does not deal adequately with these factors, or with the question of inequality in voter influence.[85]

Contextual Factors in Presidential Elections

The belief that the present electoral system ought to be retained because it produces inequalities in voter influence may in part reflect a

84. Ibid. (Sept. 18, 1969), p. H8105.

85. A contextual weakness of the populistic case different from those treated below is discussed in Dahl, *Preface to Democratic Theory*. In Chapter 3, Dahl elaborates on the point that populistic choice in an election is only significant if certain preelection and postelection conditions are met. The preelection conditions, in their most extreme form, are that any voter can schedule his own preferred alternative for voting, and that all voters have equal information about available alternatives. This has, inter alia, important implications for the presidential nominating process and the nature of presidential campaigns. I have dealt with these in brief, speculative fashion in "The Logic and Illogic of the Case for Direct Popular Election of the President" (paper delivered at the 25th annual meeting of the Western Political Science Association, April 8–10, 1971).

sincere adherence to the premise of political equality. From this perspective, the problem with direct election is that it abstracts presidential elections from the context of American government and politics.
Disproportionate influence for large-state voters in presidential elections, it is argued, balances the advantages accruing to small-state
voters in electing members of the Senate, in legislative apportionment,
and in the internal structure and workings of Congress.[86]

There are, however, a number of reasons why this analysis does
not adequately delineate the issue. The dispute is not only, or even
primarily, a disagreement between those who seek equality among
voters within a narrow context and those who believe that such
equality is meaningful only if the larger context is taken into account.

First, so far as I am aware, no proponent of the electoral college
has argued that it precisely or measurably balances other inequalities
in voter influence to produce demonstrable overall equality. "Equality," in other words, is not specified, as it is by advocates of direct
election.

Second, it is not always clear that defenders of the electoral college
mean to stop at advocating overall equality. Some emphasize strongly,
and in their own right, the advantages accruing to urban and minority
groups. The impression that overall inequality is intended, favoring
urban-ethnic voters, has been reinforced by the reluctance of electoral
college supporters to accept the idea that the "reapportionment revolution" has removed the need for "balance."[87] If this impression is
well grounded, the conflict concerns not merely approach, but fundamental values as well.[88]

Third, there is a considerable division of opinion among contextualists—if they may be so designated—about just whose influence is
enhanced by the present system. Some hold that particular groups of
"swing voters"—ethnic minorities, organized workers, inner-city
dwellers, the "disadvantaged" generally—gain special influence.[89]
Others, finding this view empirically difficult to support, content
themselves with the argument that large-state voters, and among them

86. Sayre and Parris, *Voting for President*, pp. 44–48; Bickel, *New Age of Political Reform*, pp. 5–14; Nelson W. Polsby and Aaron B. Wildavsky, *Presidential Elections:
Strategies of American Electoral Politics* (2d ed., Scribner's, 1968), pp. 242–50.

87. See, for instance, the summary of Albert J. Rosenthal's views above.

88. Supporters of the district and proportional reform plans have more or less openly
admitted favoring a different kind of overall inequality—an overall advantage for residents
of smaller, sparsely settled states.

89. See, for instance, Allan P. Sindler's remarks, above.

residents of the metropolitan areas, whoever they are, benefit from the present system.[90]

To summarize, it may be charged that the populistic argument is weakened by its abstraction of the presidential election process from the larger context of American politics. In this view, political equality requires some inequality in presidential elections. Some opponents of direct election go further, holding that even in broader terms voter inequality is justifiable. However, all these arguments lack a specific standard of "equality" to set against that used by populists. The contextualists, in short, have not produced empirically derived measures of relative influence to set against those developed in the deductive approach of the populists.[91]

The American party system is a major element of the context within which presidential elections take place. In arguments opposing direct popular election one finds at least three points at which it is held that abstract populistic logic fails to come to terms with the importance of the system.

First, as noted, sweeping statements of the populistic case—those relying on the full implications of the populistic model—hold only in two-way contests. Advocates of direct election, in other words, assume two-party competition without asking how their proposals are related to it. They tend to ignore the logical problems of multi-candidate contests and to respond in an ad hoc and tentative way to charges that the 40 percent rule violates the majority principle.

Second, populistic logic is abstract in that it assumes, in evaluating electoral rules, that all combinations of votes or preferences are equally likely. John F. Banzhaf makes this explicit:

> A critical distinction must be drawn between inequalities in voting power which are built into the system . . . and those which result either from the free choice among citizens as to how they use their voting power . . . or from factors outside the legal rules governing the process. . . . It is only . . . those inequalities which result from the rules of a particular system of voting on which we may properly focus attention in determining the basic "fairness" of the system itself.[92]

90. Sayre and Parris, *Voting for President*, p. 46, and Bickel, *New Age of Political Reform*, pp. 7–8, are among those who disavow specific "swing voter" arguments.

91. Two opponents of the present system have tried to specify relative voter influence empirically. See Kallenbach, "Our Electoral College Gerrymander," and Sterling, "Failure of Bloc Voting."

92. Banzhaf, "One Man, 3.312 Votes," p. 308.

The contextualist may argue, of course, that all combinations of preferences are not equally likely to occur. Since large blocs of American voters adhere firmly, election after election, to long-standing partisan preferences,[93] some voters are more likely than others to be pivotal—to cast decisive votes—no matter what electoral system obtains. This is clearly what Sindler, Bickel, and others are trying to make clear in their arguments about the types of voters that, under various arrangements, candidates and party leaders will seek to propitiate. From this perspective, abstract equality is not "real" equality, even if the former is elegantly measured while the latter is, as yet, unspecified.

Third, defenders of the present system argue that the electoral system is a causal factor in determining the pattern of party competition. Experience with the electoral college has shown that the mechanism, together with a two-party pattern of competition, produces reasonably satisfactory results, while direct election would either lead to multipartyism or remove a principal support for two-party competition. The result would be, from the point of view of political stability and presidential legitimacy, little short of disastrous.[94] Note, by the way, that if the assumed link between electoral systems and party competition exists, so that multiparty competition must follow from the adoption of direct election, all the populists' problems with multicandidate elections are accentuated.

Empirically, this third argument deserves more analysis than it has had. There is considerable evidence that electoral systems do not "cause" patterns of party competition;[95] in any case, the evidence that the electoral college system is a principal determinant of the two-

93. This has been documented amply by the Survey Research Center at the University of Michigan. See Angus Campbell and others, *The American Voter* (Wiley, 1960); and Campbell and others, *Elections and the Political Order*, Chap. 2.

94. Sayre and Parris, *Voting for President*, Chap. 4; Bickel, *New Age of Political Reform*, pp. 14–20; Kristol and Weaver, "A Bad Idea," pp. 152–54.

95. The argument that the electoral college system causes two-party competition—stated most boldly by Kristol and Weaver, "A Bad Idea," p. 153—depends on an analogy with Maurice Duverger's argument that a single-member, simple-plurality electoral system causes two-party competition. See his *Political Parties* (London: Methuen, 1964), pp. 216–28. Contrary evidence has been advanced by John G. Grumm, "Theories of Electoral Systems," in Andrew J. Milnor (ed.), *Comparative Political Parties: Selected Readings* (Crowell, 1969), pp. 230–50; Rae, *Political Consequences*, p. 83; and W. Phillips Shively, "The Elusive 'Psychological Factor': A Test for the Impact of Electoral Systems on Voters' Behavior," *Comparative Politics*, Vol. 3 (October 1970), pp. 115–25.

party pattern is mixed.[96] Moreover, empirically minded opponents of the populistic view here find themselves on difficult terrain. They must speculate, without adequate evidence, about how party leaders, candidates, and voters would behave under hypothetical circumstances.

Finally, there is the matter of presidential legitimacy. To some extent, both sides in the dispute operate on empirical grounds here, although perhaps without adequate evidence. Populists appear to believe that presidential legitimacy depends on the presidential election's being demonstrably democratic—that is, meeting populistic criteria. Thus their fear that the winner of a plurality of popular votes might be defeated in the electoral college or that the contingent election procedure might be necessary.

It is not always clear, however, to what extent proponents of direct election impute to the minds of their fellow citizens what is transparently legitimate in their own minds. To be sure, they cite public opinion polls favoring direct election and other evidence of public feeling; still one suspects they believe that what is logically democratic, and therefore legitimate, must sway the public at large.

Supporters of the present electoral college system, on the other hand, argue that the procedure has produced strong presidents whose right to exercise their office has not been challenged.[97] With less evidence, they contend as well that because it maintains "balance" between urban and rural interests and shores up the two-party system—which they take as the principal basis for legitimacy in American politics[98]—the electoral college is the key to presidential legitimacy.

All of which is another way of saying that the nature of the office to be filled is a contextual factor of great importance. Here we have come full circle. If the presidency is the focus for and instrument of the basic democratic values of popular sovereignty and political equality, it follows logically that the office should be filled by means that maximize these values. But, empirically, does this follow? First, is this an adequate description of what the presidency is believed to be? Or is it much more, as many political scientists argue?[99] Second, even

96. I have examined the case for the causal relationship more fully in "A Theoretical Analysis of the Electoral College," Chap. 6.

97. Sayre and Parris, *Voting for President*, pp. 56–57.

98. For a lucid argument that the two-party system serves a "constituent" function in American politics, see Lowi, "Party, Policy, and Constitution," pp. 238–76.

99. For instance, Sayre and Parris, *Voting for President*, pp. 4–5, stress the president's executive capacity and ability to act decisively.

if the description of the office underlying populistic beliefs is accepted, does the electorate generally follow the populists' reasoning? That is, does the public generally believe that the office must be filled strictly according to rules guaranteeing popular sovereignty and political equality, even if it is the principal focus for these values?

These are, I submit, the paramount contextual questions with which the deductive and abstract case for direct election must come to terms. For it is upon the grounds of the legitimacy of presidential succession that the decision for or against electoral reform is likely to be based.

A Concluding Note

Giovanni Sartori has drawn an insightful distinction between two modes of political thinking, the "empirico-pragmatic" and the "rational-deductive." In an often-quoted passage, Sartori says:

> While the empirical (empirico-pragmatic) mentality stays . . . close to what can be seen and touched, the rationalist mentality soars to a higher level of abstraction and hence tends to be far removed from facts. While the former is inclined to accept reality, the *raison* tends to reject reality in order to re-make it in its own image; while empiricism tends to be anti-dogmatic and tentative, rationalism tends to be dogmatic and definitive; while the former is eager to learn from experience and to proceed by testing and re-testing, the latter goes ahead even without tests; while the empiricist is not deeply concerned with rigorous coherence and distrusts long chains of demonstration, the rationalist is intransigent about the necessity for deductive consistency—and therefore, in the summing up, while the former prefers to be reasonable rather than rational, the latter puts logical rigor above everything and thus is rational even if it means being unreasonable.[100]

Sartori argues that the empirico-pragmatic *forma mentis* characterizes Anglo-American political life, while the rational-deductive mode is typically Continental.

While conceding that Sartori's distinction is cast in extreme terms, juxtaposing ideal types, one must nonetheless wonder whether American scholars and politicians are still predominantly in the empiricist camp. Clearly the case for direct election of the president, which has widespread adherence, closely approximates Sartori's rationalistic model. Moreover, the case against the electoral college is related

100. *Democratic Theory* (Praeger, 1965), pp. 232–33.

closely to that against malapportionment of congressional and legislative seats, whose elaboration is deductive, abstract, and rigorous.[101]

Defenders of the electoral college system (many of whom do accept the "one man, one vote" principle in legislative districting) carry on the empirico-pragmatic tradition. They cite experience and the complex relations among political institutions and practices. They insist that electoral reform must be considered in the context of American politics, and that direct election proposals ought to be evaluated in terms of their effects, not of their logic.[102]

The current debate about electoral reform ought to be regarded as symptomatic of a larger, perhaps growing division within the politically active public. One side interprets the basic legitimacy of political institutions in pragmatic terms; the other views it as stemming from the logically correct application of first principles.

To be sure, the distinction is not absolute. Populists deal with such practical problems as the 40 percent minimum requirement in a reformed presidential election. The empirically minded are concerned with first principles and their application. To some extent, they clearly believe that inequality in voter influence, favoring urban and minority group voters, is justifiable in principle.

The latter point raises an interesting question. At best, the electoral college system realizes the desired inequalities imperfectly and approximately; its exact impact has proved very hard to measure. Why not argue, instead, that black voters or residents of inner-city areas should have two votes for president? This would realize the goals deemed desirable in a clear, measurable, rational way.

In part, the answer is simply that this entails a rationalistic mode of looking at the problem which is uncongenial to those, usually pragmatic in outlook, who support the present system. But I would suggest that the absence of such arguments is also indicative of the ascendancy of populistic values.

Under the present electoral college system, populistic principles are on the whole fulfilled at each stage of voting; the requirements of the populistic model are met in each state in the election of electors, and in voting among electors. No reform proposal that has gained

101. See Dixon, *Democratic Representation*, Chap. 11; and for a critical view of the "one man, one vote" crusade, Alfred de Grazia, "The Applied Science of Equality: The Case of Apportionment, with Special Attention to the Idea of Equi-Populous Districts," in Robert A. Goldwin (ed.), *Representation and Misrepresentation* (Rand McNally, 1968), pp. 169–89.

102. Sayre and Parris, *Voting for President*, p. 147.

serious consideration since the early 1820s has suggested the further departure from populistic conditions of formalizing individual voter inequality, whereas a system of plural voting such as that suggested above certainly would. Populistic logic has such widespread acceptance that any such proposal would be without political appeal. Defense of voter inequality, or other values besides popular sovereignty and political equality, now depends on empirico-pragmatic analysis rather than on deductive arguments.

The pragmatists will be allowed to have the last word; these remarks by Irving Kristol and Paul Weaver illustrate clearly the nature of the electoral college debate:

> [House Judiciary Committee] members showed a profound reluctance to appreciate the importance and seriousness of the criticisms of direct Presidential election. They kept coming back to a single, abstract political dogma; one man, one vote, and each vote to be weighed in the same balance. The anticipated consequences of direct popular election seemed unable to affect their judgment; it was as if it had been divinely ordained that only one factor, only one criterion was properly involved in deciding how we, as citizens of a democracy, should elect our President.
>
> This obsession—it can hardly be called anything else—testifies to the extent to which, in recent decades, the democratic idea has been vulgarized and trivialized. From being a complex idea, implying a complex mode of government, appropriate to a large and complex society, the idea of democracy has been debased into a simple-minded, arithmetical majoritarianism—government by adding machine.[103]

To be fair, the case for direct election of the president entails more than "government by adding machine." But there is no doubt that it stresses logical consistency over experience and first principles over consequences. In the end, the debate over electoral reform is not so much a controversy over specific issues as a clash of philosophical perspectives. Perhaps this explains why the debate has not been resolved in more than 180 years, and why, even if reforms are enacted, the controversy is unlikely to end.

103. "A Bad Idea," pp. 154–56. This "vulgarization" or "debasement," if it is so considered, is not necessarily a phenomenon of recent decades. One is struck by the similarity between the views of Kristol and Weaver and the barbs hurled at the French revolutionaries by Edmund Burke (*Reflections on the Revolution in France*, ed. by Thomas H. D. Mahoney [Bobbs-Merrill, 1955], pp. 59, 216):

> It is said that twenty-four millions ought to prevail over two hundred thousand. True; if the constitution of a kingdom be a problem of arithmetic. This sort of discourse does well enough with the lamppost for a second.
> They have attempted to confound all sorts of citizens as well as they could, into one homogeneous mass. . . . They reduce men to loose counters, merely for the sake of simple telling, and not to figures whose power is to arise from their place in the table.

Index

239